4th Dimension

A Complete Guide to Database Development

Tim Knight

Scott, Foresman and Company

Glenview, Illinois   London

Library of Congress Cataloging-in-Publication Data

Knight, Timothy Orr.
    4th dimension.

    Includes index.
    1. Macintosh (Computer) — Programming.   2. Data base management.   3. 4th dimension (Computer program)
I. Title.   II. Title: Fourth dimension.
QA76.8.M3K685   1989   005.75'65   88-18431

    2   3   4   5   KPF   94   93   92   91   90   89

ISBN 0-673-38172-2

Notice of Liability

The information in this book is distributed on an "As Is" basis, without warranty. Neither the author nor Scott, Foresman and Company shall have any liability to customer or any other person or entity with respect to any liability, loss, or damage caused or alleged to be caused directly or indirectly by the programs contained herein. This includes, but is not limited to, interruption of service, loss of data, loss of business or anticipatory profits, and consequential damages from the use of the programs.

Scott, Foresman professional books are available for bulk sales at quantity discounts. For information, please contact Marketing Manager, Professional Books Group, Scott, Foresman and Company, 1900 East Lake Avenue, Glenview, IL 60025.

*This book is dedicated
to my father, Delos Knight, Jr.*

PREFACE

WHAT THIS BOOK IS ABOUT

This book will help you learn how to use the database development package 4th Dimension. This program, written for the Macintosh and introduced in the middle of 1987, is one of the most powerful and versatile database development programs in existence. Because of its power, however, it can sometimes be challenging to learn how to make use of all of the features of 4th Dimension. This book should help make the learning process much easier for you, through detailed descriptions of features and how to use them and through dozens of examples.

The book is broken down into three parts. Part 1 describes how to create "flat" databases, which are the easiest to understand and to create. Part 2 explains how to link files together to create relational databases for greatly added power and flexibility. Finally, Part 3 shows you how to create custom applications so that the databases you create (and perhaps even sell) are indistinguishable from stand-alone applications.

ORGANIZATION

Part 1, "The First and Second Dimensions," tells you how to create a flat database. Chapter 1, "Flat Files in the First Dimension," describes how to create single-file databases for such applications as mailing lists and membership rosters. Chapter 2, "Database Editing and Data Entry," shows you how to enter information in a database, modify it, and then display it. Chapter 3, "Isolating Information: Searches and Subfiles," tells you how to perform searches on the data in a database, how to sort the data, and how to use subfiles to store variable lists of data. Chapter 4, "Multiple Files," describes how to store multiple files in a database to contain a wide variety of information.

Part 2, "The Third and Fourth Dimensions," shows you how to create and relate to relational databases. Chapter 5, "Linking Files," tells you how to relate files to one another so they can share information and provide new views of data. Chapter 6, "Using the Layout Toolbox," shows you how to make the most of the powerful layout editor that comes with 4th Dimension. Chapter 7, "Components of the Layout," discusses advanced topics on how to create and use layouts effectively. Chapter 8, "Variables and Operators," gives basic information on the variables and operators of 4th Dimension's procedural language. Chapter 9, "Procedures and Menus," describes how to create menus that will activate procedures you have written for a database.

Part 3, "Beyond the 4th Dimension," describes how to create a stand-alone application from start to finish. Chapter 10, "Graphics and the User Interface," discusses the graphing and graphics capabilities of 4th Dimension in a database. Chapter 11, "Sets, Subrecords, and the Execution Cycle," shows you how to use sets, which are a different form of records selection, and subrecords in data storage, analysis, and retrieval. It also describes the execution cycle in a custom application. Chapter 12, "Printing, Debugging, and Customizing a Database," shows you how to finalize a custom application to make sure it prints and works properly. The appendix, "Quick Reference to Procedural Language Keyboards," lists the latest enhancements to 4th Dimension.

After reading just the first few chapters, you will be able to create a working, usable database. By the time you finish this book, you should be knowledgeable enough about 4th Dimension to create useful, feature-packed applications that can take advantage of practically all of 4th Dimension's potential. The manuals that accompany 4th Dimension are, of course, packed with useful references, but this book will make learning 4th Dimension easier and more enjoyable.

CONTENTS

Chapter **2**

DATABASE EDITING AND DATA ENTRY   21

Chapter **3**

ISOLATING INFORMATION: SEARCHES AND SUBFILES   41

Chapter **4**

MULTIPLE FILES   65

PART **2**

THE THIRD AND FOURTH DIMENSIONS OR Learning to Create and Relate to Relational Databases 83

Chapter **5**

LINKING FILES 84

Chapter **6**

USING THE LAYOUT TOOLBOX 107

Chapter **7**

COMPONENTS OF THE LAYOUT 125

Chapter **8**

VARIABLES AND OPERATORS 146

Chapter **9**

PROCEDURES AND MENUS   163

PART 1

The First and Second Dimensions

or How to Create a Flat Database and Live to Tell about It

1

Flat Files in the First Dimension

4th Dimension is a relational database for the Macintosh that has two distinct advantages over other similar programs. First of all, it was developed from the ground up as a true Macintosh program that obeys all the interface guidelines of the Mac and that makes use of the strong graphics orientation of the computer. The second advantage is that, while 4th Dimension has all the basic functionality of simple programs to suit everyday needs, its complex array of features and programmability make it the most powerful Macintosh database available.

Of course, any time you want to use a powerful program, you can expect learning that program to be a challenge. Sophisticated word processors, for instance, require the user to learn about block moves, headers and footers, character formatting, and ruler settings. With 4th Dimension, besides exploring the commands and techniques of the application itself, you'll probably also want to learn how to use 4th Dimension's programming language so you can access even more power. So you can see that mastering 4th Dimension isn't something you'll do overnight.

Nevertheless, reading this book makes the going a lot easier. This first chapter allows you to start working with 4th Dimension immediately. The reasons you can jump right in is because not everything you do is explained in full detail (that comes a little later), and because you are creating the simplest type of database: a flat file. A "flat" database, as opposed to a relational one, holds basic information like mailing addresses, names and phone numbers, and index card information.

Some very simple file management programs, such as pfs:file, can handle only this type of database. Despite its simplicity, this type of database can be useful, and it will teach you some of the important basics about 4th Dimension.

BOOTING UP

If you have not done so already, you need to install 4th Dimension on your hard-disk drive. After you have started your system and the Finder desktop is on the screen, follow these steps:

1. Type Command-N to create a new folder and name that folder **4th Dimension**.
2. Put the *4th Dimension program* disk into the floppy drive.
3. Type Command-A to select all the files from the program disk, then drag them to the folder you just created on the hard drive. All of the 4th Dimension files will be copied into this folder.
4. Follow the same procedure for the *4th Dimension Utilities* and *Examples* disks. Copy all of the files from these floppies into the 4th Dimension folder.

3

5. Once you are through copying the floppies to the hard drive, you may want to reorganize the 4th Dimension folder to suit your preferences. You might want to create a number of folders to hold examples, utilities, and databases separate from the program itself. This is completely up to you and does not affect how 4th Dimension performs.

It is highly recommended that you have a printer and a hard-disk drive. If you must run 4th Dimension off floppy disks, the preceding process is, of course, irrelevant. You only need to have a system disk in one drive and the 4th Dimension program disk in the other drive to run the program.

A NEW DATABASE

Double-click the 4th Dimension icon. In a few moments, the Welcome Screen, shown in Figure 1-1, should appear. This screen shows you any databases currently on the system and lets you either open an existing database or create a new one. Notice that the database names are followed by an italic *f*. This indicates that this is the database folder, and not the database itself. You are going to create a new database, so click the New button.

FIGURE 1-1. Click the New button to create a new database.

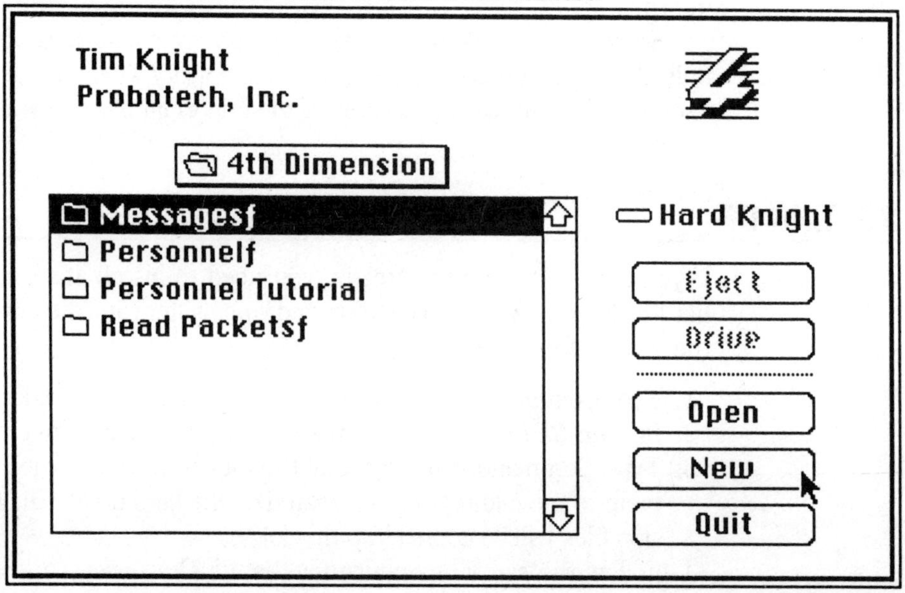

4th Dimension now needs to know the name of the database. Call this database Students, since it will list the names and other information about students in a hypothetical school. Type **Students** and click the Save button. 4th Dimension automatically creates a folder called Students with the necessary files, and you are ready to create the database.

PUTTING THE STRUCTURE TOGETHER

A window called Structure is currently on the screen. This Structure window is where you build your database. Think of the structure as a blueprint. It is something critical to the builder (yourself), but not readily visible to the user. Just as homeowners usually are not aware of the plans that went into the blueprints of their houses, the users of the database you create probably will not be aware of the structure behind it. The structure window is the assembly area for your database, which you can create and modify.

As shown in Figure 1-2, there is a graphic called File1. Because this is a flat database, File1 is the only file you will use. If more than one file on the screen were connected or *linked* together, you would be creating a relational database. For now, though, it's time to concentrate on the basics.

FIGURE 1-2.   File1 is an empty file in the Structure window.

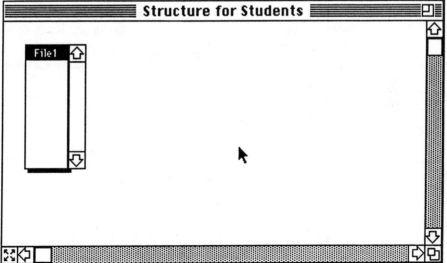

FIELDS

The file in the Structure window does not hold any meaningful information on its own. Instead, you put all the *fields* you want included in this file while you are in the Structure window. A field is a certain type or category of information. A field can be as simple as an employee number or as complex as several paragraphs of descriptive text. What goes into a field is completely up to you.

Several good "real life" examples make understanding fields easier. A phone book, for instance, contains line after line of valuable information. Each line usually has three distinct parts: the name of a person, the address, and the phone number. If you were to create a database with these categories of information, you would include three fields in a file, and you might name that file "Telephone Numbers."

You might want the fields to be broken up into more pieces to make the database more flexible. For instance, you might have fields called Last Name, First Name, Address, Prefix Number, and Suffix Number. This would let you access a very specific piece of information, like a last name or every person with a certain phone number prefix (the first three digits of a phone number).

Addresses on envelopes could also be broken up into fields. Obvious field names might include First Name, Last Name, Address, City, State, and ZIP Code. You might include another field called Business for those envelopes that require a business name. If some addresses were to individuals and not to businesses, the business field could be left blank.

As you can see, you create fields to generate space for certain types of information. Sometimes it is not easy to determine how many fields to have and what to name them, but it is always a good idea to break down the information enough so you can locate very specific types of data and to give the fields meaningful names so users know what to enter for each field.

FIELD TYPES

As mentioned earlier, this database will hold information about students. After some thought, we can anticipate that several fields will be needed: Last Name, First Name, Student Number, Date Enrolled, GPA (grade point average), and Major. You need to enter these fields one at a time, and for each field you need to tell 4th Dimension what type of field it should be.

To add a field, select the New Field option from the Structure menu. (As you can tell from the menu, you can type Command-F for the same result.) A new dialog box appears on the screen with a large number of options. This dialog box lets you establish the *field type* and the *field attributes* for each field you create. You will learn more about these different types of fields and attributes later, but a brief description of each item in the dialog box follows.

Field name. This is set automatically to Field1, Field2, Field3, and so on, as you create new fields. You will probably want to change the name to something meaningful, so simply type the name in this box.

Alpha. This field type is used for relatively small amounts of alphanumeric data (basically anything you can type on the keyboard). If you select this field type, enter a number from 2 to 80 in the box next to it to specify the maximum number of characters allowed in this field. Data such as last names, addresses, phone numbers, identification numbers, and brief comments are appropriate for the Alpha field type. Just make sure you allow the user enough characters for the data being entered (last names, for instance, are often longer than 10 characters).

Text. This field type is for much longer strings of text, such as lengthy descriptions or comments. The data entered here can be anywhere from a single character to 32,767 characters (which would be pages of information), but you should use this field only if you expect the data entered to be typically longer than the 80 characters allowed in the Alpha field. In databases, a good rule is to give users plenty of room for all possibilities, but not to be wasteful (a text field for a last name, for instance, would be inefficient).

Real. This field type is for real numbers, that is, for numbers that will always or occasionally require decimal points. Use Real fields for salaries, prices, and other information where decimal points may be entered.

Integer. If a field will always be a whole number between 32,767 and −32,767 (for example, an employee number or a ranking), use the Integer field type.

Long Integer. For large whole numbers between 2,147,483,647 and −2,147,483,647, use the Long Integer field type. Incidentally, the ranges for the Integer and Long Integer field types are not arbitrary. They are powers of 2, because most computer technology is based on the binary number system.

Date. Use the Date field type for fields that require a month, day, and year in the format mm/dd/yr. 4th Dimension recognizes whether the date is valid (23/46/87, for instance, would not be accepted) and makes sure the entire date string is entered correctly.

Picture. 4th Dimension was designed as a Macintosh database, and this is a good example of why this design orientation is an advantage. The Picture field can contain a graphic such as an office layout, a picture of a product, or a digitized picture of a person for an employee file.

Subfile. This is a unique field type, since it acts as a file within a field. It is most useful when you want a field devoted to several separate fields of information, especially when that information varies greatly in length. Later, when you add a subfile to the database you are about to create, you will better understand the significance of this field type.

FIELD ATTRIBUTES

The attributes of a field are not field types themselves, but they do help further define each field. They are as follows:

Mandatory. If you select this check box, the database requires that the field be entered before the user can complete the record. If the user tries to go to the next field without entering this field, 4th Dimension displays a dialog box telling the user that the field is mandatory. This is a useful attribute for fields like Last Name and ID Number, where the database is not much good without those critical pieces of information in every single record. Some fields, of course, don't have to be entered every time (a Comments field is a good example).

Display only. If a field will be displaying an item that does not have to be modified (the result of a calculation, for example), there is no reason that the field should be modifiable by the user. The Display only attribute would be appropriate for such a field.

Can't modify. This attribute should be used spartanly, since the field cannot be changed once the record is entered. For example, a person's Social Security number for a person will never change, thus, that field should not be alterable. The danger, of course, is that should the user make a mistake, he or she can't go back to that record and provide the field with the correct entry.

Indexed. This attribute is used for fields that are key for sorting and finding particular records. It makes 4th Dimension keep an index file of all entries in the field so they can be quickly arranged or located. Last names, identification numbers, and other common search fields should be indexed, because searching and sorting a non-indexed field is much slower. This does not mean all fields should be indexed, however. Indexing would not be appropriate for a field with comments, for instance, since it is unlikely that would be a desirable field for either sorting or searching for data.

Unique. This attribute is available only if you have selected the Indexed attribute. Choosing the Unique attribute ensures that when the database is used no two records will have the same entry in a particular field. For example, if you were trying to think of code names for a wide assortment of products in development, you wouldn't want to use the same code name for two different products. The field—which might be named Code Name—could be given the Unique attribute so that 4th Dimension would not allow duplicate entries in that field.

Standard Choices. This is a time-saving attribute for fields that will contain one item from a rather small list of possibilities. In the Students database you are about to create, for instance, there will be a small list of possible majors, so the Major field will be given the Standard Choices attribute. You will then enter the choices available (that is, the different majors). Information that has a wide range of possibilities (such as a person's first name or exact salary) isn't appropriate for Standard Choices, since it would be much faster to enter the data directly instead of choosing one item from a very long list.

ENTERING THE FIELDS

Just as determining what fields you will need to use takes some forethought, it also takes time to figure out what name to give each field, what type it should be, and what attributes it should have. For the first field, which will contain the student's last name, type **Last Name** in the Field Name box. Keep in mind that you can call a field anything you want, but it's a good idea to use a name that suggests the field's contents. Calling this field Social Security Number, for instance, would be ridiculous, even though 4th Dimension would still accept it.

Any last name will consist of text, and it is unlikely that any last name will be over thirty characters long. The Alpha field type is already selected, so type the number 30 in the box next to Alpha. The last name should also be Mandatory and Indexed, so select both of these attributes, as shown in Figure 1-3. If this was the last field you wanted to enter, you would click just the OK button. However, there are several other fields to go, so click the OK button and the Next button to enter the next field.

There are five more fields to enter: First Name, Student Number, Date Enrolled, GPA, and Major. Use the following steps to finish entering the fields. In each case, type the name of the field in the Field Name box, then click OK and Next when you are ready to enter the next field.

1. **First Name.** This is also an Alpha field. Twenty characters should be sufficient, so there is no need to change the default number. This field should be Mandatory.

2. **Student Number.** Because only integers less than 32,767 are necessary for this field, select the Integer type, then make the field Mandatory Indexed,

FIGURE 1-3.   Enter the field name, type, and attributes for Last Name.

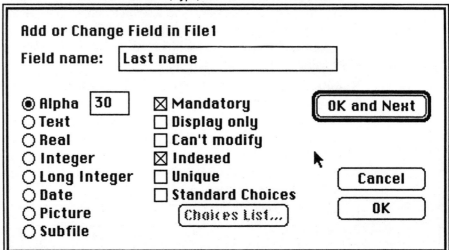

and Unique. Notice that Unique is not available for selection until you have first clicked the Indexed check box.

3. **Date Enrolled.** Select the Date field type and make this field Mandatory.
4. **GPA.** This field will probably contain decimals, so select the Real field type. There is no need to set any attributes, since a newly enrolled student would not have a GPA, and it probably won't be used as a standard search item.
5. **Major.** This is a good example of a Standard Choices field. First, select the Alpha type, because in every case the major will be only a short word or two. Now check the Standard Choices attribute, and the Choices List button becomes highlighted. Click the Choices List button so you can list the various choices.

   Now enter the majors Marketing, Management, Finance, Accounting, and Decision Information and press the Return key after each entry. When you're through, click the Sort button. The choices will be instantly sorted in alphabetical order. Later on, you might want to type in another major, so click on the check box that indicates the Choices can be modified.

   Before clicking the OK button, take a look at the dialog box, also shown in Figure 1-4. The buttons you have not yet used are easy to understand. The Insert button makes a space in the list for another choice entry. By pressing the Return key after each entry, you automatically make space for the next entry. If you want to insert an entry in the middle of the list, you can move to that point and click on Insert to make room.

FIGURE 1-4.   Standard choices can be entered, sorted, and removed.

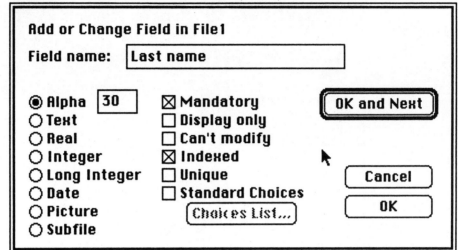

Add or Change Field in File1

Field name: | Last name |

- ◉ **Alpha** `30`
- ○ **Text**
- ○ **Real**
- ○ **Integer**
- ○ **Long Integer**
- ○ **Date**
- ○ **Picture**
- ○ **Subfile**

- ☒ **Mandatory**
- ☐ **Display only**
- ☐ **Can't modify**
- ☒ **Indexed**
- ☐ **Unique**
- ☐ **Standard Choices**

(**Choices List...**)

▶

(**OK and Next**)

[**Cancel**]

[**OK**]

Clicking on Append is the same as pressing the Return key. If you click on Append, the entry you have just entered will be accepted, and the cursor will be on the next line of the choices list. If you want to remove a choice you have entered, select that choice, then click the Delete button.

GETTING BACK TO STRUCTURE

You are now through entering the standard choices and the fields. Click the OK button on the Choices List, and you will return to the New Field dialog box. Since Major is the last field to be entered, click on the OK button to return to the Structure window.

The name of the file, like the name of fields, should describe its contents. Select the Rename File option from the Structure menu and type in the word Students. Click the OK button. Notice that the file is renamed Students, is resized to fit its new name, and contains all the fields you entered, as shown in Figure 1-5.

Next to each field name is a letter that represents the type of field. The Last Name, First Name, and Major fields have the letter A next to them, for Alpha. The Student Number, Date Enrolled, and GPA fields have the letters I (Integer), D (Date), and R (Real), respectively, next to them to show their field types. This allows you to see the types of fields in a file without having to open up each field.

FIGURE 1-5. Rename File with all six fields listed.

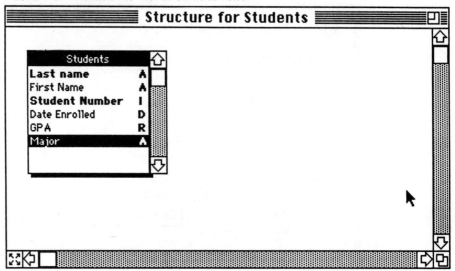

Notice that the Last Name and Student Number fields are in bold text rather than plain text. This indicates that those two fields are indexed, while the others are not.

CHANGING AND DELETING FIELDS

There are a couple of other commands on the Structure menu that you should understand: Change Field and Delete Field. These are available as menu items, and they do just what they say. Change Field lets you alter a field's characteristics, while Delete Field removes a field from a file.

If you want to delete a field, select that field and then the Delete Field command. The program then asks if you are sure you want to delete the field. If you are sure, click OK.

Changing a field is just as easy and can be accomplished in one of two ways. One way is to select a field and then choose the Change Field command from the menu. Another way is to double click the field you want to change. In either case, the Field Types and Attributes dialog box appears on the screen so you can make any changes to the characteristics of that field. If you want to save your changes and alter the next field, click OK and Next. To save your changes, click OK; to cancel your alterations, choose Cancel.

LAYOUTS

You have now finished creating the structure of a very simple database. Your Students database consists of a single file with six fields. Because there are no links and no subfiles, this is the simplest type of database possible. Now you need to design the graphics that will be used to receive data from the user and to display those data later.

The input and output displays are called a layout. A layout is a collection of MacDraw-like objects (including variables that represent fields, graphics, and text) arranged in a way that is appropriate for the data. An output layout, for example, usually differs from an input layout, since it is more important to be able to view a list quickly in output mode than in input mode.

4th Dimension has eight preprogrammed layouts to choose from, and a custom layout is available if you want to assemble a layout one object at a time. For the simple example in this chapter, you will create the most basic input and output layouts and then use this database to enter information for a few students.

THE INPUT LAYOUT

To create any layout, you first have to choose the Layout option from the Design menu. This switches you from Structure mode to Layout mode. The Layout dialog box appears, and the first thing you should type is the name you want to give the layout. Type *Input*, as shown in Figure 1-6. The rectangular area on the left displays the files available. In this case, Students is the only existing file. The rectangular area on the right side shows a miniature version of the layout; because none exists now, it is blank.

There are other parts in this dialog box that you will learn about shortly. For now, click the New button to tell 4th Dimension you want to create a new layout called Input (again, you can name the layout anything you want, but it's best to give it a short, descriptive name).

The New Layout dialog box appears, showing the various fields available for inclusion in the layout, the font sizes you can choose, and the layouts available. Later in this book, you will learn how to select only certain fields for inclusion in the layout. For now, just leave this area as it is, so that all the fields will be used in the layout. As shown in Figure 1-7, click the 9-point font size and leave the layout selector where it is. You can choose any layout graphics by clicking on it, but the one already selected is ideal for this simple database.

The name you have given this layout, Input, is already in the Layout name box. You could change the name at this point, but there is no need to do so, so click the OK button.

FIGURE 1-6.   The Layout dialog box lets you choose a file and name a layout.

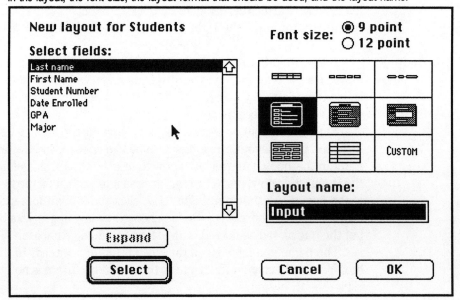

FIGURE 1-7.   In the New Layout dialog box, you can tell 4th Dimension which fields to include in the layout, the font size, the layout format that should be used, and the layout name.

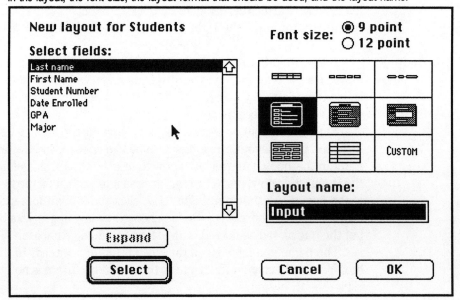

In an instant, 4th Dimension displays the Input layout for the Students file. The field names (shown in bold) and the field name variables (shown enclosed in boxes) are in the layout, and the tools on the left side of the screen can be used to modify or add to this layout. As you can see in Figure 1-8, this looks like an appropriate layout to enter student data, so click on the Close box to remove the layout from the screen. The layout is automatically saved.

You are now returned to the Structure window. To prepare the Output layout, select Layout from the Design menu. Type in the name **Output**, and click the New button. A New Layout dialog box appears on the screen, with Output in the Layout name box.

Again, you will be using all the fields in this layout. The default layout style is not appropriate, since you will want to see many names at once. Pick the layout style in the upper left corner, as shown in Figure 1-9, and once again choose the 9-point font size.

When the Output layout appears on the screen, as in Figure 1-10, you can see right away that something is wrong: there isn't enough screen to show all the fields. Because so much room is allocated for the different fields, they can't all be

FIGURE 1-8.   4th Dimension automatically created this layout with just a few parameters. In upcoming chapters, you will learn the details of the layout toolbox and how you can create customized layouts.

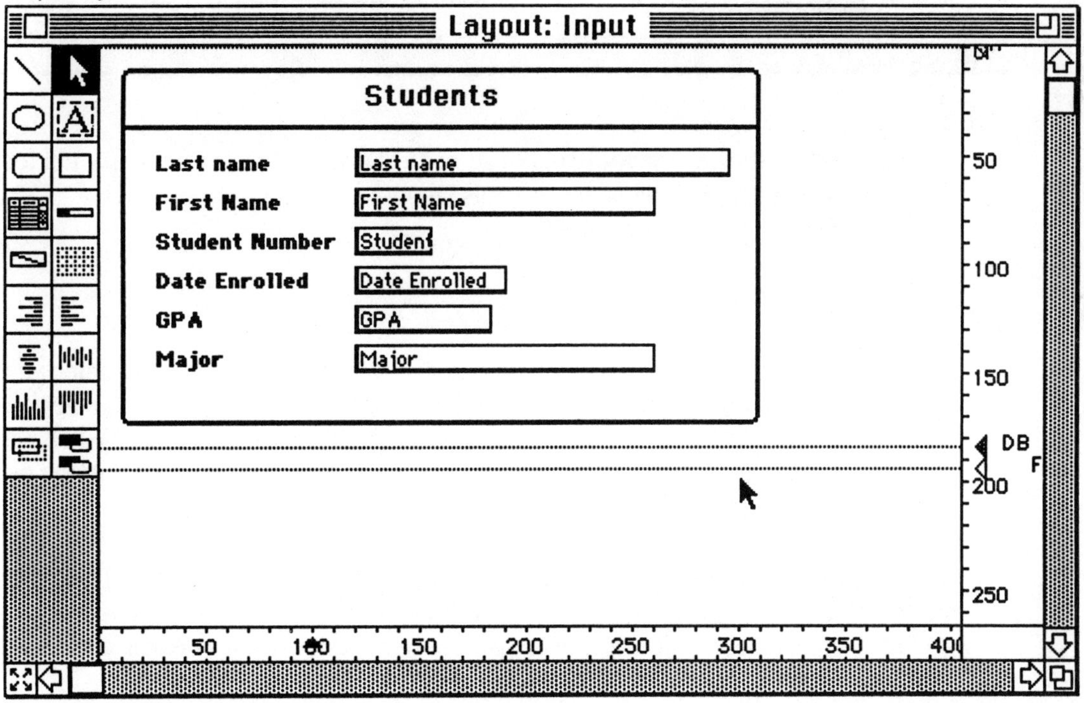

FIGURE 1-9.   The top three layout styles are best for output, while the middle three layout styles are best for input.

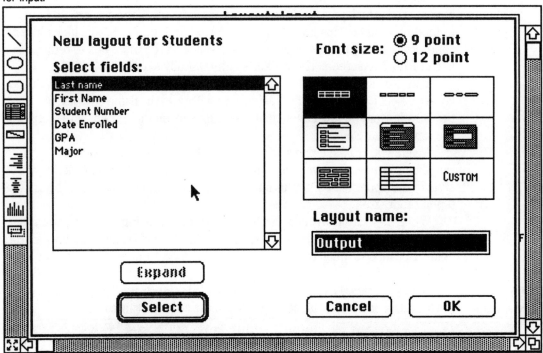

displayed in the narrow width of the screen. There are ways around this, but for now click on the Close box to save this layout.

REVIEWING LAYOUTS

Some of the other elements of the Layout dialog box are useful for examining and perhaps modifying layouts that already exist. Choose Layout from the Design menu. The bold file name Students is on the left side of the dialog box. You have created two layouts for this file, but their names will not be displayed until you expand the file.

There are two ways to expand and contract the file. The first is to double-click on the file you want to expand. The first double-click expands the file so that all of its layout names are visible. Another double-click makes those layout names disappear. Clicking the Expand button in the dialog box has the same toggling effect.

FIGURE 1-10.   The layout for Output has all the fields included, but there isn't enough room on the screen to show them simultaneously.

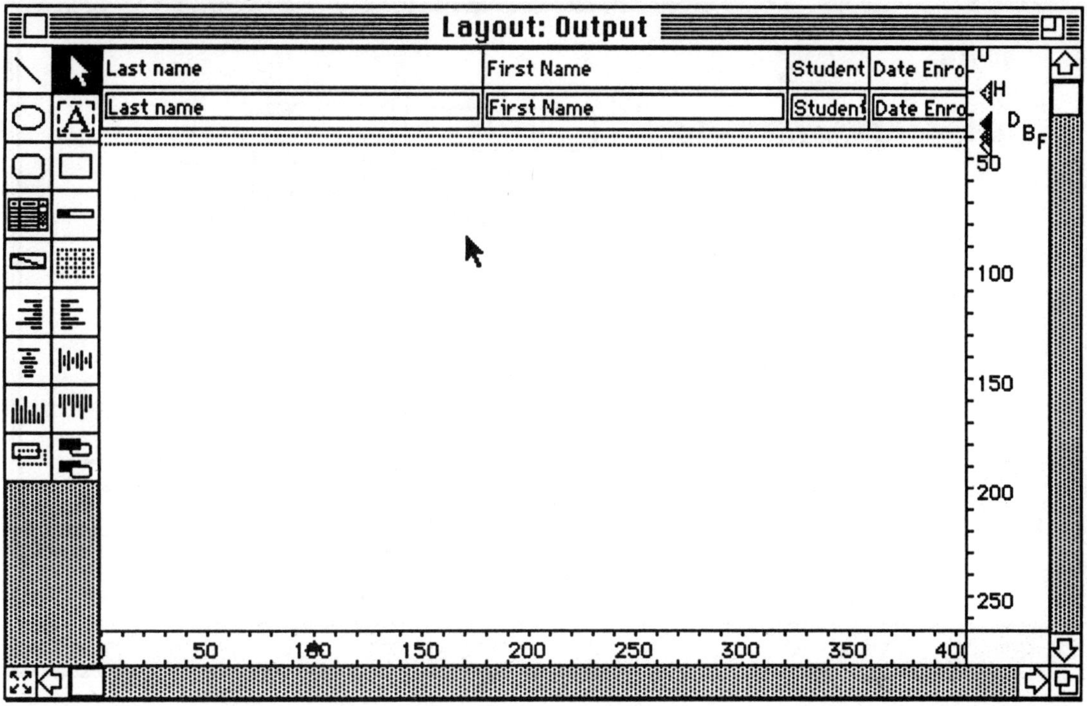

When the layout names are visible, you can select any of them to see a small graphic representation of a layout on the right side of the dialog box. For instance, select the Output layout. Now look at the right side of the screen, where the Output layout is shown in miniature form. To examine and possibly modify it in the Layout: Output window, you would double-click the Output name.

When you select a layout name, you can also check either the Input box or the Output box to indicate for what that layout is to be used. With names as descriptive as these, it may seem pointless to specify which is for input and which for output, but for practice, go ahead and make those settings. With Output still selected, click the Output check box. A capital O appears next to the Output layout name, indicating it is an output layout.

Now choose the Input layout name. Click the Input check box, and the letter I appears next to its name, as in Figure 1-11. You can set any layout to either input or output. You can even set a layout for both by checking both Input and Output check boxes; in that case, the letter B appears next to the layout name.

To delete a layout, select that layout's name and click the Delete button. Before 4th Dimension deletes a layout, it checks to make sure that there are at

FIGURE 1-11.   The letter next to the layout name indicates the purpose of the layout: I means Input, O means Output, and B means Both.

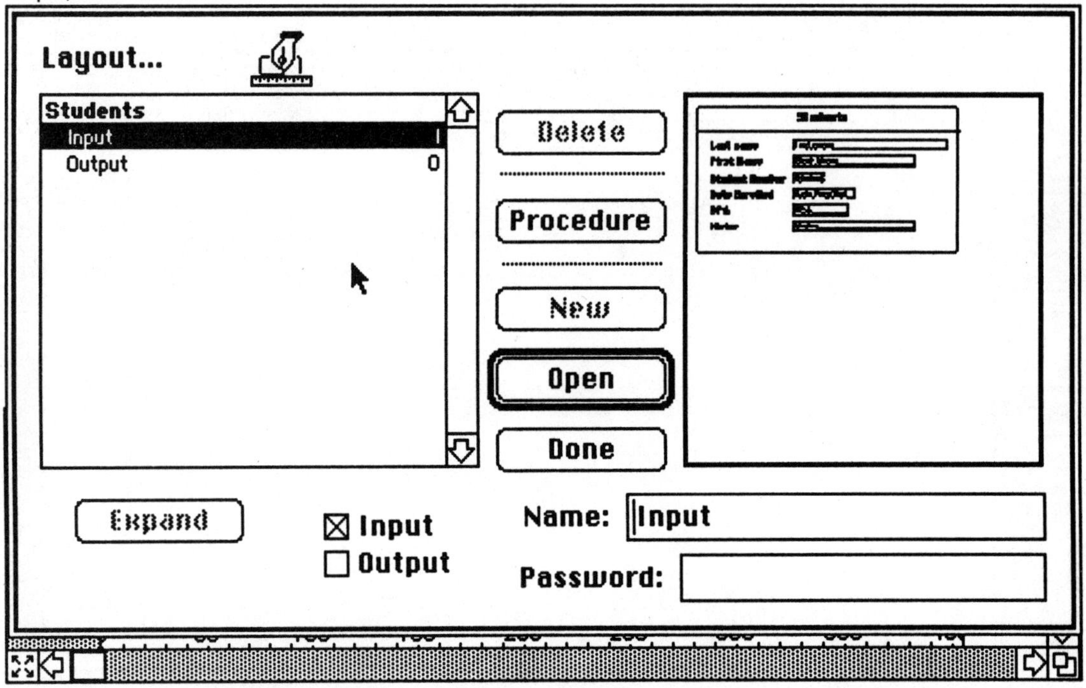

least one input and one output layout available (which might be a single layout used for both input and output). If not, the Delete button is not even highlighted, meaning you can't delete that layout.

For example, suppose you had three output layouts (Outone, Outtwo, and Outthree) and one input layout (Inputone). You could delete one or two of the output layouts, since there is at least one output layout remaining. However, you could not delete the input layout, since that is the only means of input available. To get rid of that input layout, you would first have to create a new layout and then return to the Layout dialog box and delete the unwanted input layout.

USING THE DATABASE

You are going to be developing this simple database a lot more to explore other aspects of 4th Dimension. But for now, try entering just a few names to see how the input and output process functions within the confines of the layouts.

To get from Design mode to User mode, select the User option in the Environment menu. 4th Dimension will tell you that there are no records in the file, since of course you haven't entered any names yet. Select the New Record command in the Enter menu (or press Command-N, the keyboard equivalent) and enter the first student record. Type the last name, *LaBatt*, and press Tab. Now enter the first name, *Darren*, the student number, *1*, the date enrolled, *9/15/85*, and the GPA, *3.5*, and press Tab after each entry.

When you press Tab after entering 3.5, the Choices for Major list appears, as shown in Figure 1-12. This Standard Choices field allows you to select a major without having to type it, thus reducing the risk of a spelling error. Select Decision Information, and that Major is instantly included for that field.

You're now finished with this record, so click the Enter button on the left side of the screen. Enter this next student record: Huang, Chi, 4, 9/16/84, 3.87, Management. Click Enter. Type in the third student record: Bruck, Timo, 9, 4/1/83, 3.43, Marketing. Even though this is the last record you'll enter in this chapter, click Enter. When the fourth, blank Input layout appears, click Cancel to stop the input process.

FIGURE 1-12.   The Standard Choices list appears when the cursor reaches the Major field. By clicking on any of these majors, you can instantly enter it into the field.

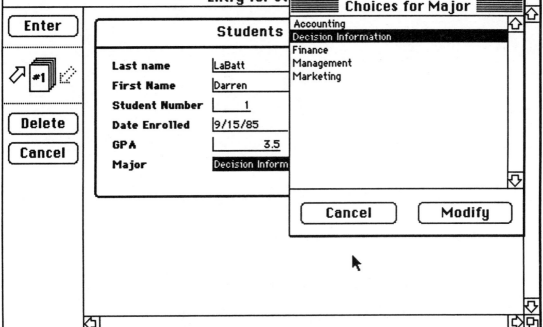

USING OUTPUT

Before finishing this chapter, take a quick look at the output for the three names in your database. When you clicked Cancel from the Input layout, 4th Dimension automatically showed all the records you had entered so far in the Output layout. (This layout extends beyond the right edge of the screen, but you'll learn how to remedy this situation later on.)

In this first chapter, you created a simple database from the ground up, and you now have a basic understanding of how to enter and display data. As you go through each chapter, you will build on what you have learned already. So far, you've discovered some of the basics of structure, the layout window, and input/output in the database. The next chapter will help you understand more of the details behind these components of 4th Dimension, so you can modify layouts and make the input and output screens easier to use.

2

Database Editing and Data Entry

In chapter 1, you constructed a simple database that kept track of students and information about them. The one-dimensional database called Students would be adequate for some simple record-keeping, and it would not be difficult to add on to that database so it could support more information.

In this chapter, you will create a somewhat more sophisticated database to keep track of a customer list. In upcoming chapters, you will build an increasingly complex database from this foundation. An easy way to create this customer database would be to start from scratch, because, as you learned in chapter 1, "flat" databases take very little time to create in 4th Dimension. It would be more enlightening, however, to take the database you already have and to edit it to transform it from a student database to a customer database.

Naturally, most databases are not made that way, but we are going to do it this way for two reasons: (1) the database you have is quite simple and won't take much time to edit and (2) more importantly, you can learn how easy it is to change fields, choices, and the layout of a database. By changing Students to Customers, you can better understand how to edit within 4th Dimension.

USING THE RENAMER

4th Dimension depends on a variety of files for each of its databases. Return to the Finder and locate the folder called Students. You'll want this folder to be renamed Customers, so select the name Students by dragging the I-beam over it, then type **Customers**.

Once you have changed the name of the folder, find the 4th Dimension utility called 4D Renamer (which will be on the hard disk or, if you haven't copied it there yet, the 4th Dimension Utilities disk). This simple program renames all the files within a 4th Dimension folder. Double-click the 4D Renamer icon and follow these steps:

1. Use the directory list that appears on the screen as you would any other. Find the folder called Customers, then double-click that folder to open it and reveal the Students database. All the file names in the Customers folder are still some variation of Students, and they all have to be renamed.
2. Double-click the Students database name.
3. The Renamer dialog box is now on the screen. Type in the new name you want to give this database (in this case, type Customers, as shown in Figure 2-1).

FIGURE 2-1.   The 4D Renamer dialog box accepts the new database name.

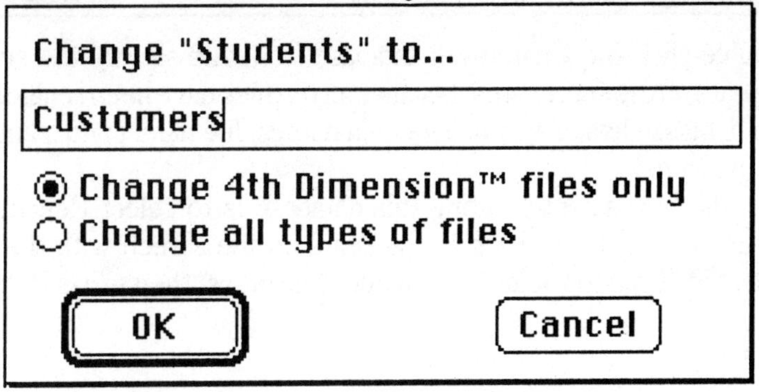

Change "Students" to...

Customers|

◉ Change 4th Dimension™ files only
○ Change all types of files

OK   Cancel

4. You want to change all the 4th Dimension files, so leave the radio button as it is. If you wanted to change all the files in the folder with the old name of the database to the new name (whether they were 4th Dimension files or not), you would click the "Change all types of files" radio button.
5. Click OK. The program asks you to verify that you want the changes made. You do, so click OK.

Now that 4D Renamer is through, select Quit from the File menu. Double-click the Customers folder, and notice that all the file names have been changed, as shown in Figure 2-2. You could have changed these names yourself, but 4D Renamer changes the names more quickly and ensures that there are no misspellings.

FIGURE 2-2.   All the 4th Dimension files have been renamed.

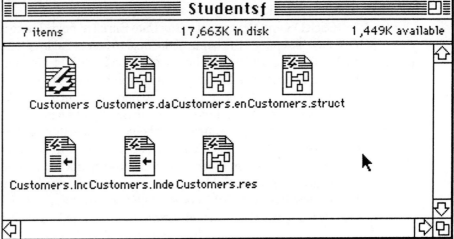

CHANGING THE FILE

Double-click the Customers database icon, and shortly the structure window appears on the screen. Just because all the files have been renamed doesn't mean the database has changed. The field names, file name, and standard choices are all the same.

The first step to editing this database is to select Rename File from the Structure menu. A dialog box appears on the screen with the name Students selected. Type in the new file name, Customers, then press Return.

CHANGING THE FIELDS

Altering the field takes a little more time. This involves changing not only each field name, but in some cases requires changing field attributes. To begin, double-click the first field in the file, Last Name.

The dialog box for the Last Name field appears. Because this field is appropriate for the Customers database, there is no need to change it. Therefore, click the OK and Next buttons so that the First Name field dialog box appears. Again, this field will be necessary in the Customers file, so click OK and Next.

The customers in this database will need numbers, but the Student Number field is inappropriately named. Move the cursor up to the word Student in the field name and double-click the mouse button. Type the word Customer to replace it, as shown in Figure 2-3. The Integer field type is appropriate, as are the Indexed and Unique attributes, since the customer number will be a number less than 32,767 and should not be shared by any two records.

Click OK and Next to get to the Date Enrolled field. There is no need for this field now, so change the name of the field to Street Address and the field type to Alpha. The Mandatory radio button can remain clicked, but there is no reason for this field to be indexed. You can anticipate that the street address will probably not be used often to sort records or to find a particular record.

Click OK and Next, then change the GPA field's name to City. The field type should be Alpha, and the attributes should be Mandatory and Indexed, as shown in Figure 2-4. You can see already how easy it is to access a 4th Dimension database in the Design mode and to alter the characteristics of the fields.

There is only one field left, and you should change its name from Major to State. Click the Standard Choices check box so that the last field is no longer selected. You could have listed all fifty states as standard choices, but this would

FIGURE 2-3. Change the name from Student Number to Customer Number.

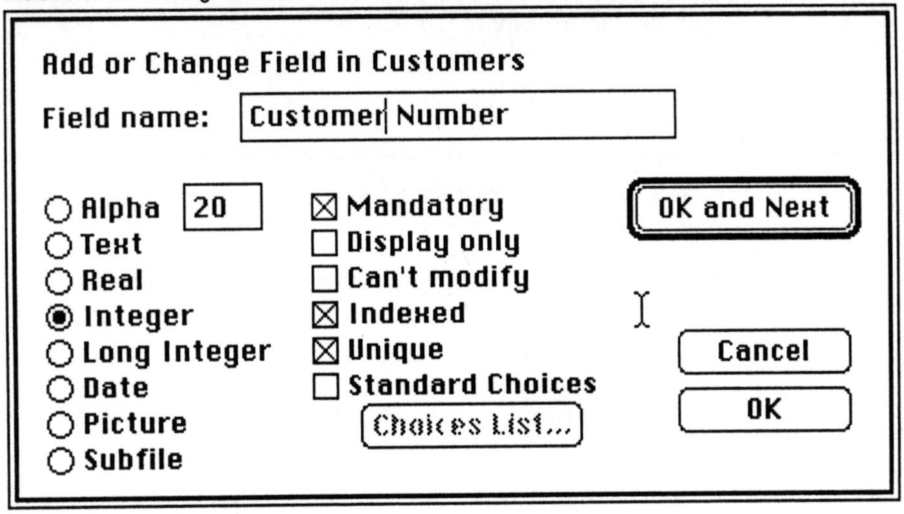

```
┌──────────────────────────────────────────────────────────────┐
│  Add or Change Field in Customers                              │
│                                                                │
│  Field name:  │Customer| Number                    │           │
│                                                                │
│  ○ Alpha  │20 │      ☒ Mandatory        ╭─────────────────╮   │
│  ○ Text              ☐ Display only      │  OK and Next    │   │
│  ○ Real              ☐ Can't modify      ╰─────────────────╯   │
│  ◉ Integer           ☒ Indexed         I                       │
│  ○ Long Integer      ☒ Unique            ╭─────────────╮       │
│  ○ Date              ☐ Standard Choices  │   Cancel    │       │
│  ○ Picture           ╭──────────────╮    ╰─────────────╯       │
│  ○ Subfile           │ Choices List...│   │    OK      │       │
│                      ╰──────────────╯    ╰─────────────╯       │
└──────────────────────────────────────────────────────────────┘
```

FIGURE 2-4. The fifth field is City, which is Alpha and Mandatory.

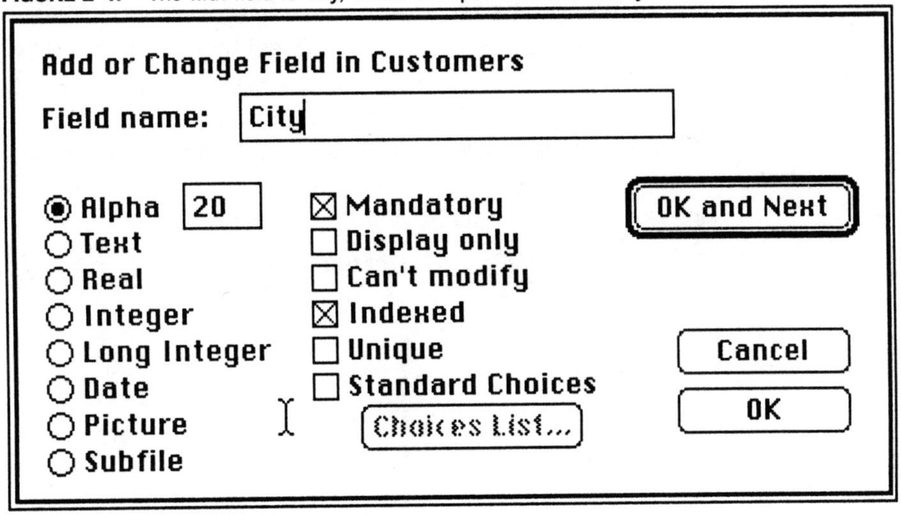

```
┌──────────────────────────────────────────────────────────────┐
│  Add or Change Field in Customers                              │
│                                                                │
│  Field name:  │City|                               │           │
│                                                                │
│  ◉ Alpha  │20 │      ☒ Mandatory        ╭─────────────────╮   │
│  ○ Text              ☐ Display only      │  OK and Next    │   │
│  ○ Real              ☐ Can't modify      ╰─────────────────╯   │
│  ○ Integer           ☒ Indexed                                 │
│  ○ Long Integer      ☐ Unique            ╭─────────────╮       │
│  ○ Date              ☐ Standard Choices  │   Cancel    │       │
│  ○ Picture      I    ╭──────────────╮    ╰─────────────╯       │
│  ○ Subfile           │ Choices List...│   │    OK      │       │
│                      ╰──────────────╯    ╰─────────────╯       │
└──────────────────────────────────────────────────────────────┘
```

be time consuming and not very efficient for the end user. Instead, click the Mandatory and Indexed field attributes, then click the OK and Next buttons.

You have now altered the six original fields, but you still need another field for the ZIP code. 4th Dimension recognizes that you are out of fields, so it creates a new one called Field7, which you should rename ZIP Code. Make it an

Integer field that is Mandatory and Indexed. Click OK, and your structure window should resemble Figure 2-5.

EDITING THE LAYOUTS

Now you have to create a new input layout and a new output layout. Follow these steps:

1. Select the Layout environment from the Design menu.
2. Double-click the filename Customers so you can see the associated layouts. There are currently Input and Output layouts, but neither is appropriate for the new database.
3. Type Customers Input as the name for the new input layout, then click the New button.
4. You can now choose what layout style you want to use and which fields should be included. The layout style selected is fine, but click on the 9-point radio button so that the text will be smaller.
5. When you want the fields to appear in a particular order in the layout, you can select them in the order that you want them to appear. The easiest way to do that is to double-click the field names in the appropriate order (or you could just as easily select each field and click the Select button every time). In this case, put the fields in this order: Last Name, First Name, Street Address,

FIGURE 2-5.   The structure window after the field changes.

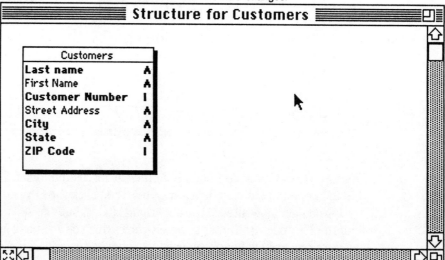

City, State, ZIP Code, and Customer Number. The Customer Number field comes last since it should not be embedded in the address. As shown in Figure 2-6, numbers signifying the order of the fields appear to the right of the field names. Click OK when you're through.

On the screen is the Customer Input layout. The name at the top of the layout is Customers (the name of the file), and each field is on a line of its own, as shown in Figure 2-7. 4th Dimension has no way of knowing how you want the fields arranged (except the order of the fields, which you set), so it places all of them on different lines. Part of your work as a database designer is positioning the elements of a layout in the most sensible, easy-to-read places.

TOOLS AND OBJECTS

The layout screen has a lot of tools available for you to use, but for now you need to understand only a couple. The first tool is the pointer, which is the left-pointing arrow in the upper right corner of the tool section. You use the pointer to select

FIGURE 2-6. The layout type, point size, and field order are selected.

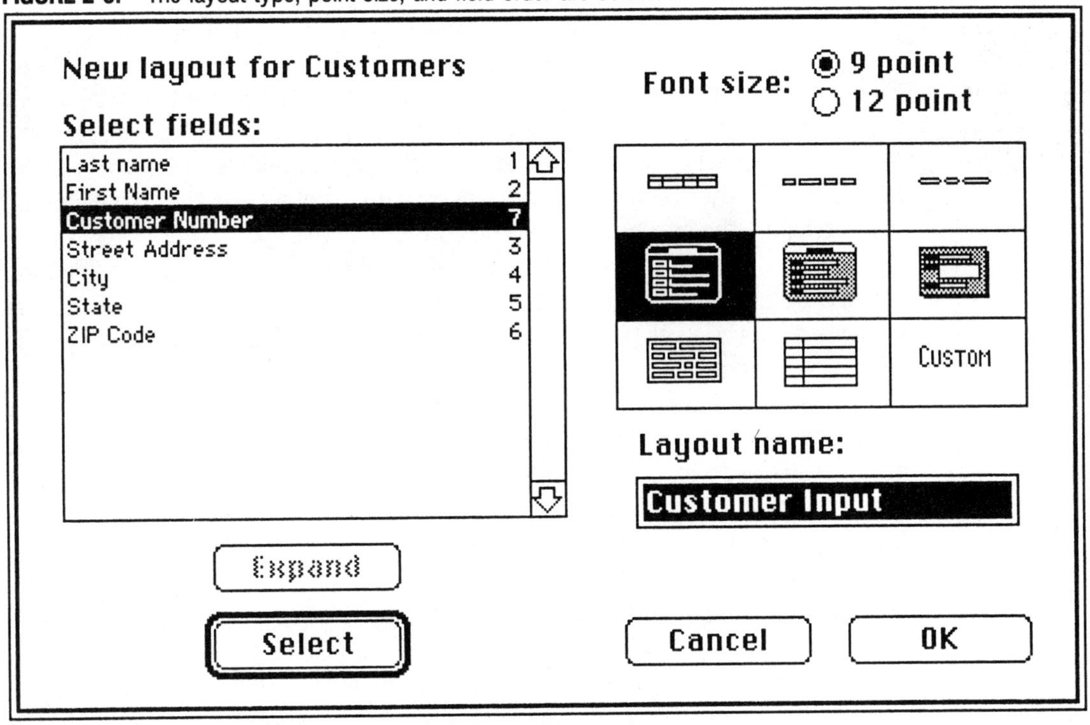

FIGURE 2-7.   The fields are in the order you designated, but each field is on a separate line.

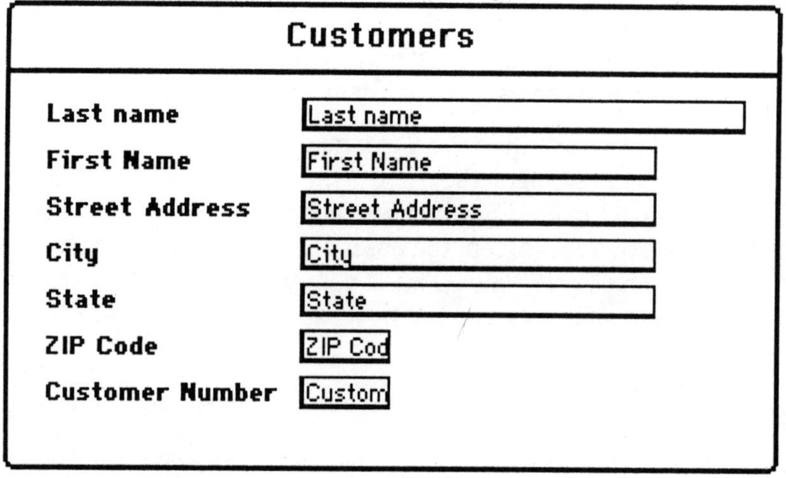

```
┌─────────────────────────────────────────────────────────┐
│                      Customers                            │
│  ┌──────────────────────────────────────────────────┐    │
│   Last name        │Last name                         │   │
│                                                           │
│   First Name       │First Name              │             │
│                                                           │
│   Street Address   │Street Address          │             │
│                                                           │
│   City             │City                    │             │
│                                                           │
│   State            │State                   │             │
│                                                           │
│   ZIP Code         │ZIP Cod│                              │
│                                                           │
│   Customer Number  │Custom│                               │
│                                                           │
└─────────────────────────────────────────────────────────┘
```

objects in the layout window, move them, and resize them. The other tool you'll use now is the text tool, which is represented by the capital A in the tool box. With the text tool you can enter and modify text in the layout.

Before you use either of these tools, you need to understand the objects on the layout screen. Each piece of text, each variable, and each graphic in the layout is an object. If you have ever used MacDraw or any other object-oriented program, you know that objects are independent of one another, although you can move or delete them as a group. By working with the objects in the layout screen, you can adjust the appearance and the contents of the final layout.

The first thing you'll want to do with this layout is change its title. Changing the title (which is now Customers) does not affect the name of the file. It just changes what the user sees at the top of the Customer Input layout when it is displayed.

If it isn't selected already, click the pointer tool and move the pointer over the title Customers. Click the mouse button once. Four black handles appear around the title, which indicates that this object has been selected. Now select the text tool and drag the I-beam over the title Customers. Replace the title by typing Customer Input. Your screen should now resemble Figure 2-8.

The whole title does not appear, since the size of the object is not wide enough. Select the pointer and point to either of the handles on the right side of the selected object. The pointer becomes a four-directional arrow, which indicates that you can resize the object in any direction. Hold down the mouse button and drag the handle far enough to the right so that the whole title can be seen. Try not to resize it vertically; just drag the handle to the right so the object is wider.

FIGURE 2-8.   Replace the title Customers with Customer Input.

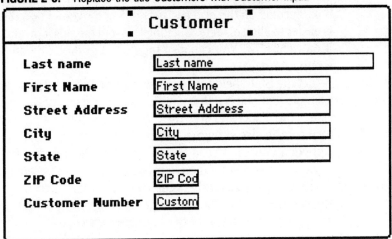

Now that you can see the whole title, move the pointer to the white area of the layout screen outside the border of the layout. Click the mouse button so none of the objects is selected. You have entered a new title by following a simple three-step process:

1. Select the object with the pointer and select the text with the text tool.
2. Type in the new text to replace the old text.
3. Resize the object so that all the text is visible.

MOVING OBJECTS IN THE LAYOUT

Moving and modifying objects like titles is easy, but altering objects like field variables is somewhat more complex. The reason is that the fields are actually represented by two objects. The first object is the field variable itself, which holds information like last names (Smith, Jones, Brown, and so on). Beneath that object is a graphic rectangle, so that when the layout is displayed, there are boxes on the screen for entry and modification of the field names. Without these boxes, the user's only indication of field positions would be the names of the fields on the screen.

Because there are two objects for each field, you should modify both to rearrange the layout. A good place to start would be the State field. Assume the user wants to use standard state abbreviations (like CA, LA, and OH), which are only two letters long and which require very little screen space. Follow these steps to narrow this field in the layout:

1. Click on the grid tool, which is the fifth tool down on the right side of the tool box. Turning on the grid restricts object movement on the screen so that it is easier to align objects. Clicking this tool toggles it on and off, and you want it on right now. You can also toggle the grid on and off under the Layout menu.

2. Select the State field (not the field name, which is to the left of it and is just a simple text object). Position the pointer on one of the handles on the right side of the object and drag the mouse to the left so that the width is reduced to about the size shown in Figure 2-9.

3. Although you can't read the name of the field in the field variable object anymore, it will still function properly. Select the graphic rectangle that is filling the space formerly occupied by the State field.

4. Reduce the size of the rectangle by dragging a handle to the left so it is approximately the size of the State field variable.

There is now enough room to the right of the State field to put the ZIP Code title and field. Click on the ZIP Code title, and notice that the object is much wider than necessary. Drag one of the handles to the left so that the object size is just wide enough to show the words ZIP Code, as shown in Figure 2-10.

Now drag the title up to a point just to the right of the State field. The title should be aligned evenly with the State field and should allow enough room so that the ZIP Code field can be moved up to that line as well. Aesthetics like this are important in databases, especially when they affect the user's understanding of how to use the database.

FIGURE 2-9.   Shorten the State field to just a few characters wide.

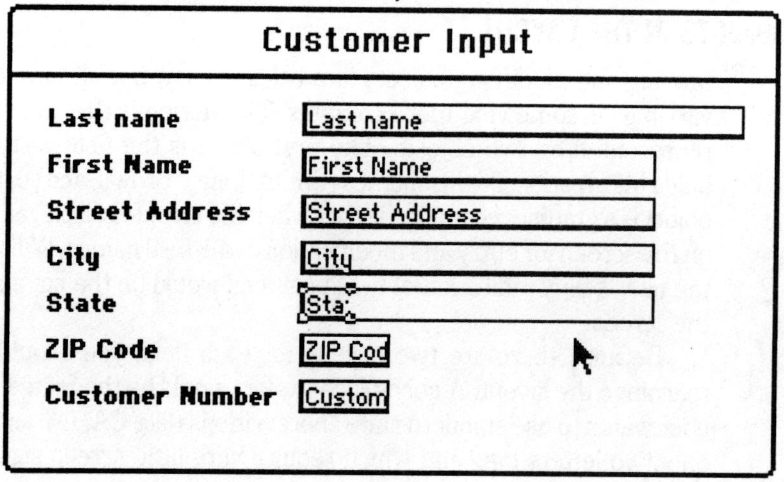

FIGURE 2-10.   Reduce the length of the title to a manageable size.

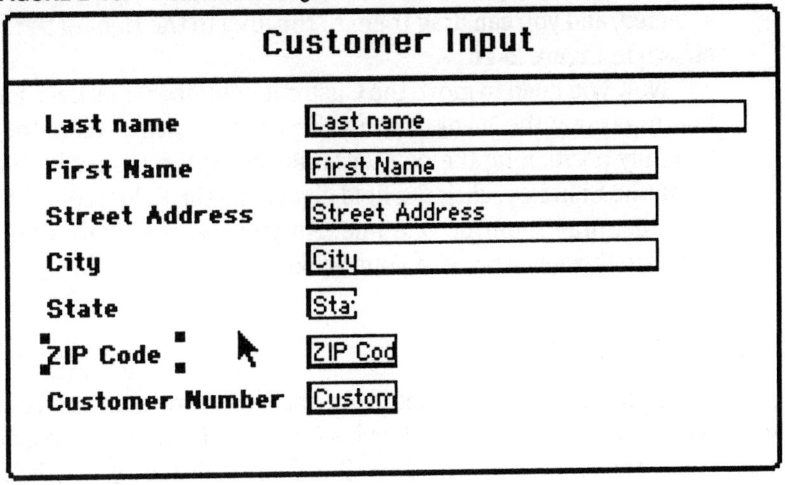

SELECTING MULTIPLE OBJECTS

An important skill to learn when using an object-oriented window like the Layout screen is how to select more than one object. On the surface, it's easy: select the first object, then hold down the Shift key and select any other objects you want. Each one object will be marked, and you can move or delete objects as a group.

In some cases, though, selecting multiple objects can be difficult. A good example is selecting a field and its accompanying graphic, since they are usually so close to each other. For example, you need to move the ZIP Code field and its graphic to the right of the ZIP Code title. There are several ways you could do this:

- You could first drag the field to the left to get it out of the way, then drag the graphic to the appropriate spot on the layout, and then drag the field on top of that graphic.
- You could resize the field so that the graphic underneath could be selected easily, select the graphic, and then select the field. With both selected, you could then drag them to the right spot and resize the field to return the field to its original size.
- You could carefully position the pointer to select the graphic underneath and then select the field on top.

In this exercise, try the third method in the preceding list. Although it is difficult to point to the one-pixel-wide area of the graphic "peeking out" from underneath the field, you can do it with a little practice. Once it is selected, hold down the Shift key and click on the field object. Now both objects should be selected, and you can drag them to the area to the right of the ZIP Code title, as shown in Figure 2-11.

Now you need to move the Customer Number title, field, and graphic up one line to occupy the blank area in the layout. Again, select the graphic first by carefully positioning the pointer and clicking the mouse button. While holding down the Shift key, click the field object and the field title. With all three objects selected, drag them up one line. As you can see, with a little time, you can improve the appearance of your layout.

CREATING THE OUTPUT LAYOUT

Select the Layout command from the Structure menu to return to the list of layouts you have created. Double-click the file name to expand the list, then select the one you just made (called Customer Input) and click the Input check box. Next, select the old input layout and click the Delete button. 4th Dimension confirms that you want to delete this old layout. Click the Yes button.

You have now removed the old input layout from memory and have replaced it with a new default input layout (notice the letter *I* next to the name Customer Input). Select the file name Customers again and do the following:

1. Type in `Customer Output`, which is the name of this new layout, then click the New button.
2. Click the layout style in the upper left corner of the layout dialog box.

FIGURE 2-11. Position the ZIP Code field and graphic on the same line.

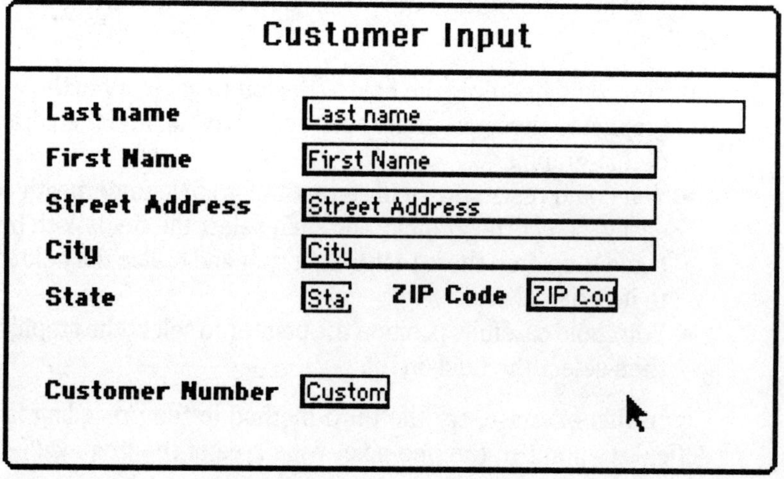

Customer Input	
Last name	`Last name`
First Name	`First Name`
Street Address	`Street Address`
City	`City`
State	`Sta` **ZIP Code** `ZIP Cod`
Customer Number	`Custom`

3. Select the fields you want in the output in the order you want them by double-clicking Customer Number, Last Name, First Name, and then ZIP Code. For now, these are the only fields that will be in the output, and they will be in the order denoted by the numbers to the right of the fields.
4. Select the 9-point type size. Your screen should resemble Figure 2-12. Click the OK button.

Now you have both the Customer Input and the Customer Output layouts made. Remember, though, that you still need to delete the old output layout. Select the Layout command again and make the new output layout the default, then delete the old output layout. There should be an *O* next to the name Customer Output and an *I* next to the layout name Customer Input. These should be the only two layouts existing within the Customers file.

FIGURE 2-12. Format parameters for the new output layout.

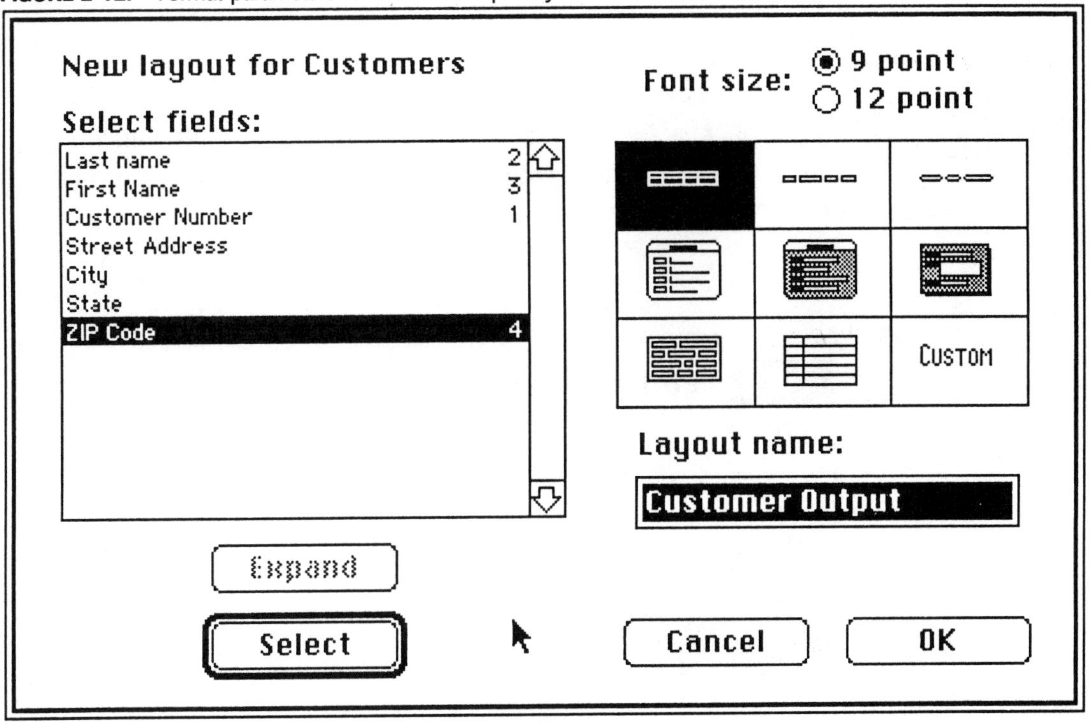

MORE ON THE INPUT PROCESS

You have now constructed a second database. It's not much different from the first one, but you had more of a hand in constructing the layout, and both the input and output layouts will be fully visible on the screen. Now is a good time to put this database to use and discover some effective techniques for data input and output.

Select the User environment from the Environment menu. The first thing you see on the screen is the three student names you entered in the last chapter displayed in the Customer Output layout. These data are now erroneous, so you should remove these names. Holding down the Shift key, click each of the three names, then choose Clear from the Edit menu, as shown in Figure 2-13. Click the Yes key when 4th Dimension asks if you really want to remove those records.

4th Dimension displays a graphic of a drawer and states that there are no records for the Customers file. Now you can begin entering customer names in the Customer Input layout. Select the Enter a New Record command from the Enter menu. The Command-N symbol next to this option indicates that you can also start record entry by pressing Command-N. As the Customer Input layout appears on the screen, recall the purpose of the following keys:

Tab.   Pressing the Tab key signifies the end of a field entry. For each field, type in the contents, then press Tab.

Shift-Tab.   Holding down the Shift key and then pressing Tab tells the computer to back up one field. It does not erase any fields, but it will go one step backward instead of forward.

FIGURE 2-13.   Choose the old records then select Clear from the Edit menu.

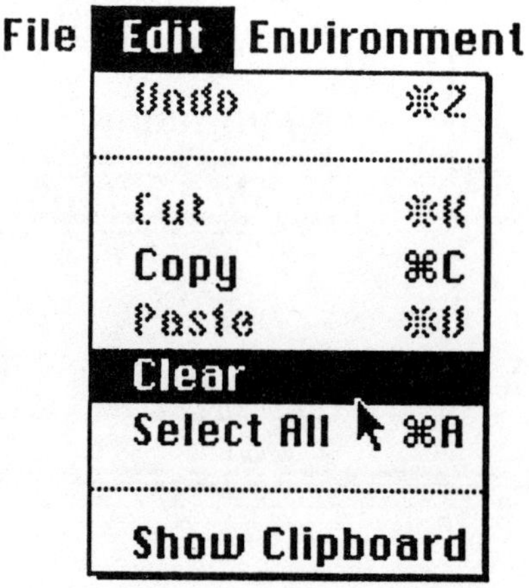

Enter. Pressing the Enter key signifies that you are through entering a record. Press Enter (or click the Enter button on 4th Dimension's control panel) each time you finish typing in a record, even if it is the last one for entry.

Now type in the following customer information. Each comma separates a field, so remember to press the Tab key each time you complete a field entry.

```
Wellhouse, Max, 76 Park Street #10, Baton Rouge, LA, 70815, 12
```

Before you complete this first entry, you will encounter a problem. When you try to enter the 70815 ZIP Code, 4th Dimension displays a dialog box stating that integer values must be between 32,767 and −32,768. This is one reason the User mode is so useful: you can experiment with the database and discover any errors that might be in it.

One thing you might do is change the ZIP Code field from an Integer type to a Long Integer type (which would make codes greater than 32767 acceptable). When you encounter an error, however, you should take a minute to make sure your correction will be appropriate. There are some ZIP codes that begin with a zero (like 02342). Neither the Integer nor the Long Integer will retain the zero, since any zeros that begin a number are truncated (cut out). Therefore, a number like 02342 would automatically be made 2342, which is not the ZIP code you entered.

A better choice for the ZIP Code field would be Alpha, since that will not alter the digits or have any numeric limits:

1. Click the Cancel button to get out of Entry mode, then select the Design mode from the Environment menu. The Structure window for the Customers file will be displayed.
2. Double-click the ZIP Code field, then change its type to Alpha. In the box to the right of Alpha, enter the number 10, since no ZIP codes will be more than 10 characters long.
3. Click the OK button to complete the change, then return to the User environment.

Now you're ready to enter the records again. You have to start at the beginning since you cancelled the entry of the first record, so press Command-N to begin entering new records. Here are the sixteen records to enter:

```
Wellhouse, Max, 76 Park Street #10, Baton Rouge, LA, 70815, 12
Fresco, Al, 56 El Camino Real, Sunnyvale, CA, 95423, 5
Pending, Pat, 5000 Laura Street, Minneapolis, MN, 45623, 9
Atrick, Jerry, 8000 Stinson Way, Palos Verdes, CA, 90023, 82
Baum, Alice, 76 Boston Way, Tigard, OR, 97223, 34
Smith, John, 4 Plain Blvd., Davenport, IA, 54023, 6
Smith, Sam, 700 Pensacola Lane, Sarasota Springs, FL, 32311, 21
```

```
Kay, Otis, 3 Main Street, Belford, MO, 52367, 64
Syrup, Mabel, 7 Smokey Way, Burlington, VT, 23418, 44
Teak, Anne, 71456 Billway, Otis, MD, 04556, 2
Board, Bill, 10 Fieldbrook Place, Morgana, CO, 87232, 7
Byrne, Tina, 21 Turner Hall Lane, New York, NY, 10023, 93
Smith, Fran, 23 Appian Way, Fairbanks, AK, 99234, 66
Jenkins, Anthony, 44 Millhouse Row, St. Louis, MO, 45221, 17
Brown, William, 9823 Leslie Lane, Biloxi, MI, 74133, 105
LaFrance, Viva, 4 Aloha Way, Beachtown, HI, 99872, 51
```

When 4th Dimension displays the input layout for the seventeenth time, click the Cancel button. The program now shows you the information you entered with the Customer Output layout, as shown in Figure 2-14. Not all the fields are displayed, of course, since this output does not contain all of the fields.

MODIFYING RECORDS

Now that the basic information for the sixteen records is displayed, you can modify any of them. The modification process is quite simple: (1) select a record

FIGURE 2-14.   All the records for Customers are displayed in order of entry.

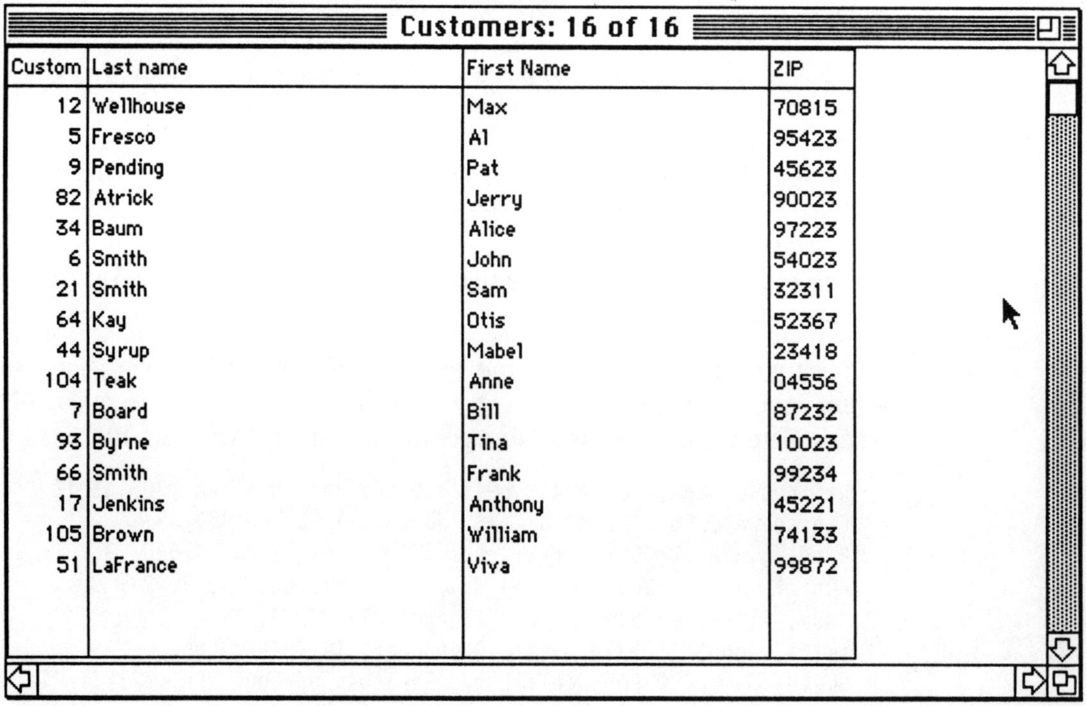

Custom	Last name	First Name	ZIP
12	Wellhouse	Max	70815
5	Fresco	Al	95423
9	Pending	Pat	45623
82	Atrick	Jerry	90023
34	Baum	Alice	97223
6	Smith	John	54023
21	Smith	Sam	32311
64	Kay	Otis	52367
44	Syrup	Mabel	23418
104	Teak	Anne	04556
7	Board	Bill	87232
93	Byrne	Tina	10023
66	Smith	Frank	99234
17	Jenkins	Anthony	45221
105	Brown	William	74133
51	LaFrance	Viva	99872

Customers: 16 of 16

by pointing to it and clicking the mouse button, (2) choose the Modify Record command from the Enter menu or press the keyboard equivalent, Command-M, and (3) that record is then displayed in the input layout format.

Suppose you have discovered that Anne Teak lives in Otisburg, not Otis, and that her Customer Number is wrong. Select Anne's record, then choose Modify Record from the menu or keyboard. The Customer Input layout is used as the modification form, as shown in Figure 2-15, and Anne Teak's information is loaded into memory.

There are two ways to get to the field you want to modify: you can use Tab or Shift-Tab until you reach the City field, or you can point to that field and click the mouse button. Use either way to get there (remember that either technique can also be used when you are entering new records).

There are also two ways to change the contents of this field. You can now type Otisburg from the keyboard, which eliminates the old city name and replaces it with the new one. Or you can point to the part of the field you want to change and click the mouse button. In this case, point to the end of the name Otis and click the mouse button once. A text cursor should now be at the end of the field, and you can type in **burg** at the end of "Otis" to make the name correct. As you can see, all the text-editing capabilities you are familiar with on the Macintosh apply in 4th Dimension.

Now move down to the customer number. Change the number 2 to **105**, then press Enter. 4th Dimension displays an alarm box that states, "This key already exists," which means that customer number 105 is taken. Remember that customer numbers have the Unique field attribute, which allows only one

FIGURE 2-15.   You can modify any record within this layout.

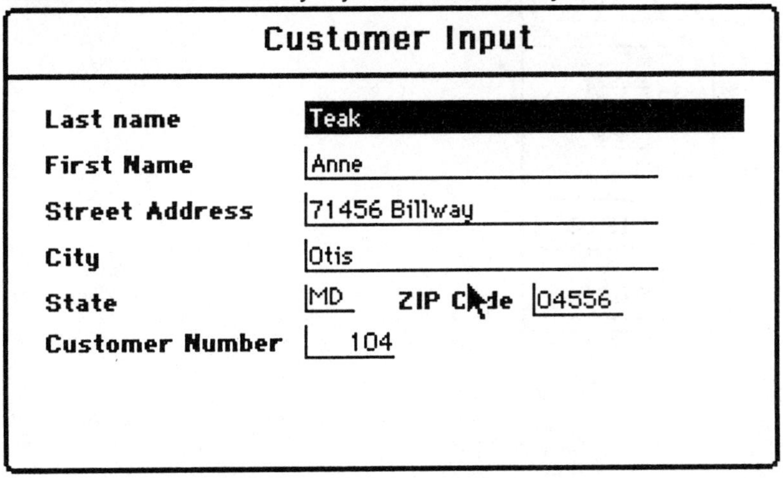

unique customer number per record. This safety check has warned you to use a different number, so click OK and enter the number 104.

Before pressing Enter, take a look at the control panel on the left side of the screen. When you were entering records, not all of the control panel was highlighted. Now that it is, take a look at each element, as shown in Figure 2-16:

Enter. The equivalent of the Enter key on the keyboard, this button lets you complete a record entry.

Right-pointing arrow. Clicking this element moves you forward one record in the database.

#1 icon. Clicking this element moves you to the first record in the database.

Left-pointing arrow. Clicking this element moves you backward one record in the database.

Delete. Clicking this element deletes the current record.

Cancel. This element cancels the dialog box. If you click Cancel, the contents of the layout on that screen (whether they are modifications or a new entry) will not be saved.

Click the right-pointing arrow to move one record ahead, and Bill Board's record should appear. Use the arrows and the #1 icon for awhile to understand how to move through the records. When you are through, click the Cancel key to get back to the output display of all the records.

FIGURE 2-16.   The control panel is highlighted when you modify records.

SORTING RECORDS

Sorting is one of the easiest to use and most powerful features in 4th Dimension. You can sort records based on the contents of individual fields, and those sorts can be in ascending or descending order. An ascending sort of the alphabet would be A, B, C . . . and of numbers would be 1, 2, 3. . . . A descending sort, conversely, would be B, C, A for the alphabet and 3, 2, 1 for numbers.

You can sort based on the contents of more than one field, which is extremely useful for large databases. Sort doesn't seem terribly useful with only sixteen records entered, but you can get a good idea how to use it.

First, choose the Sort command from the Select menu. The Sort dialog box appears, displaying the field names on the left and a set of empty sort field cells on the right. Within those sort field cells, you can tell 4th Dimension which fields to sort, whether the sort should be ascending or descending, and the precedence of the fields during the sort.

Point to the field name Last Name and click the mouse button. Last Name appears in the top sort field cell, and an upward-pointing arrow is next to it. This ascending symbol indicates that the sort of the last names will be in ascending order. Point to the arrow and click the mouse button a few times. The arrow toggles between pointing up and pointing down each time you click it. Make sure it is back to upward-pointing when you are through.

Click the Customer Number field so it appears beneath Last Name, and your Sort dialog box should resemble Figure 2-17. This ensures that if there are several customers with the same last name, they will be sorted by Customer Number. There are several Smiths in this database, so when 4th Dimension encounters those names, it will apply this second sort criterion and sort those names by customer number in ascending order.

You can add as many fields as you want in these cells, and any one of them can have an ascending or descending arrow. Since there are only sixteen records in the file right now, there's no need to have more than two fields used as sort fields. Click the Sort button, and 4th Dimension displays the sorted list of records using the output layout, as shown in Figure 2-18.

This reorganization of the file makes it much easier to examine. Try using the Sort command several more times with different sort fields. The ZIP Code and the Customer Number, for example, would be two different sorts that might be helpful. Experiment with Sort to understand how the ascending and descending arrows work and how useful certain fields can be to information organization.

FIGURE 2-17.   The Sort dialog box contains two fields that will be used to sort the file in ascending order.

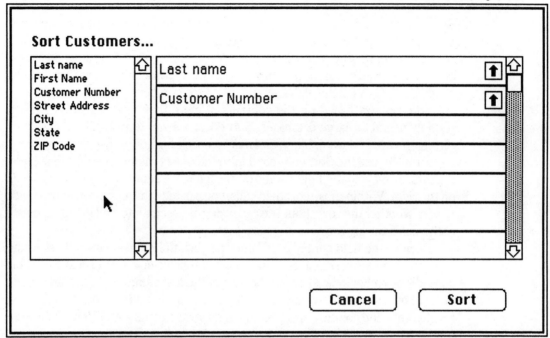

Sort Customers...

| Last name |
| First Name |
| Customer Number |
| Street Address |
| City |
| State |
| ZIP Code |

Last name

Customer Number

Cancel   Sort

FIGURE 2-18.   All the records have been sorted based on the contents of the sort fields. Notice in particular the three Smith records.

Custom	Last name	First Name	ZIP
82	Atrick	Jerry	90023
34	Baum	Alice	97223
7	Board	Bill	87232
105	Brown	William	74133
93	Byrne	Tina	10023
5	Fresco	Al	95423
17	Jenkins	Anthony	45221
64	Kay	Otis	52367
51	LaFrance	Viva	99872
9	Pending	Pat	45623
6	Smith	John	54023
21	Smith	Sam	32311
66	Smith	Frank	99234
44	Syrup	Mabel	23418
104	Teak	Anne	04556
12	Wellhouse	Max	70815

Isolating Information: Searches and Subfiles

In this chapter you will learn how to isolate information from the main file. This isolation can take two forms: the information can be contained in a subfile, or you can give 4th Dimension instructions for which data to isolate by performing a search on the data. These are two very different types of isolation, so they will be examined one at a time.

SEARCHING IN 4TH DIMENSION

On the 4th Dimension screen, you should see all sixteen customer records listed in the output file. At the top of the screen is the title Customers: 16 of 16, which indicates that all sixteen of the sixteen records in the file Customers are being displayed.

When you have a large amount of data, it is useful to extract data that meet certain criteria. For example, if you have a list of thousands of customers, you might want to send customers in New York a special catalog featuring products that would appeal to people living in that state. On the other hand, if your database had the salaries of all your customers, you might want to send information only to customers who earn a salary above a certain amount.

4th Dimension makes it easy to select records from a database based on a multitude of criteria. You can specify conditions that any of the fields must meet, and you can link together conditions with logical operators. For instance, you might instruct 4th Dimension to select all the records with the Last Name field equal to "Smith" *and* the ZIP Code greater than 5000 *or* the Salary less than 40,000. You will learn more about how this logic works shortly.

PERFORMING A SEARCH

Move the pointer to the Select menu, where there are three Search commands. This section deals with the *Search..* command and the *Search and Modify..* command. Later you will learn how to use the more complex *Search by Formula..* command. Choose Search, and in a moment the Search editor appears on the screen, as shown in Figure 3-1.

Before exploring this editor fully, try doing a simple search. Suppose you wanted to find all customers whose last name was Smith. You would do the following:

1. Click the Last Name field in the Customers list. The name of this field appears in the editor text area.

FIGURE 3-1. The Search editor lets you establish search criteria.

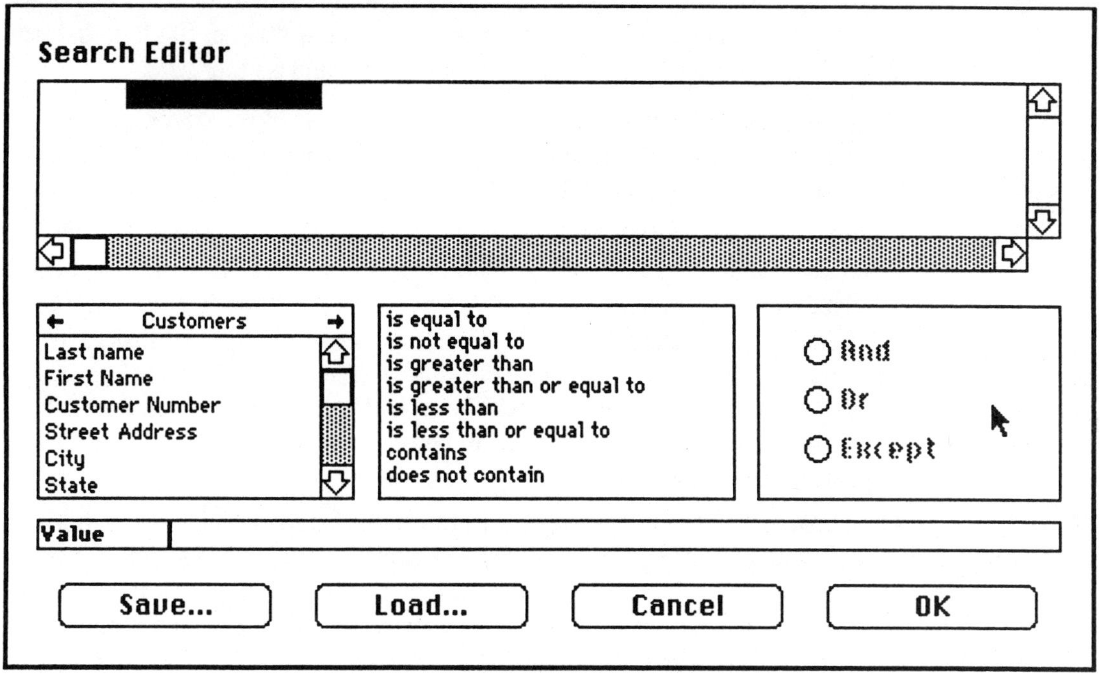

Search Editor

← Customers →	is equal to	
Last name	is not equal to	◯ And
First Name	is greater than	
Customer Number	is greater than or equal to	◯ Or
Street Address	is less than	
City	is less than or equal to	◯ Except
State	contains	
	does not contain	

Value

[**Save...**] [**Load...**] [**Cancel**] [**OK**]

2. Click the is equal to operator in the middle box. Again, what you click appears in the text editor area.
3. Type in Smith. This name appears in the Value box.

Your Search editor should resemble Figure 3-2. You have entered the field name, the operator, and the value by clicking and typing, and the resulting search function is in the Editor text window.

Click OK. 4th Dimension displays the three customers it found with Smith in the Last Name field: John Smith, Sam Smith, and Frank Smith.

FIGURE 3-2. The search function after entry.
Search Editor

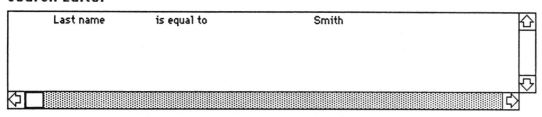

Last name	is equal to	Smith

COMPONENTS OF THE SEARCH EDITOR

There are six main areas in the Search editor: the text area, the field list, the operator list, the conjunction area, the value area, and buttons.

Text area. Also known as the criteria area, this part of the editor displays the criteria you have created or loaded from the disk. In this part of the screen, you enter and edit text as you normally would. You can also watch your criteria for the search develop as you select and type in different items from the editor.

Field list. This area lists all the field names in the file. For the Customers database, it includes Last Name, First Name, Customer Number, Street Address, City, State, and ZIP Code. You can scroll this list if there is not enough room to show all the fields and you need to select one that is not visible. You cannot select a field from subfiles, which you will learn about later in this chapter. Searches can be performed only on fields within the parent (that is, the main) file.

Operator area. Click on one of the items in this list to establish restrictions on the search. Each operator is fairly self-explanatory: *is equal to*, *is not equal to*, *is greater than*, *is greater than or equal to*, *is less than*, *is less than or equal to*, *contains*, and *does not contain*. These work with both text and numbers, so Jones *is less than* Smith, and ABCDE *contains* ABC. Here are a few examples of these operators:

- *is equal to*
  SMITH is equal to Smith
  123 is equal to 123
- *is not equal to*
  Jones is not equal to Harrison
  540 is not equal to 539
- *is greater than*
  Zebra is greater than Alphabet
  500 is greater than 100
- *is greater than or equal to*
  Hello There is greater than or equal to Hello There
  600 is greater than or equal to 10
- *is less than*
  Cow is less than Kangaroo
  12 is less than 15

- *is less than or equal to*
     Bridge is less than or equal to Broom
     5000 is less than or equal to 5001
- *contains*
     New York contains New
     70815 contains 81
- *does not contain*
     Minneapolis does not contain Old
     3001 does not contain 6

As with the field list, you only have to click the operator you want for it to be selected and to appear in the text area.

Conjunction Area. You can click a radio button in this area for one of the three conjunctions, *And*, *Or*, or *Except*. These conjunctions connect sets of criteria. Suppose you want to select all the customers with the last name James and the first name Edward. Enter

```
    Last Name is equal to James
And First Name is equal to Edward
```

If you want to add everyone with the last name of Brown to this list, the text area would look like this:

```
    Last Name is equal to James
And First Name is equal to Edward
Or  Last Name is equal to Brown
```

4th Dimension uses the conjunctions to select the records that have

- a last name equal to James *and* a first name equal to Edward
                              OR
- a last name equal to Brown

Notice that the two logical constructs are considered separately: the Or *separates* the second and third logical decisions, whereas the And *combines* the first and second logical decisions.

Value area. This is where you enter the values that you are using to restrict the search. The value follows the operator, so that 4th Dimension looks for the value in the field you specified using the operator you specified.

Buttons. There are four buttons near the bottom of the search editor:

- SAVE. . . saves the search criteria you have entered. If you create an especially complex set of criteria, it might save you time and effort later to save the string under an appropriate name.
- LOAD. . . loads in a set of search criteria from the disk.
- CANCEL removes the Search editor from the screen and eliminates any search criteria you have entered.
- OK tells 4th Dimension to proceed with the search that you have programmed.

PUTTING SEARCH TO WORK

The sixteen records you have entered so far are really insufficient to give you an understanding of the Search command. So load the Personnel database provided with the 4th Dimension package. When you open the Personnel database, the Customers database will be closed, but any changes you have made will be saved. Do the following to load the Personnel database:

1. Choose the Show All command from the Select menu so that all of the records are displayed again.
2. Choose Open Database from the File menu and find the Personnel folder. Double-click Personnel to open that database.
3. When 4th Dimension asks for the password, type Manager, then press Return. Passwords are case sensitive, so make the M uppercase and all the other letters lowercase.
4. Select Quit from the file menu to get from Custom mode to User mode. A list of seventy-six names will be on the screen.

You can now make selections from these seventy-six names. Say you want to get a list of all the employees with employee numbers greater than or equal to 50 who have salaries of $35,000 or less and who do not work in the department named ACCT2. To commence this search,

1. Choose the Search command. The box around the list of fields is blinking on and off, indicating that you should click in that box. Point to the field name Employee Number and click the mouse button once.
2. Click is greater than or equal to in the operator area, then type **50** and press Return.

3. Click the conjunction button And to logically pair the criteria you just entered and the criteria you are about to enter.
4. Click the field name Salary, then the operator is less than or equal to. Enter **35000** and press Return.
5. Since you don't want employees in the ACCT2 department included, click on the Except conjunction, Department Code, then the operator is equal to. Enter **ACCT2**.

Your search text editor should resemble Figure 3-3. Notice that when you click on a conjunction button, 4th Dimension automatically goes to the next line. This is to make the text easier to read and the logical flow easier to understand. In this case, the first and second lines are connected with the logical And, and the third line modifies the second line by telling the editor not to include employees whose field name is equal to ACCT2.

Click the OK button, and the search begins. A "thermometer" appears on the screen to indicate how far in the search 4th Dimension has progressed. For complex searches in large databases, the thermometer is a helpful indicator of how much longer you have to wait until the search is through. Most of the time, it will be on the screen for only a few moments. Your screen should now have fifteen of the seventy-six names listed, all of which met the criteria you gave the computer.

Choose the Search command again from the Select menu. Notice that your old search string is no longer there. You can see why the Save and Load buttons might be helpful if you are performing complex searches, because 4th Dimension does not retain old criteria after a search has been performed.

Now you are going to enter a more complex search string. Use the following table to enter the criteria:

FIGURE 3-3. This search function uses two conjunctions to connect three lines of criteria.

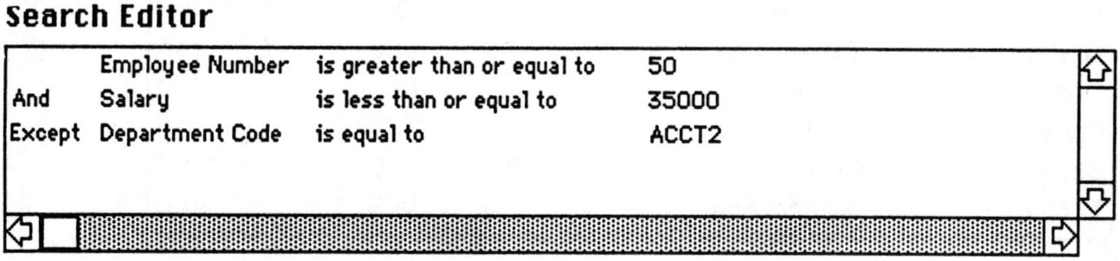

Search Editor

	Employee Number	is greater than or equal to	50
And	Salary	is less than or equal to	35000
Except	Department Code	is equal to	ACCT2

Conjunction	Field name	Operator	Value
	Department Code	is equal to	DES
And	Salary	is greater than	25000
Or	Department Code	is equal to	ADMN
And	Salary	is greater than	25000
Except	Employee Number	is less than or equal to	3

This search string will find employees who (1) are in the DES department and who earn greater than $25,000, along with (2) employees in the ADMN department who earn more than $25,000, except for those with employee numbers 1, 2, or 3. Notice that the Or separates the first two lines from the last three lines. 4th Dimension selects employees who meet the criteria in lines 1 and 2 *or* those who meet the criteria in lines 3, 4, and 5.

Now that the string is entered, click the OK button. In a few moments, eighteen of the seventy-six employees will be listed, as shown in Figure 3-4.

FIGURE 3-4.   List of the eighteen out of seventy-six employees who meet the criteria entered.

First Name	Last Name	Empl. Number	Dept. Code	Salary
Wanda	Matthewson	26	ADMN	$25,260
Dave	Walden	27	DES	$27,250
Tyler	Williams	10	DES	$41,550
Bill	Donaldson	11	DES	$31,500
John	Jorgenson	14	DES	$27,545
Frank	Adler	19	DES	$29,750
Jonathan	Patell	30	ADMN	$31,100
Andy	Brown	34	DES	$28,750
Frederich	Burgess	38	ADMN	$28,000
William A	Crown	40	DES	$27,060
Carl Z	Edwards	46	DES	$25,850
Susan R	Fennel	49	ADMN	$25,330
Sally E	Fell	51	DES	$35,250
Thomas C	Hildebrand	58	DES	$33,250

Employees: 18 of 76

SEARCH AND MODIFY

The Search command selects those records that meet certain criteria. The Search and Modify command lets you modify any of those records. Search and Modify lets you perform a basic search on the file, then it gives you access to the same window encountered with the Modify command, in which you can change any of the information in the record.

Choose the Search and Modify command. The Search and Modify dialog box appears. This box shows all the indexed fields, in this case, Employee Number, Last Name, and First Name. You can enter what you are looking for in any of these fields. For example, suppose you want to modify the record of a man with the last name Brown. Type the name **Brown** in the Last Name field box, as shown in Figure 3-5, then click OK.

Soon an Entry dialog box appears on the screen. Change this record so that Andy Brown's salary is $33,000, as shown in Figure 3-6. In this case, there is only one employee named Brown. Had there been more, you could have sorted

FIGURE 3-5.   Entering the name Brown will bring up all the records with Brown in the Last Name field.

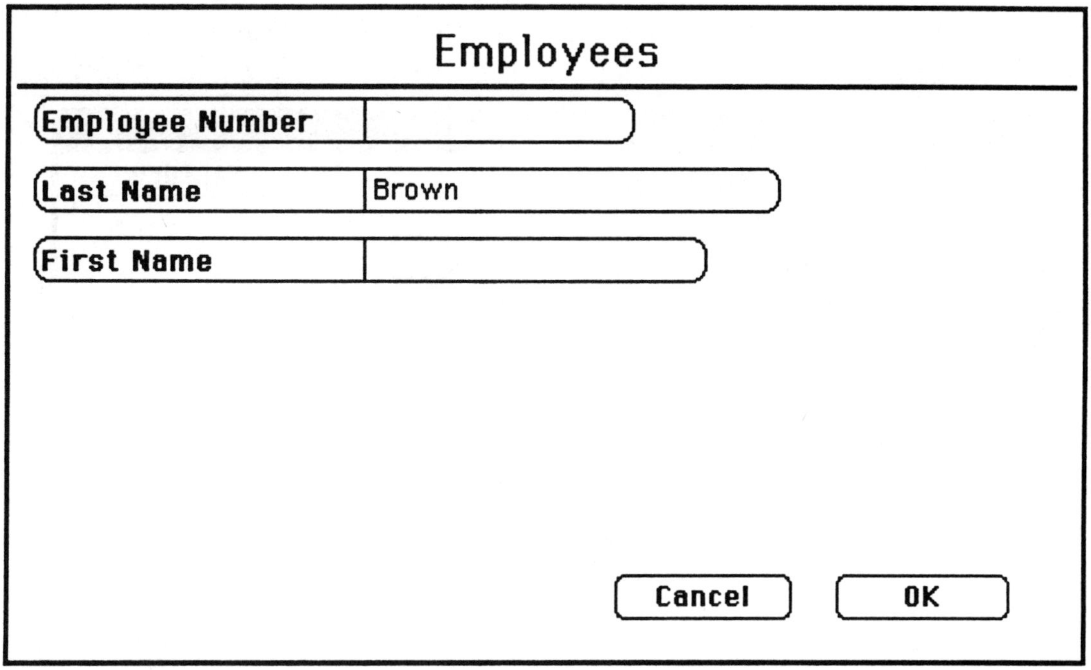

through the records using the record selection arrow icons. Because Andy Brown is the only employee named Brown, click Enter. You are returned to the output list, which now has only one name in it: Andy Brown.

WILDCARD AND OTHER NOTES ABOUT SEARCHING

Up to now, you have told 4th Dimension exactly what you wanted to find by typing in the contents you were looking for in a certain field. There is a "wildcard" character in 4th Dimension that is helpful if you are uncertain how to spell what you are looking for or if you want to make a broader search. The at character (@) is the wildcard, and by entering it by itself or in conjunction with other characters, you can make the search process easier.

For instance, suppose you want to search through all of the records whose city names began with the word New. By entering **New@** in the City field, you instruct 4th Dimension to locate all the records with names like New York, New Haven, Newport News, and Newton. Any names in that field that begin with the three letters New qualify. The wildcard character *cannot* be used with integer, long integer, or real fields.

FIGURE 3-6. You can modify this record that has been retrieved by the Sort and Modify command.

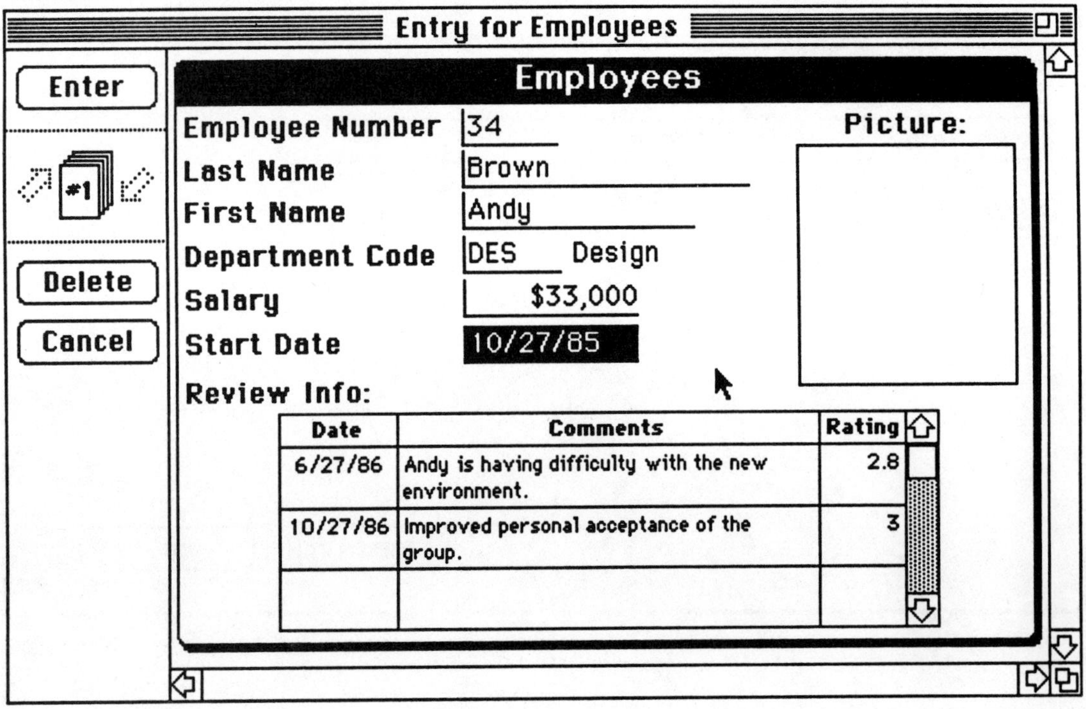

If the wildcard is used by itself, every record will be selected (assuming, of course, there are no other criteria for other fields). You can use @ to replace any character or characters — Br@, Minn@s, and @burg are all examples of acceptable field entries. The wildcard has many applications, both when searching and in other areas of 4th Dimension:

- Wildcard is helpful if you aren't sure how a word is spelled. For example, say you are looking for someone named Carrie in the employee's file First Name field, and you're not sure if her name is spelled Carrie or Cary. An easy way around this is to enter **Ca@** in the first name field so that 4th Dimension will find everyone with first names that begin with Ca. Of course, Calvin, Carl, and other names meet that criterion, so narrow the search further by entering **Car@** instead.
- If for some reason you want to make a very broad search (like the New example given earlier), place the wildcard in the spot where the character content does not matter. For instance, to get the records of every person whose last name begins with O', enter **O'@**. O'Connor, O'Malley, and all the other O' names will be displayed or ready for modification (depending on the command you chose).
- In different parts of 4th Dimension, such as linking fields and procedure programming, the @ wildcard symbol can be a useful tool if you need help looking for a particular name or function.

When you are searching in 4th Dimension, keep in mind that there is no difference between uppercase and lowercase letters. Some aspects of 4th Dimension are case sensitive (such as passwords), but when searching, it doesn't matter what case you use. Entering the name JONES in a Last Name field, for instance, retrieves JONES, Jones, jones, joNES, and any other combination of uppercase and lowercase letters as long as those letters are j, o, n, e, and s.

Finally, when you are using the wildcard character on indexed fields (as in the Search and Modify dialog box), use it only at the end of the text you enter, since that is all 4th Dimension allows. The wildcard entry West @, for example, would be fine, but Por@and would not be acceptable in an indexed field search.

SUBFILES

The Customers database currently is made up of a single file called Customers, which contains basic data about some imaginary customers. Now you are going to add another part to this database called a subfile, which is a file separate from Customers that will contain fields of its own.

First, you need to get back to the Customers database. Choose Open Database from the File menu, then find Customers and double-click it. The Structure window on the screen shows the Customers file and all of its fields. You are going to add a new field to the customers file, so select the Customers file by clicking it, then select New Field (or press the keyboard equivalent, Command-F).

To add a subfile to Customers, follow these steps:

1. Select the field type Subfile. Notice that all of the attribute radio buttons become gray, indicating that none of them can be selected for this field type.
2. Type Meetings, which will be the name of this subfile. The purpose of this subfile is to keep a history of meetings with customers made in the process of selling or maintaining equipment.
3. Click OK. In the Structure window, you will see the Meetings field name in the Customers file and an asterisk next to it, indicating it is a subfile. Descending from that asterisk is a line that goes down to the box representing the subfile.
4. The subfile box Meetings is empty, as shown in Figure 3-7, since there are no fields in it yet. If you can't see all of the subfile, select it and drag it to a position where you can see both Customers and Meetings.

FIGURE 3-7.   The subfile is attached with a line to the parent file. You can reposition any file in the Structure window by dragging it.

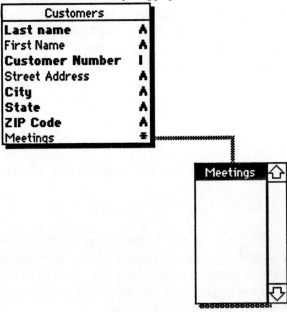

You have just created a subfile called Meetings, which, as already mentioned, will keep a history of the meetings your imaginary company has with customers.

Before going on, you should understand what it is you have just created. A subfile is not an independent file; instead, it is attached to a parent file, which in this case is Customers. In fact, a subfile can have a subfile of its own, and there can be as many as five subfiles attached in a chain descending off the parent file. In actual use, it's unlikely that you would ever need a multitude of attached subfiles like that, but that feature is available if you need it.

Creating a subfile consists simply of making a field type Subfile. After a subfile is created, you must create fields for it and include the information in the subfile within the layouts of the main file. The subfile is best suited for keeping information where the number of items is uncertain (a list is a good example). In this case, the subfile will be used to keep a history of meetings. Some customers may have never met with you before, whereas others might have ten, twenty, or even more meetings on record.

It would be impractical and inconvenient to make a series of fields dedicated to a list like this (with text fields Meeting One, Meeting Two, Meeting Three, and so on), so a subfile is a convenient solution. There are disadvantages to subfiles, however. They can consume a lot of memory, and you can access them only through the parent file (which means you can't perform a search on a subfile). The best practice is to create subfiles only for information that demands multiple entries.

FIELDS IN THE SUBFILE

Adding fields to a subfile is just as easy as adding fields to a regular file. Just click the subfile and select New Field, then put these fields into the subfile:

Name	Type	Attributes	Other
Date	Date	Mandatory	
Purpose	Alpha (15)	Mandatory	
		Standard Choices:	Cold Call
			Referral
			Maintenance
			Information
			Training
			Closing
Notes	Text		

When you enter the Standard Choices, check the Choices can be modified box and click on the Sort button. After entering the Notes field, click OK. Your subfile should have the three field names in it with their respective field types: D (Date), A (Alpha), and T (Text).

MAKING SUBFILE LAYOUTS

Subfile layouts are created for inclusion in normal file layouts, but creating the subfile layouts properly is important to easy data entry and readable data output. Select Layout from the Design window, and the Layout dialog box appears on the screen with the name of the file Customers in bold letters. Double-click this file name, and below it will appear the names of its two layouts, Customer Input and Customer Output.

Also notice that a third item is on the list in bold characters: the subfile name Meetings. Select this name, then type in the name for the first layout you will create: Mtg. Input. If the dialog box resembles Figure 3-8, click the New button to create the new layout.

FIGURE 3-8.   Select the subfile name, type in the layout name, then click New.

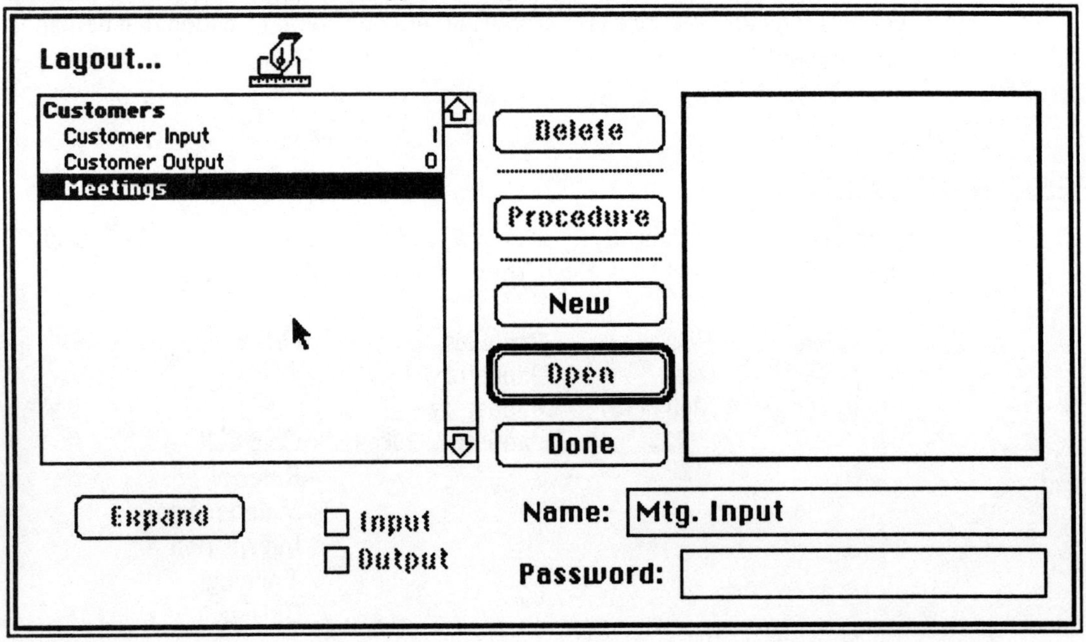

The defaults in the new layout box are adequate for this layout, so click OK. The layout window appears with the Meetings layout window in place. This layout will be used each time you want to enter information about an individual meeting. Unfortunately, the area allocated for the Notes field isn't very big. Even though you enter plenty of text in this field, it will be cumbersome to enter notes properly when you can see only one line at a time. Therefore, you should expand the area for Notes:

1. Select the rounded rectangle that is the border of the layout. Drag the bottom so the border is about one inch taller.
2. Next, select the rectangle that is underneath the Notes field. Remember that this can be difficult, so position the pointer carefully, click the mouse button, then drag the bottom of the rectangle so it is about one inch taller.
3. Finally, click the Notes field and drag the rectangle that defines it so it matches the rectangle beneath it. The rectangle graphic underneath the field should "peek through" a little on the left edge and the bottom edge so that when this layout is on the screen, you know where the field is located based on the rectangle. Your layout should closely resemble Figure 3-9.

You are through with the Mtg. Input layout for now, so click the Close box. Now it's time to create the output layout, so select Layout from the Design menu again, then expand the list of layouts so you can select the Meetings subfile. Enter the name of the new layout, Mtg. Output, and click New.

FIGURE 3-9.   The Mtg. Input layout now has an expanded Notes field for easier data entry.

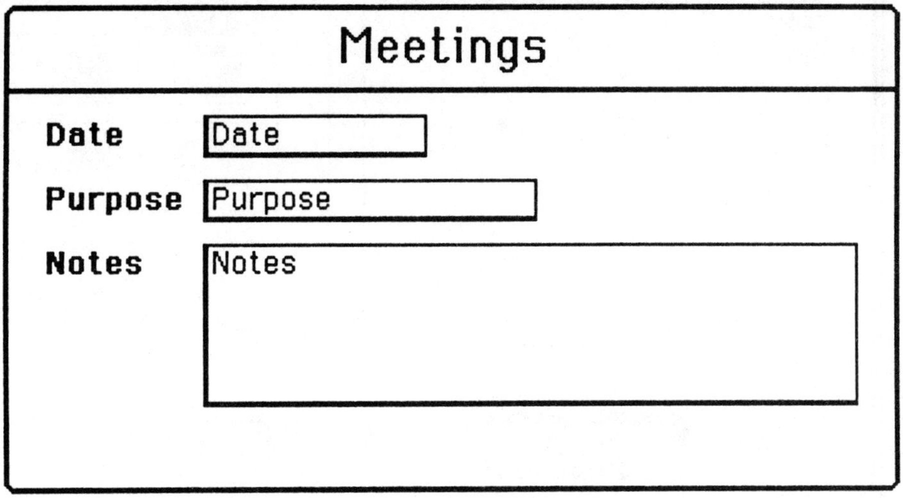

This time you have to make a few changes to the new Layout dialog box. First, select the 9-point font size so this layout is as compact as possible. Next, choose the selection in the upper left corner for the layout type and double-click the Date field name, then the Purpose field name. Your new Layout dialog box should look like Figure 3-10. Click OK to proceed.

When the Mtg. Output layout appears, you will see it is very small. The reason for making it small is because it will be part of the Customer Input layout, and you don't want to crowd out the other elements already there.

INCLUDED LAYOUTS

An included layout is a layout that is made a part of another layout. Included layouts are important for subfiles, since you will want the information from subfiles to be entered (input) and displayed (output) from the parent file's layout.

FIGURE 3-10.   The output layout will be more compact than the input layout.

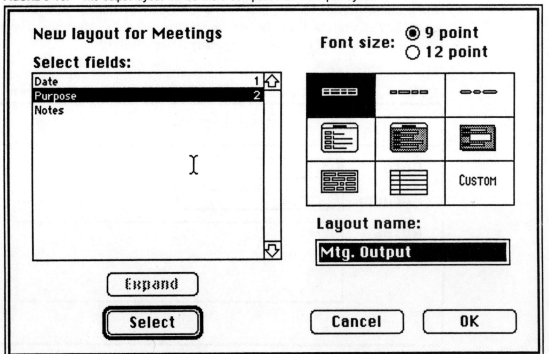

In this case, you are going to include both the Mtg. Input and the Mtg. Output layouts in the Customer Input layout. They will not be side by side. Instead, only one of them will be displayed, based on the following rules:

- When the Customer Input layout first appears on the screen, the Mtg. Output layout is included. This means that the dates and the purposes of all the meetings are immediately visible in the Customer Input layout, and the user can scroll up and down this list to see the date and the purpose of any meeting. This is called a multi-line layout, since multiple lines (that is, a scrollable list) is on the screen.
- If the user points to the area of the included layout and double-clicks the mouse button, the Customer Input layout disappears and is replaced by the Mtg. Input layout. This is called a full-page layout, since the whole page of Mtg. Input is on the screen. Once information has been entered into this layout, the user clicks Enter and is returned to the Customer Input layout.

In general, the user inputs information by double-clicking the included layout and entering the information on the full-page layout, and the user can view the output of previous meetings by using the scrollable list.

CREATING AN INCLUDED LAYOUT

The first thing to do when including a layout is to allocate enough space for it. One fast and easy way to do this is to draw a rectangle over the layout that will be displayed, copy that rectangle to the main layout, and then create the included layout using that much room.

Follow these steps to include the Mtg. Output layout in the Customer Input layout:

1. Load the Mtg. Output layout into memory and select the rectangle icon (the third icon down on the right side of the tool box).
2. Position the crosshairs so they are exactly in the lower right corner of the Mtg. Output layout and draw a rectangle so it completely covers this layout, as shown in Figure 3-11. The rectangle should be as close to the size of the Mtg. Output layout as possible so it is an accurate representation of the layout's size.
3. Press Command-X on the keyboard so that the rectangle is cut from the layout and moved to the Macintosh's Clipboard.
4. Close the Mtg. Output layout and open the Customer Input layout.
5. Drag the three arrows on the right side of the layout down to about 250 so there is enough room to expand this layout.
6. Select the rounded rectangle that forms the border of this layout, and drag its bottom down so that the layout resembles Figure 3-12.

FIGURE 3-11.   Make the rectangle exactly the same size as the layout so the layout is completely covered.

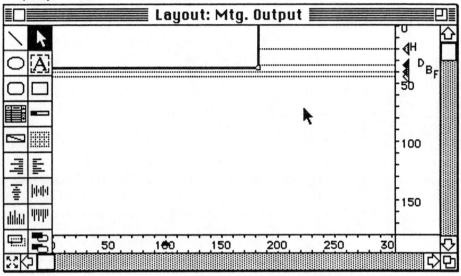

FIGURE 3-12.   Drag the arrows down, then increase the height of the rounded rectangle.

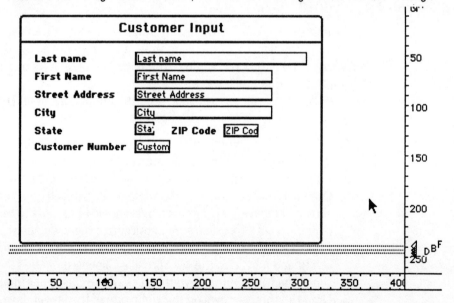

7. Press Command-V to make the rectangle appear in the layout. Drag the rectangle to the empty space you just created by expanding the Customer Input layout.
8. Now you are ready to set up the included layout. Select the Include Layout icon in the toolbox (as shown in Figure 3-13) and position the crosshairs in the upper left corner of the rectangle you just pasted onto the layout.
9. Hold down the mouse button and drag the mouse so that a rectangle is formed that perfectly covers the graphic rectangle. When you release the mouse button, the Include Layout dialog box appears.

THE INCLUDE LAYOUT DIALOG BOX

Now that you are in the Include Layout dialog box, you can tell 4th Dimension which layouts to include and what formats they should take. The only subfile you have created in this database is Meetings, so that subfile name appears in bold at the top of the list.

FIGURE 3-13.   Select the Include Layout icon, which is the fourth one down on the left side of the toolbox, and position the crosshairs as shown.

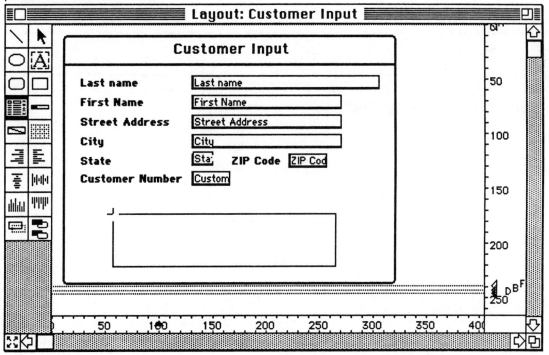

Point to the Select button and click the mouse button. An asterisk appears next to the subfile name Meetings, indicating that the layouts of this file will be included in another file. Double-click Meetings (or click the Expand button) to see the layouts available, which are Mtg. Input and Mtg. Output.

First, select Mtg. Input. This will be the full-page input so that clicking the included layout area will make the Mtg. Input layout replace the Customer Input layout during data entry. Therefore, click the Full Page check box. The letter F appears next to Mtg. Input.

Now select the name Mtg. Output. This will be the multiple-line layout so that a scrollable list of meeting dates and purposes is available. Click Multi-line, and the letter M appears next to Mtg. Output, as shown in Figure 3-14.

You are now through with this dialog box, so click OK. When you are returned to the Customer Input layout, your included layout box has the word Meetings in it, indicating that the subfile Meetings is included in the Customer Input layout in that location.

When a person is actually using the database, there will be nothing in the layout box except a blank listing (or nonblank, should there be subrecords in it).

FIGURE 3-14. The layouts have been designated as Full Page and Multi-line in the Included Layout dialog box.

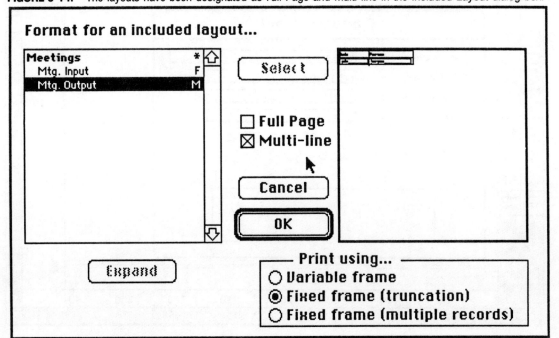

Nevertheless, it will not be clear what the purpose of the list box is. To alleviate this, add the title Past Meetings: just about the included layout, as shown in Figure 3-15. To do this,

1. Select the text icon, which has the capital letter A in it.
2. Hold down the mouse button and drag the crosshairs over the area where the Past Meetings: title will be to form a rectangle. The rectangle should be big enough to enclose the entire title.
3. Point inside the rectangle you just formed and click the mouse button once. Select Bold from the Style menu so the text will be boldfaced.
4. Enter the title Past Meetings:.
5. Reposition the title by dragging it around the screen until you are satisfied with its position.

You have now finished including the subfile's layouts in the Customer Input layout. As you can see, it isn't that difficult to do, and the applications for subfiles can be numerous. Before completing this chapter, give your new subfile a try.

FIGURE 3-15. Position the title Past Meetings: above and to the left of the included layout box.

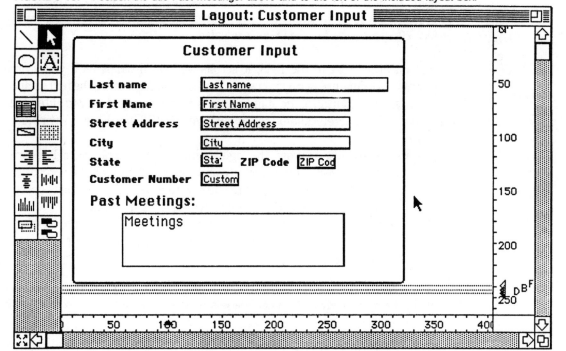

USING THE SUBFILE

Switch to the User environment, then select the record for Max Wellhouse (which should be at the top of the customer list). Press Command-M to modify this record, and you will see the Customer Input screen with a blank list at the bottom. Eventually this list might be full of meeting information, but now there are no subrecords in it. (A complete set of information in a file is called a record; a complete set of information in a subfile is called a subrecord.)

To get to the subrecord, press Command-Tab. You can get to the subrecord with Command-Tab no matter which field the cursor is in. When you do, the date 00/00/00 should be displayed and selected.

Since you want to input some information, point to this date (this is the subrecord you want to input) and double-click the mouse button. The Mtg. Input layout appears on the screen, and you can enter information in all three fields. Had you stayed in the Customer Input layout, you could still have input the date and the purpose of the meeting, but you could not have entered any notes.

Type in a date, such as 8/14/87, and press Tab to get to the next field. The Standard Choices list appears, so point to the word Information and click the mouse button. Press Tab again and enter these notes:

```
Went to Max and told him about our new desktop communications
system. He said he might be interested in a month. Their company
has 20 employees but will be expanding.
```

As you enter text in the field, it scrolls and word-wraps as if you were working with a miniature word processor. You can edit text, move the text up and down, and select text in all of the standard ways, which makes it easy to enter and modify notes. Your screen should resemble Figure 3-16. Click Enter to complete the subrecord entry.

Use the left-pointing arrow, the right-pointing arrow, and the #1 record icons on the entry screen to move forward and backward through the records or to the first record. Click the right-pointing arrow to move to the second record, then click it again to get to the third record, which is Pat Pending.

Press Command-Tab to enter a new subrecord and double-click the 00/00/00 default date. Enter the date 10/15/87 and press Tab. Choose the purpose of Training, then enter these notes:

```
Pat needed some assistance with our new networking program. After
about half an hour, the problem was solved.
```

FIGURE 3-16.   Click Enter after you have finished typing in the subrecord.

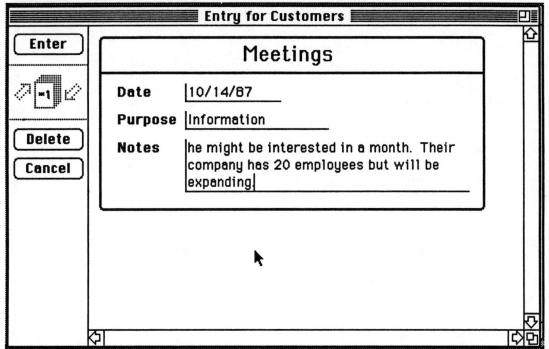

Press the Enter button to finish the subrecord. Press Command-Tab again and double-click the new date to enter the second subrecord. Its date should be 10/17/87, and it should also have the purpose of Training. Type

```
Still problems with the software. We discovered a minor bug in the
system.
```

Press the Enter key. Your screen should resemble Figure 3-17. The dates and the purposes of the two subrecords are visible, and you could select either one by pointing to it and double-clicking. If you have a lot of subrecords (say, ten or twenty, you can scroll through the list until you find the one you want to examine or modify.

This gives you a small sampling of how to use subrecords and what their purpose is. The keyboard is especially useful when you are examining or modifying subrecords, so here are the functions of the important keys that you should remember:

FIGURE 3-17. You can scroll through a list of multiple entries and select any one by double-clicking it.

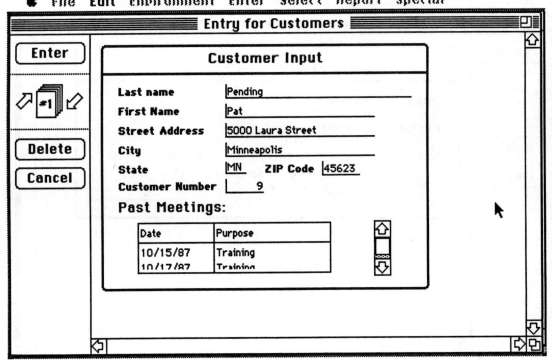

Command-Tab. Enter a new subrecord.

Tab. Move to the next field. If there are no subrecords, you cannot get to the list by pressing Tab. If there is at least one subrecord, pressing Tab when the cursor is on the last field of the parent file will get you to the first subrecord. Pressing Tab also moves you from one field to the next in the subrecords.

Enter. Completes entry or modification of the subrecord.

There is a lot of flexibility between using the mouse and using the keyboard in 4th Dimension. For every mouse function, there is almost always a keyboard equivalent. You can experiment by entering more subrecords into different records to understand how to enter, modify, and scroll information. Later chapters give you more in-depth instruction on data entry, but for now practice is the best teacher.

4

Multiple Files

In this chapter, which is the last one in the first section, you will learn how to add more files to the database, how to enter data more efficiently, and how to access the layouts of any of the files. Even though none of these files is linked to another (which you will learn how to do in the next section), you can begin to build a more diverse collection of information by having a group of separate files with distinct information and layouts.

ADDING ANOTHER FILE

Go back to the Design environment's Structure window for Customers. Currently, there is a file called Customers, which contains seven fields, and an eighth field, which is a subfile. Graphically, the Customers file is in a box of its own, and the subfile called Meetings is in a separate box, connected to the first by a shaded line.

The Structure window is your design tablet for the database. As you add files, links, and subfiles to the database, the Structure window will become more complex. In fact, this window has a logical size that is much bigger than its physical size. To see this, point to the lower left corner of the window where the Show Page box is and click the mouse button once. Your screen should now resemble Figure 4-1, which shows the entire database structure in miniature form.

FIGURE 4-1. Show Page reveals the entire structure of the database.

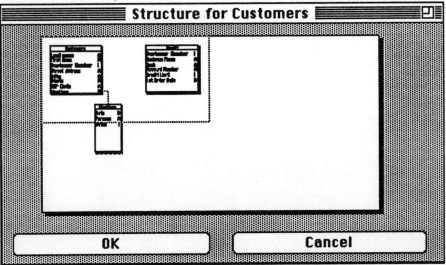

The dotted box shows the portion of the database structure you will return to when you click OK. Before you do that, move the dotted box around to see how you can shift from one part of the window to another. When you are through moving the box around, return it to the upper left corner and click the OK button.

You are going to create a new file called Credit, which will keep records of financial information for each customer. This file will be separate from Customers for now, and it will contain six fields. To create it and position it in the Structure window, choose New File from the Structure menu (or press Command-N), then move the file icon to the right of the Customers box. It doesn't really matter where the file is placed, but put it far enough away from the other graphics so it will be clear what the structure is. Now click the mouse button, and a blank file box called File2 will be in place.

Select the Rename File command from the Structure menu, then type in the new file name Credit. After you click OK, press Command-F to add a new field and add the following six fields with their attributes. After you enter the characteristics of each field, click OK and Next. After you have entered the sixth field, just click OK.

Field	Attributes
Customer Number	Integer (20), Mandatory, Indexed
Business Name	Alpha (30)
Bank	Alpha (20), Mandatory, Standard Choices (these choices are Bank of America, CitiBank, First Interstate, Home Savings, and Wells Fargo, as shown in Figure 4-2). Check the Choices Can Be Modified box and sort these bank names.
Account Number	Alpha (20), Mandatory
Credit Limit	Integer, Mandatory
1st Order Date	Date, Can't modify

Now that you've entered these six fields into the new file, your Structure window has a new file box with the field names, as shown in Figure 4-3. The Customer Number field name is boldface because it is indexed, and although the Credit file isn't linked to any other file right now, you can still use it independently. If you want to reposition either of the two files or the subfile in the Structure window, point to the file's name and drag the box around while holding down the mouse button. When you are satisfied with the file's new position, let go of the mouse button.

FIGURE 4-2.   Each customer has to have a bank name from this list, which should be modifiable and sorted.

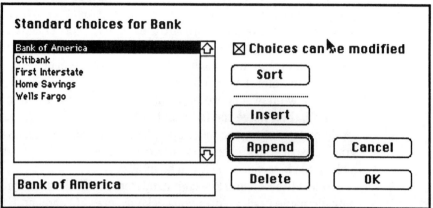

FIGURE 4-3.   A new file has been added to the structure window. Any element in this window can be repositioned for easier viewing.

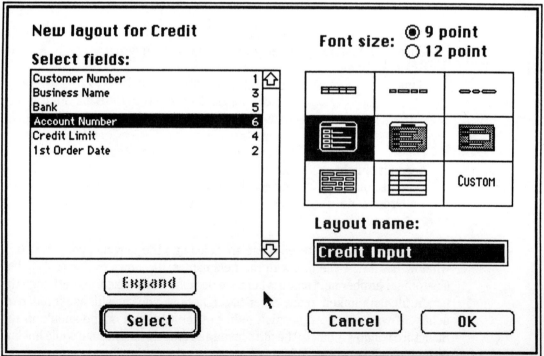

CREATING THE LAYOUTS

As with any new file, you have to create at least one layout for this one. For the Credit file, you will have separate input and output layouts. Select Layout from the Design menu, then select the boldfaced file name Credit. Since no layouts exist for this file yet, type in the file name `Credit Input` and click the New button.

The default layout 4th Dimension uses is fine for this file, but choose the 9-point font size to be sure the layout fits on the screen. Now click OK, and your layout appears on the window.

Since you can use any of the tools in the Layout Design window, it would be worthwhile to embellish this layout somewhat. To start, you can change the title at the top of the layout from Credit to Credit Input, and you can add a double border around the title. Follow these steps:

1. Point to the title and click the mouse button to select it.
2. Choose the text tool (whose icon is a capital A) and select all the text within the object you've just selected.
3. Select the Center option from the Style menu. Now type `Credit Information` to replace the old title Credit.
4. Select the pointer from the toolbox and click on the title object. The object isn't big enough to show all of the text, so point to the lower right handle of the object and drag it far enough to the right so that the entire title (Credit Information) shows.
5. This object is not centered with the rest of the layout, but there's an easy way to fix that. The icon on the left side of the toolbox and third from the bottom is the horizontal centering icon. It's easy to spot because it consists of several horizontal lines centered relative to each other. To use this icon, select whatever objects you want horizontally centered, then click the icon.

   In this case, select the outside border of the layout and the title Credit Information. Point to the horizontal centering icon and click the mouse button. These objects will be properly aligned, as shown in Figure 4-4.
6. Now you can add a double border around this title. Select the rectangle icon (right side, third one down in the toolbox) and position the crosshairs in the upper left area near the title. Hold down the mouse button and drag the mouse so that a rectangle forms around the title.
7. Once you release the mouse button, this rectangle will be filled with the default white pattern, which means the title is now hidden. You don't want the rectangle to be filled at all, so pull down the Layout menu and select the

FIGURE 4-4. Clicking the icon horizontally centers the selected objects.

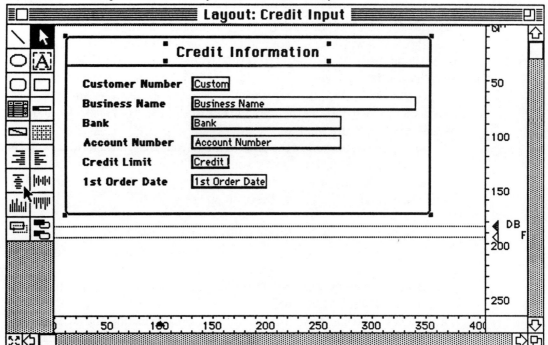

Fill option. All the different fill patterns are now on your screen, as shown in Figure 4-5. When you choose one of these, the currently selected object will be filled with that pattern. In this case, you don't want any fill at all, so choose None.

8. Now you can see through the rectangle object so that the title shows through. Add another rectangle so that a double border surrounds the title. Choose the rectangle tool again and drag a slightly larger rectangle around the first.

9. Once again, the rectangle is filled with white. To access the Fill selection a little more quickly, point to the rectangle and double-click the mouse button. Choose None. When you return to the layout window, you should see a transparent double border surround the title, as in Figure 4-6.

Of course, when you are using the database, this border will appear around the title just as you have created it. Anything you create within the layout design will appear when you are using the layout. With that in mind, you should add one more thing to this layout to enhance it. Next to the Account Number field, add a warning that the account number should be verified. It's helpful to remind the

FIGURE 4-5.   Click on any of the fill patterns to fill selected objects with that pattern.

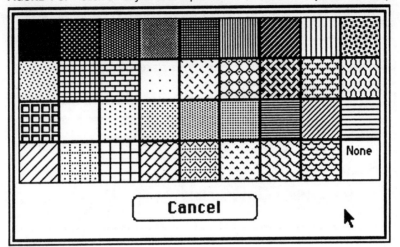

user entering the data to be especially careful about a field that is prone to mistakes. To add this reminder,

1. Select the text icon and draw a text box in the area next to the Account Number field. Remember that the Account Number title is different than the Account Number field, since the title is the text object on the far left, and the field is the boxed variable name near the center of the layout.
2. Type in the reminder Verify! in this text box.
3. Select the text you just typed and change the font to Times and the style to Bold. Both the font and the style changes can be accessed through menus.
4. Now choose the rounded rectangle icon (left side of the toolbox, third one down) and draw a rounded rectangle around Verify! The graphic is filled, of course, so double-click it and choose None for the fill pattern. Your layout should now resemble Figure 4-7.

You are through creating the Credit Input layout, so now you can do Credit Output. Close the Credit Input window and choose the Layout item from the Design menu. Select the Credit file name and type in the name of the new layout, Credit Output. Now click the New button to create the new layout.

You will be using only three fields in this output layout: Customer Number, Business Name, and Credit Limit. Therefore, 12-point text is probably all right to use, since these three fields shouldn't take up more room than the width of the screen. Of course, it would be all right even if they did, but to avoid horizontal scrolling, it's often a good idea to design the layouts to be compact.

FIGURE 4-6.   Two transparent rectangles make up the double border.

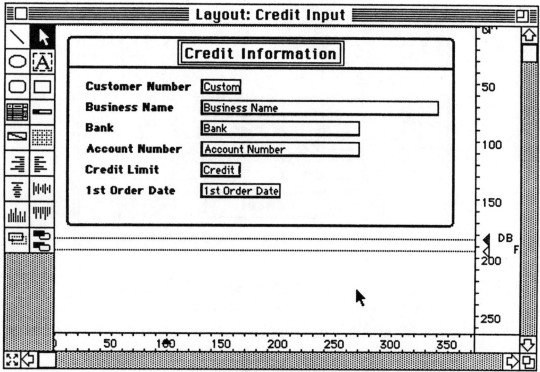

FIGURE 4-7.   The warning is surrounded by a transparent graphic object.

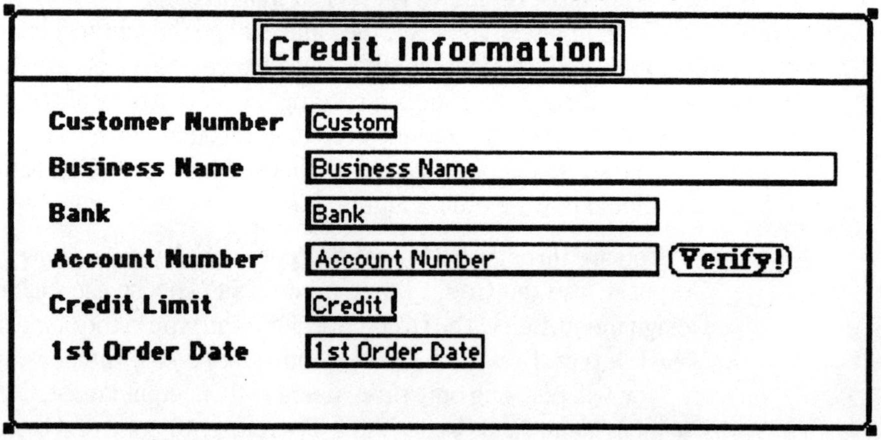

Choose the layout in the upper left corner of the layout designs available and select the three fields Customer Number, Business Name, and Credit Limit. Selecting is done either by double-clicking the field name or by selecting the field name and clicking the Select button. Now that all three fields are selected, as shown in Figure 4-8, click the OK button.

Even though it took much less time to create this layout than it did to create the first one, you are through. Point to the Close box in the Credit Output window and click the mouse button.

ACCESSING DIFFERENT FILES AND LAYOUTS

Now that you have more than one file to work with, you need to know how to access any given file or layout for input or output. Select the User option from the Environment menu so you can see how to switch between files and layouts. Once you are in the User environment, you should have a list of the sixteen records you have entered.

FIGURE 4-8. The Credit Output layout will use 12-point text and the three fields you have selected.

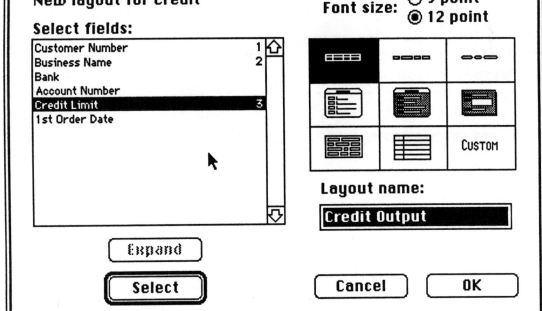

The file you created first and have used so far is Customers, so 4th Dimension is using the default input/output layouts from the Customers file (that is, Customer Input and Customer Output). However, no matter how many files or layouts you have in a database, you can access any of them with the Choose File/Layout command in the File menu. This command lets you select the file you want to be using (at this point, you are using the Customers file) or what layout you want to use (which currently is the default output layout, Customers Output).

Select Choose File/Layout, and a list of the files available appears. Since there are only two files in this database, Customers and Credit, those are the only two shown. Point to the Customers file name and double-click the mouse button. The names of the layouts in the Customers file, Customer Input and Customer Output, now appear beneath the file name. Double-click the Credit file now too (or select the name and click the Expand button), and that file's two layout names appear, as shown in Figure 4-9.

You can select any layout name and see a miniature picture of that layout in the box on the right. Right now, instead of using any particular layout, select the file Credit and click the Choose button. This shifts you over from the Customers file to the Credit file, so that the records you add, delete, modify, or list now will be strictly within Credit. You are still in the same database, but you are working in a different part of that database.

FIGURE 4-9. Use this dialog box to access any file or layout.

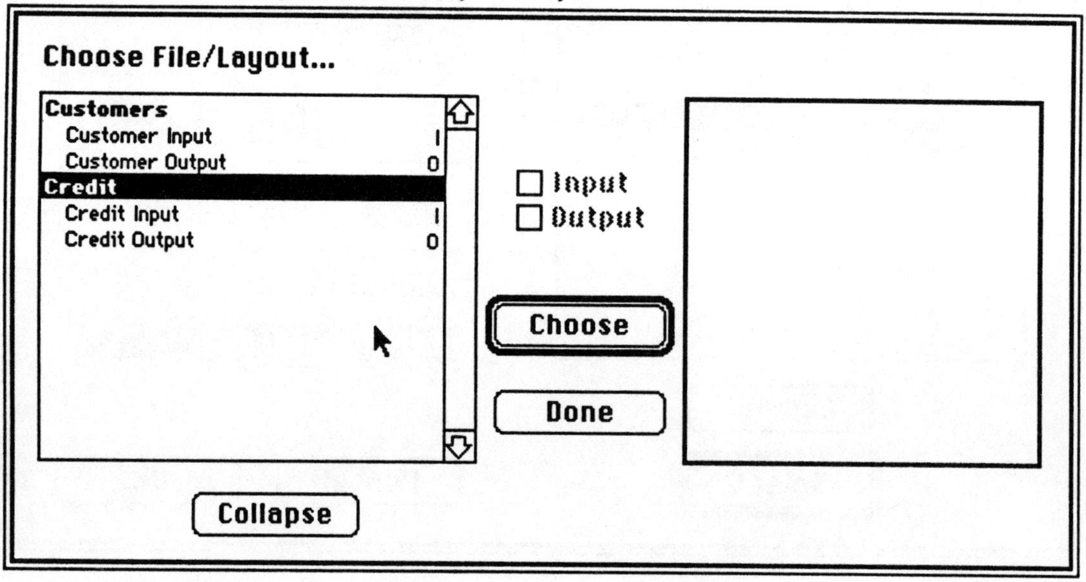

Because you have not put any information in the Credit file, a graphic of a drawer appears and 4th Dimension tells you that there are no records in the Credit file. You're going to change that now by giving all sixteen of your customers credit information.

ENTERING THE CREDIT DATA

Press Command-N (or select the command New Record from the menu) to enter the first record in the Credit file. The Credit Input layout you designed appears on the screen, and you can enter your first record as follows:

Customer Number:	12
Business Name:	Coffee Importers, Inc.
Bank:	First Interstate
Account Number:	0499-898027
Credit Limit:	2000
1st Order Date:	12/4/85

As you can see in Figure 4-10, all the embellishments you added to the Credit Input layout are there, and the data was entered in the same way you already know. Once you enter this record by clicking the Enter button or by pressing the Enter key on the keyboard, you can't go back to it and change the 1st Order Date field, since that field has the Can't be modified attribute. Try changing that field later, and you'll discover that 4th Dimension won't let you.

Now enter a couple of other records:

Customer Number:	5
Business Name:	Al's Deli
Bank:	Wells Fargo
Account Number:	4523-193000
Credit Limit:	1450
1st Order Date:	4/5/79

Customer Number:	9
Business Name:	Inventions by PP
Bank:	Home Savings
Account Number:	7293-124909
Credit Limit:	4000
1st Order Date:	4/5/87

Figure 4-11 shows a helpful technique in entering a choice from the Standard Choices list. You already know a couple of ways to get a standard choice: you can

FIGURE 4-10. This is the first record in the Credits file. Be careful to enter all the data correctly.

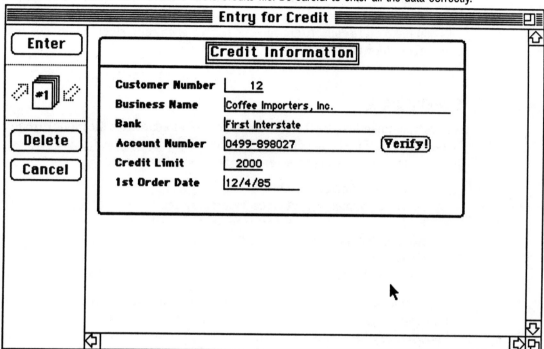

point to the choice and double click it, or you can use the arrow keys to move up and down through the list and hit Select when you want to choose one.

An easier, faster way to get to an item in a list is to type the first character of that item. Because there are only a few banks listed here, and because there's only one that begins with the letter H, a user who wants to enter Home Savings as the bank can simply type H and press the Return key. When you type a letter, 4th Dimension automatically goes to the first item on the list that begins with that letter. This is especially helpful if you have dozens of possible choices, since you can instantly go to the area of the list you want.

Now add a few more names to the Credit file:

Customer Number: 82
Business Name: Senior Achievers
Bank: Citibank
Account Number: 0012-233912

FIGURE 4-11.   Pressing the first letter of the bank name instantly selects that bank for you.

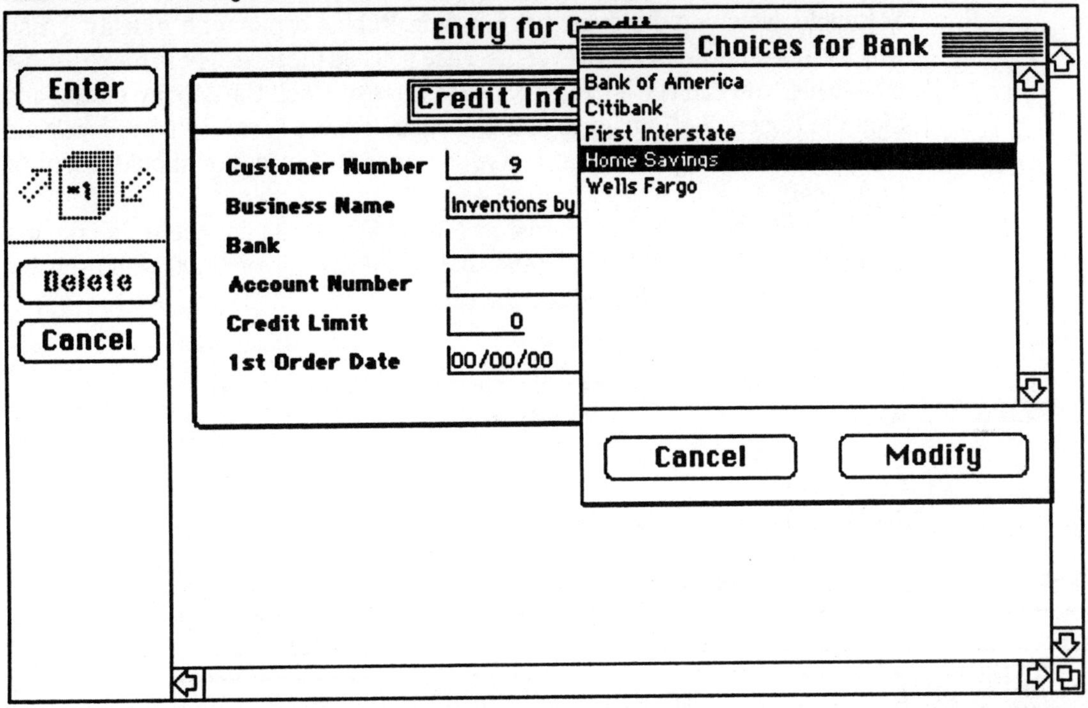

```
                          Entry for Credit
                                          Choices for Bank
  ┌─────────┐                             Bank of America
  │  Enter  │              Credit Info    Citibank
  └─────────┘                             First Interstate
                                          Home Savings
     ▱ ◿ ◹ ◺                              Wells Fargo
       ×1                   Customer Number        9
                           Business Name    Inventions by
  ┌─────────┐              Bank
  │ Delete  │              Account Number
  └─────────┘              Credit Limit           0
  ┌─────────┐              1st Order Date   00/00/00
  │ Cancel  │
  └─────────┘
                              ┌──────────┐      ┌──────────┐
                              │  Cancel  │      │  Modify  │
                              └──────────┘      └──────────┘
```

Credit Limit:	7000
1st Order Date:	12/4/82
Customer Number:	34
Business Name:	Ballistics Naval Station
Bank:	Bank of America
Account Number:	0334-938031
Credit Limit:	3400
1st Order Date:	4/2/79
Customer Number:	6
Business Name:	The Smithereens
Bank:	Citibank
Account Number:	7283-239203-01
Credit Limit:	1000
1st Order Date:	6/1/84

For the next record, enter Customer Number 21 and Business Name Smith & Rubble. Now you discover that Smith & Rubble banks with Fidelity Trust, which is not on your list. However, because you had the foresight to make the list modifiable, you can add Fidelity Trust to the list. Click the Modify button and then the Append button. Type in the new bank name `Fidelity Trust`, click the Sort button to Sort the list again, and your Standard Choices box should resemble Figure 4-12.

After you select Fidelity Trust as the bank, you can complete this record. Enter the account number 8720-940203, a credit limit of 10,000, and the 1st Order Date of 3/1/81. Now add all the other records:

Customer Number:	64
Business Name:	(none: remember it's not mandatory)
Bank:	Home Savings
Account Number:	8211-189749
Credit Limit:	500
1st Order Date:	4/2/76

FIGURE 4-12.   Modifying the Standard Choices list is easy: just append the new item to the current list.

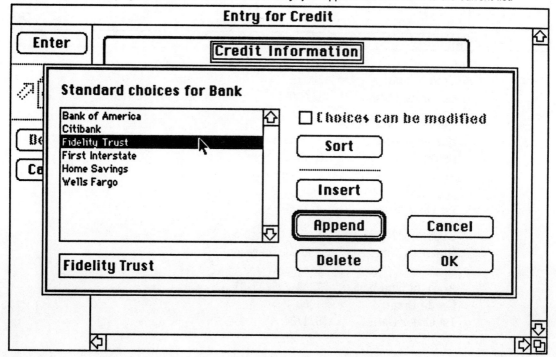

Customer Number: 44
Business Name: Confectioners USA
Bank: Bank of America
Account Number: 0488-239013
Credit Limit: 1250
1st Order Date: 8/4/85

Customer Number: 104
Business Name: Imports of Otis
Bank: Home Savings
Account Number: 0089-391039
Credit Limit: 250
1st Order Date: 5/6/74

Customer Number: 7
Business Name: Board Advertising
Bank: Citibank
Account Number: 3421-980222
Credit Limit: 3500
1st Order Date: 1/2/80

Customer Number: 93
Business Name: Singalong
Bank: Wells Fargo
Account Number: 0286-293800
Credit Limit: 400
1st Order Date: 2/2/87

Customer Number: 66
Business Name: Benco
Bank: Gibraltar (you'll have to add this bank, too)
Account Number: 0400-392809
Credit Limit: 500
1st Order Date: 4/9/76

Customer Number: 17
Business Name: Blondie's
Bank: Citibank
Account Number: 8890-293801
Credit Limit: 1000
1st Order Date: 9/9/79

Customer Number:	105
Business Name:	Legends Co.
Bank:	Wells Fargo
Account Number:	0287-898100
Credit Limit:	900
1st Order Date:	6/5/72

Customer Number:	51
Business Name:	Pineapple Imports
Bank:	Bank of America
Account Number:	9802-769120
Credit Limit:	1200
1st Order Date:	3/4/83

You are through entering the credit information for these sixteen different customers. After you press Enter to add the Pineapple Imports credit file, another blank layout appears. Click Cancel to get out of New Record entry.

A QUICK REVIEW OF DATA MODIFICATION

You have already learned a number of techniques on how to change, delete, or add records to a file. Currently, you are looking at the output of sixteen different credit records, as set up by the Credit Output layout. At this point, you could do a number of things to this data (none of which you should do right now):

Add a record. Under the Enter menu is the New Record (Command-N) command. To add a new record, select this command, type in the information, then press the Enter key. To return to the output list at any point, click the Cancel button. If you click the Cancel button, anything in the current record on the screen is not saved to disk. However, records you have already entered are saved.

Delete a record. Under the Edit menu is the Clear command, which deletes any selected record. To delete a record, point to it and click the mouse button to select it, select the Clear command, then respond Yes when the program asks if you really want to delete that record. You cannot Undo a Clear command, so use it with caution.

Modify a record. Try this on a record now just to see how the date cannot be modified. Select any record, then choose the Modify Record command from the Enter menu (or just double-click that record). The input layout (in this case, Credit Input) appears on the screen with that record's data, and you can change any of the information in that record. For this file, the date cannot be modified, so 4th Dimension won't even let you into that field area.

Move through records. While you're in the input layout, you can see the right-pointing arrow, the left-pointing arrow, and the #1 record icons on the left side of the screen. To move forward through the records in a file, click the right-pointing arrow. To move backward, click the left-pointing arrow. Of course, if you're at the first or last record of a file, 4th Dimension does not allow you to "loop back" to the opposite end of the file, so only one arrow will be darkened to show you the direction you can travel to the next record. The #1 record icon sends you to the first record in a file.

Search or **Search and Modify.** Usually you need to select a record yourself if you want to modify it or delete it. With the Search command, which is in the Select menu, you can have 4th Dimension do the selecting for you based on certain criteria. 4th Dimension will create a subset of records based on those criteria. For example, only three of sixteen files might fit a particular description, so the current selection would change from all sixteen files to just three files.

Search and Modify goes an extra step since it not only extracts a subset from the entire file, but also lets you modify any of those records, one at a time.

Sort. This command under the Select menu can sort the current selection of records based on certain fields. You can sort based on fields in either ascending or descending order, and you can rank which fields have preference over others in sorting.

THE LAST OF THE FLAT DATABASE

This completes the first section of this book. You have learned about creating files and records in a flat database and how to develop the Structure window, how to create files, fields, and corresponding layouts, and how to input the information into those files. You have also learned about 4th Dimension's powerful commands that can modify, sort, and select data.

You can create a lot of useful information storehouses using what you know now. You can create dozens of files to store just about any kind of information, and with the command tools 4th Dimension has, you could probably use this data very efficiently. In the next section, however, you will take the next step in database development: you will learn how to link together separate files in a database so that the information center you create is easier to use and far more efficient. The concepts are somewhat more difficult, but the power you can access with those relational structures makes it worth the effort, as you will see.

PART 2

The Third and Fourth Dimensions

or Learning to Create and Relate to Relational Databases

5

Linking Files

In this chapter, you will learn one of the most important concepts that make a relational database unique: linking files. The process of linking files is exactly what the name suggests. You tell the database to associate a field in one file with a similar field in another file; after the files are connected, they can share data. It's really a synergistic relationship, because the two combined files often are more useful and powerful than they were when they were apart.

The power of linking, or relating (hence the name relational database), different fields is that you can avoid a lot of unnecessary work and searching because one file can depend on the data already in another file. For instance, suppose you have a database that tracks all the students in an elementary school. The name of each student's teacher will be entered, but you also want to have the teacher's phone number, address, and picture available in that same file.

It would be tedious to enter all this information for each of the hundreds of students in the school. However, if you already have a file that contains the information and a picture for each teacher, you can link the teacher name field in the student database with the teacher name field in the teacher database. Because the two files are linked, the student file can access the data in the teacher file. If you enter the name Mary Jones into a student's file, then the information about Mary Jones and her picture will be loaded into the appropriate fields in that student's file. Thus, you don't have to find and enter all those data.

Of course, some setup is involved to get to this level of simplicity. The easy part of linking files is creating the link itself: it takes just a few moments. Modifying the layouts to accommodate the extra data is more of a challenge, as you'll discover in this chapter.

RULES FOR LINKING

It is helpful to understand a few guidelines on what fields can be linked and what the relationship between two files is after a link is made. Keep the following rules in mind:

- Link fields of the *same type*. You can link Alpha to Alpha, Real to Real, and so on. You cannot link Alpha to Date, for example.
- When you draw the linking arrow from one file to another, the field from which the arrow is drawn is the *linking* field, and the file to which the arrow is drawn is the *linked* field (the linking file and the linked file have the same correspondence). The linking field *must* have the Indexed attribute. It does not matter whether the linked field is Mandatory.

- Although the two files are connected, think of the link as a one-way street. Suppose you have two files called File A and File B, and you establish a link that goes from File A (the linking file) to File B (the linked file). The purpose of this link is for File A to get information from File B, not the other way around. Think of File A, the linking file, as the "boss"—it uses File B to get the data it wants. The arrow that establishes the link goes from the linking field in File A and points to the linked field in File B, the file from which the needed information is obtained.

When you establish a link, 4th Dimension writes a simple, automatic procedure that retrieves data from the linked file for the linking file's use. You don't have to do anything except make the link and modify the layout to support the extra data.

MAKING THE LINK

As mentioned earlier, linking two files is very simple. Bring up the Layout window in your Customers database and find the field called Customer Number in both the Customers and the Credit files. Notice that Customer Number is an indexed, mandatory field in both cases. The names of the fields happen to be the same, but this isn't necessary. As long as you are relating the same type of data and you are certain that a proper relationship is established when you link those two fields, you needn't be concerned if their names are different. It simply makes it easier to understand the link if they are.

Move the mouse pointer up to the field name Customer Number in the Customers file and hold down the mouse button. While holding the button down, move the pointer to the Customer Number field name in the Credit file. Notice that a line follows the pointer as you move it, as shown in Figure 5-1.

When you release the mouse button, the link is made, indicated by a heavy line between the two field names, as shown in Figure 5-2. The link line is easy to distinguish from the subfile line, which is a light gray line. If you move the boxes representing the files around the screen or if you move the scroll bar within a file box to see different field names, the lines are repositioned accordingly.

Now you can access any information you want in the Credit file—like Business Name, Bank, or Account Number—and display it in the Customers file layout. Later you'll learn how to modify the retrieved data in this indirect way.

FIGURE 5-1.   A line shows the connection you are making.

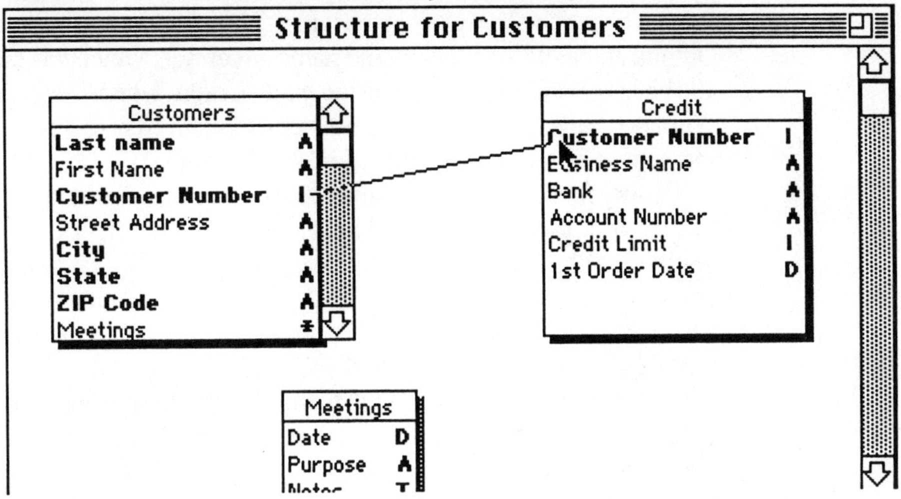

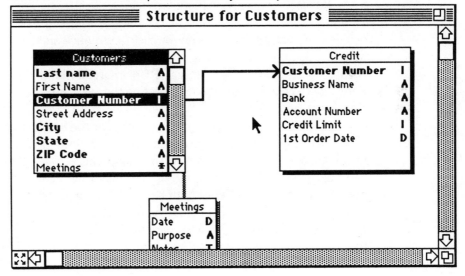

FIGURE 5-2.   A dark line represents the link you have just created.

CHANGING THE LAYOUT

In this case, probably the easiest way to get a layout that uses the linked information is to create a new one from scratch. You will make a new layout that has all the elements you want. After you make the new layout the default input layout, you can delete the old input layout you have been using up until now.

Select Layout from the Design menu and double-click the file name Customers to see the layouts that exist for it already: Customer Input and Customer Output. In boldface is the subfile name Meetings, which has layouts of its own, and below that in boldface is the file name Credit, which also has its own layouts. What you want to do is create a new input layout to replace the old one. Type in the name New Input, then click the New button.

Now you have to tell 4th Dimension which fields you want in the new layout. In this case, the first field you'll want is the linking field Customer Number. It doesn't matter where the linking field is in a layout, but in this example, it would be most convenient if it is first. Click the boldfaced field name Customer Number. Notice that the file name (Credit) is appended to it. This indicates that the field Customer Number is a field linked to the Credit file.

Try double-clicking this field name. Instead of putting a number 1 next to it, 4th Dimension lists all the fields in the Credit file. You cannot select a linking field name by double-clicking it. Instead, you have to use the Select button. Since Customer Number (Credit) is still selected, point to the Select button and click it. A number 1 should appear next to the field name, which means this will be the first field placed in the New Input layout.

Because none of the other field names are linking fields, you can either double-click them to select them or click them once and then click the Select button. Click on the names in this order: Business Name, Last Name, First Name, Street Address, City, State, ZIP Code, Credit Limit. The last name, Credit Limit, should have a 9 next to it, indicating there are nine fields selected for the New Input layout.

The layout chosen is appropriate, but click on the 9-point button. Your layout dialog box should resemble the one in Figure 5-3, with the field names selected in the same order. Notice that at this point there is no difference between selecting fields in the linking file or the linked file. The only special rule to remember is to use the Select button on the linking field; double-clicking it only expands or collapses the list of field names in the linked file.

Click the OK button. In a few moments, two windows appear on your screen: the New Layout window and a Procedure window, as shown in Figure 5-4. The Procedure window contains the information 4th Dimension needs to load data from the linked file into the linking file. Later, you'll learn how to create and modify procedures, but for now close this window.

Click the Full box, which is located in the upper right corner of the New Input layout window. Notice the two linked fields in the layout. They are called AG2 and AG9 and are represented by rectangles with a slash running through them. When you use this database, 4th Dimension automatically loads in this information and shows the business name and credit limits in AG2 and AG9, respectively.

FIGURE 5-3.   Choose the 9-point font size and select the fields in this order.

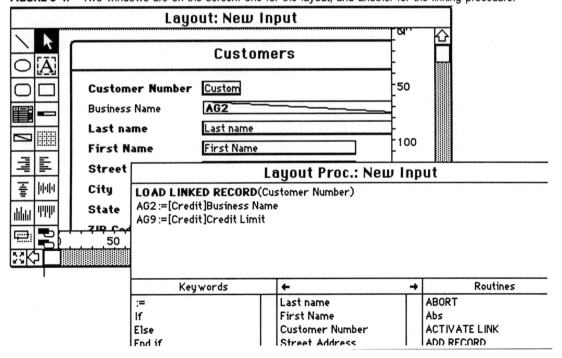

FIGURE 5-4.   Two windows are on the screen: one for the layout, and another for the linking procedure.

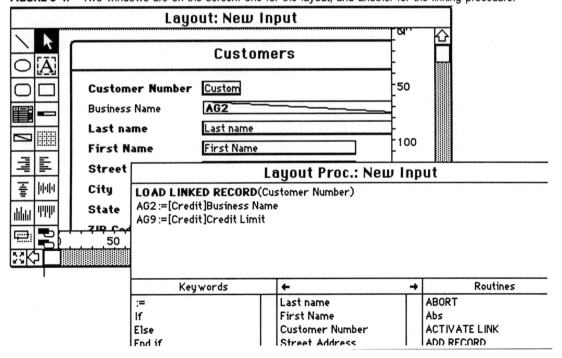

REORGANIZING THE LAYOUT

Notice also that there is a lot of room on the top line. You might want to drag the two objects at the bottom of the layout to the top of the layout to make more room. To do this, follow these steps:

1. Select the field name object Credit Limit, located at the lower left corner of the New Input layout.
2. Point to one of the handles on the right side. Hold down the mouse button and drag the handle left to eliminate the white space. There's no need for all that white space to be occupying that object. Don't obscure any of the Credit Limit name, however.
3. Drag this object up to the first line so it matches evenly with the Customer Number field, as shown in Figure 5-5. It is important that they match exactly.
4. Next, drag the Credit Limit field itself (called AG9, since it is a linked field from the Credit file) up to the same line. All four objects on that first line — Customer Number name, Customer Number field, Credit Limit name, Credit Limit field — should be even.
5. You now have more white space on the bottom than you started with, but you can add even more by expanding the rounded rectangle that is the border of the layout. There are three arrows at the bottom of the layout

FIGURE 5-5. Drag the field name to the first line of the layout after you remove the white space.

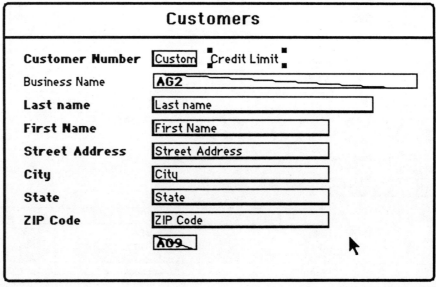

screen, denoted by the letters D, B, and F (you'll learn more about these later). Point to each arrow and drag it closer to the bottom of the screen to make more room for the layout.

6. Now that you have dragged all three arrows lower, select the rounded rectangle border. Point to one of the two handles on the bottom and hold the mouse button while you drag the mouse down. The border should be expanded as far as it can go without going below any of the three arrows, as shown in Figure 5-6.

The reason you needed to create this extra space is to make room for the included layout that contains information on past meetings. Recall that in the original Customer Input layout, you had this included layout at the bottom. Now that you are creating a new layout, you will have to paste Previous Meetings to the bottom of the layout.

Fortunately, this copy-and-paste operation is easy. Follow these steps:

1. Choose Layout from the Design menu so you can load the original input layout into memory.

2. Double-click the Customers file name (which is in bold) to see its layouts. Next, double-click the layout name Customer Input.

FIGURE 5-6. You've created more white space at the bottom by moving two objects to the top line and by expanding the size of the border.

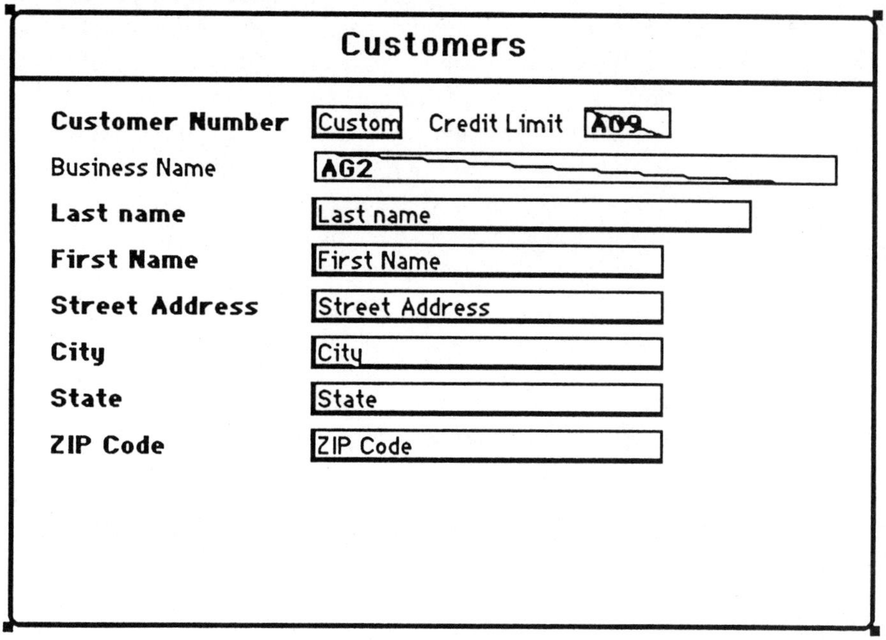

Customers
Customer Number [Custom]   Credit Limit [A09]
Business Name   [AG2]
Last name   [Last name]
First Name   [First Name]
Street Address   [Street Address]
City   [City]
State   [State]
ZIP Code   [ZIP Code]

3. You want to move the title Past Meetings and the corresponding layout to the New Input layout. Scroll down the layout until you find those two objects. Click the text object Past Meetings, then hold down the Shift key and click the included layout Meetings. Now both objects should be selected. Press Command-C to copy these two objects to the clipboard.

4. Pull down the Design menu. At the bottom of the menu are the two layout names, Layout: New Input and Layout: Customer Input. The Layout: Customer Input has a check mark next to it since it is the currently selected window. As you begin working with procedures, layouts, and other types of windows, you'll discover that using this menu is a fast and easy way to access any available windows.

   Point to Layout: New Input and release the mouse button. Now the New Input layout is selected. You could have simply pointed to that window and clicked the mouse button, of course, but it's a good habit to get into choosing the window you want with the menu.

5. Now you're ready to paste those two elements into the New Input layout. Press Command-V (or choose Paste from the Edit menu), and the text and included layout objects will be pasted into New Input. They are not in the place that you want them, so you'll have to do some more rearranging.

6. Deselect these two objects by pointing anywhere on the screen and clicking the mouse button once. Select the Meetings Included layout and drag it to the lower right corner of the New Input layout, as shown in Figure 5-7.

7. There isn't quite enough room for the text object Past Meetings to fit, so you'll have to modify it. Select the text icon (represented by the capital A) and click the Past Meetings text between the words Past and Meetings. Press the Backspace key to get rid of the space. Now press the Return key so that Past and Meetings are on separate lines.

8. The shape of this text layout is wrong since you've changed it. Choose the pointer tool and, after selecting this text object, drag the lower right handle to reshape the object. You should be able to see the words Past and Meetings, and there should be very little wasted white space.

9. Last, drag this text object to the white area in the lower left corner of the layout.

It should be easy to see why you had to make all that white space. It gave you enough room to put the text object and its included layout at the bottom of the screen. To help embellish the layout a little, select the rectangle tool and draw a couple of rectangles around the Past Meetings text icon. Use the Layout menu

FIGURE 5-7.   Drag the included layout to the lower-right corner.

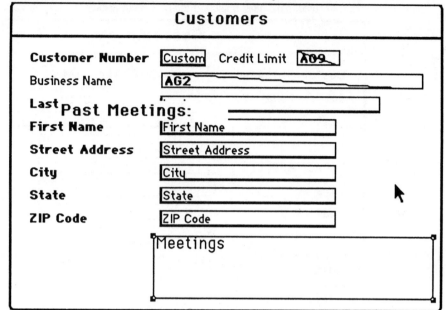

to select their Fill colors, which in both cases should be None. Try to make the rectangles look like the ones in Figure 5-8, and your layout redesign should be complete.

The old Customer Input layout still exists, so you should delete it and make New Input the default input layout. Follow these steps:

1. Choose Layout from the Design menu and double-click the Customers file name.
2. Select the layout called New Input and check the Input checkbox. Now New Input is the default input, and the letter I is next to New Input instead of Customer Input.
3. Select Customer Input and click the Delete button. When the dialog box appears asking if you are sure you want to delete it, click Yes.
4. To make things simple, select the New Input layout name and change the name to Customer Input. Do this by selecting the name inside the Name box and typing in the new name. Your layout dialog box should look like Figure 5-9.
5. Click the Done button, then click the Close box on the layout window.

FIGURE 5-8. The reconstruction of the layout is complete, now that the text object and the included layout have been copied to the New Input layout.

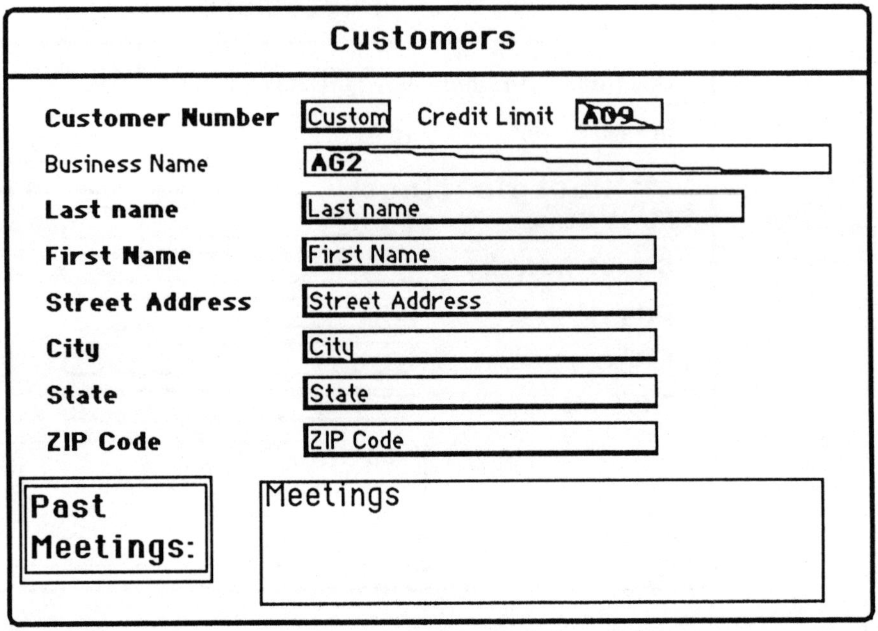

Customers

Customer Number [Custom] Credit Limit [A09]

Business Name [AG2]

Last name [Last name]

First Name [First Name]

Street Address [Street Address]

City [City]

State [State]

ZIP Code [ZIP Code]

Past
Meetings: [Meetings]

FIGURE 5-9. Your layout dialog box should look like this after you've deleted the old Customer Input layout and replaced it with the new one.

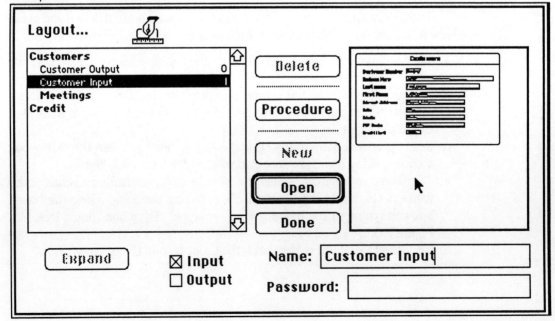

Reorganizing the layout wasn't hard, as you can see. It just takes an understanding of where the necessary elements are and how you can cut and paste them in the right order. As things stand now, you have a database with a single link and the appropriate layout to go with it. Now you can try the Customers database in its current form to see the value of the link.

USING THE LINK

Select User from the Environment menu to display the listing of customers already in the database. Nothing seems different, since the changes you made are in the input layout, and the link will be used only when you enter new data or modify a record.

Select the first record — the one for Max Wellhouse — and press Command-M (or choose the equivalent from the Enter menu, Modify Record). As you can see in Figure 5-10, the name of the business and the credit limit associated with customer 12 have been loaded into the record and are displayed in the layout.

FIGURE 5-10. The two fields from the linked file are in boldface, showing they cannot be entered or modified but only displayed.

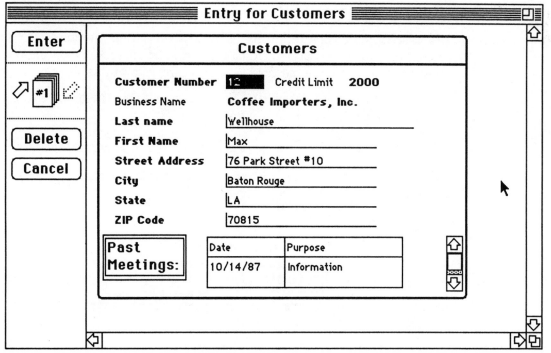

They are in boldface, showing that they are from a linked record and cannot be entered or modified from this layout.

Now go through a few of the records. Notice that for each record, the linked data are loaded into the input layout. Some of these people (like Otis Kay) don't own a business, so no business name appears in the layout. Keep moving through the records until you reach the business Board Advertising. The customer number in the layout is 7. Type the number **1** in the customer number field and press the Tab key to enter it. The dialog box in Figure 5-11 appears, indicating that the record for that customer number does not exist in the Credit file. You can create that record in the Credit File by selecting the Create It button, or you can reenter the customer number by selecting Try Again. In this case, click Try Again.

Now try typing the number **5** in the Customer Number field and pressing the Tab key. A dialog box appears that states, "This key already exists." Recall that the Customer Number field has the Unique attribute, and because a record already has that number, you cannot use it in this record as well. As you can see, you are stuck with the customer number you have. If you try to use a customer number that already exists, 4th Dimension won't allow it. If you use one that does not exist, you'll have to create that new record, which would be redundant if that information is already somewhere in the Credit file.

ENTERING A NEW CUSTOMER

Of course, creating a new record makes sense when you are entering data for an entirely new customer. Click the Cancel command, then press Command-N to enter a new record. Once the input layout appears, follow these steps:

1. Type in customer number 107. The program tells you that this record does not exist. Click the Create It button.

FIGURE 5-11. If you enter a customer number that doesn't have a corresponding record in the linked file, this dialog box will appear.

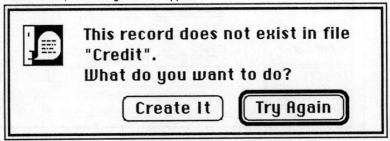

2. Enter the following data in the Credit input layout:

Business Name:　　Mad Max's Meats
Bank:　　Gibraltar
Account Number:　　0411-989000
Credit Limit:　　1000
1st Order Date:　　5/7/88

3. Click the Enter button. Notice that the business name and credit limit are loaded into the Customers input layout. Now type in the remaining data:

Last Name:　　Mansky
First Name:　　Max
Street Address:　　3200 Beef Way
City:　　Heffer
State:　　WI
ZIP Code:　　89633

4. Double-click inside the Meetings Included layout. The layout for the Meetings subfile appears. Enter the date 3/2/88, the purpose as a Cold Call, and type in the Notes area, "A friend recommended I go see Max. He has the largest cattle ranch in this country, and I'm sure he's a great prospect."

5. Click Enter to enter this information. Your complete record for Max Mansky should resemble Figure 5-12. You have entered the credit information, customer information, and meeting information all in the same procedure.

Select the Choose File/Layout command from the File menu. Double-click the Credit file name, then double-click the layout name Credit Output. Here you can see all the information from the Credit file in the Credit Output layout format. Double-click one of these records, such as the one for The Smithereens. (Note: A minor quirk of 4th Dimension is that when you double-click from an output layout, it doesn't always seem to work. Try clicking several times quickly to get the input layout for that record on the screen.)

The input layout for The Smithereens should be on the screen. You can change the data for any one of these fields, except the 1st Order Date, which cannot be modified. Notice that this input layout isn't any different from what it was before Customers and Credit were linked. Because Credit is a linked file, it isn't really affected, since data are pulled from it, not given to it.

FIGURE 5-12. The completed record has all the information about the customer, his credit, and any meetings that have taken place.

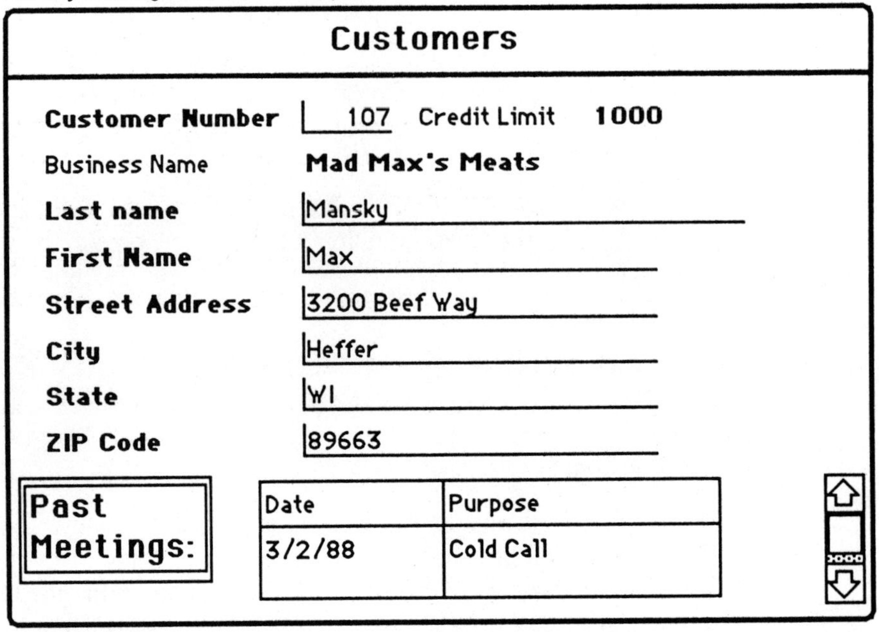

```
                        Customers

    Customer Number  |   107   Credit Limit   1000

    Business Name      Mad Max's Meats

    Last name          |Mansky

    First Name         |Max

    Street Address     |3200 Beef Way

    City               |Heffer

    State              |WI

    ZIP Code           |89663

    ┌──────────┐  ┌────────────┬──────────────┐
    │ Past     │  │Date        │Purpose       │
    │ Meetings:│  │3/2/88      │Cold Call     │
    └──────────┘  └────────────┴──────────────┘
```

If you change the information in this record, there will be an effect, of course. For example, suppose you change the name of the bank. When you examine the input layout for this customer, the different bank name is displayed instead of the original one, since the bank name is retrieved from the Credit file. If you change the Customer number, you might really cause damage to the database, since the customer record that corresponds to this credit record won't be able to find it anymore.

Given the structure of the database right now, it doesn't make sense to randomly alter the data in the Credit file. However, if a customer changes banks, or if a customer's credit line is raised, you need to choose the Credit Input layout to alter the appropriate data. The reason this link is useful is that you have to alter the data in only one place.

To see what this means, suppose that The Smithereen's credit limit is raised to 5000. You already have this record loaded into the Credit Input layout, so all you have to do is enter the new credit limit of 5000, as shown in Figure 5-13. Click the Enter button to enter this modified record.

FIGURE 5-13.   Type in the new credit limit of 5000 in the Credit Input layout.

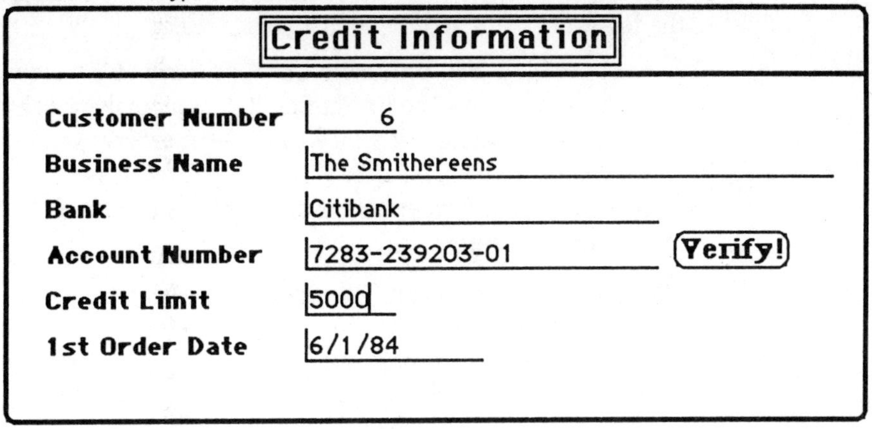

```
╔═══════════════════════════════════════════════════════╗
║             ┌────────────────────────┐                 ║
║             │ Credit Information │                      ║
║             └────────────────────────┘                 ║
║                                                         ║
║    Customer Number  │      6                            ║
║                                                         ║
║    Business Name    │The Smithereens                    ║
║                                                         ║
║    Bank             │Citibank                           ║
║                                                         ║
║    Account Number   │7283-239203-01        (Verify!)    ║
║                                                         ║
║    Credit Limit     │5000                               ║
║                                                         ║
║    1st Order Date   │6/1/84                             ║
║                                                         ║
╚═══════════════════════════════════════════════════════╝
```

Now select the Choose File/Layout command again and double-click the Customer Output layout to see the list of all customers. Double-click customer number 6, the Smithereens. Notice that this customer's new credit limit of 5,000 is displayed in the Customer Input layout. The data from the linked field is always current.

DEVELOPING ANOTHER LINK

What you have just developed is a fairly useful link that incorporates the data from the Credit file with the information in the Customers file. However, the real power of a link is evident when a field has only a few possible entries (like the names of a few departments in a company) and that field is linked to a file with a lot of information relevant to that field (like the manager of a department, the department's budget, its location, and so on). That way, you have to enter only a small amount of information in a single field to load in a lot of current information from the linked file.

To understand this better, you are going to create a new file called Banks, which contains information about the various banks in the Credit file. There are only seven banks listed in the Standard Choices list, so it won't take long to enter information about each bank. Once this is done, you can link the Bank field in the Credit file to the Bank field in the Banks file. By keeping information in the Banks file current, you can be assured that this linked information is current for the Credit file.

Start by creating the new file called Banks. You've made a few files already, so the following steps are somewhat abbreviated:

1. Select the New File command from the Structure window, then place the new field just below the Credit file. It doesn't make much difference where each file is placed, but it's nice to have an orderly window where you can easily see each file box.

2. Type Command-F to enter the first field. Enter the following fields, along with their attributes:

Bank:	Alpha (20) Indexed	Mandatory
Contact:	Alpha (20)	
Address:	Alpha (20)	Mandatory
City:	Alpha (15)	Mandatory
State:	Alpha (2)	Mandatory
ZIP:	Long Integer	Mandatory
Phone Number:	Alpha (15)	Mandatory

3. Select Rename File (or press the keyboard equivalent, Command-R) and enter the file name Banks.

4. Point to the Bank field name in the Credit file. Hold down the mouse and drag the linking line down the Bank field name in the Banks file, as shown in Figure 5-14. A dark line from the Credit file to the Banks file represents the link.

5. Select the Banks file box again and choose Layout from the Design menu. Select Banks from the list of files and type in the layout name Banks Layout. Now click the New button to create the new layout.

6. In the Layout dialog box, click the 9-point radio button, then click the OK button. Once the layout appears on the screen, shrink the ZIP Code text object somewhat so the space it occupies is reduced. Move the ZIP Code field name and the field itself up to the same line as State, then move the Phone Number field name and field up one line. Once you have slightly rearranged this layout, it should resemble Figure 5-15. Close the Layout box when you're through.

7. Select the Layout option, then select the Banks file. Type in the layout name Bank Output and click New. Choose 9-point font size, then select the fields Bank, Contact Name, and Phone Number. Select the layout style in the upper left corner, which is commonly used for output layouts. Finally, click the OK button.

FIGURE 5-14. Make the link between the two Alpha fields in the Credit and Banks files.

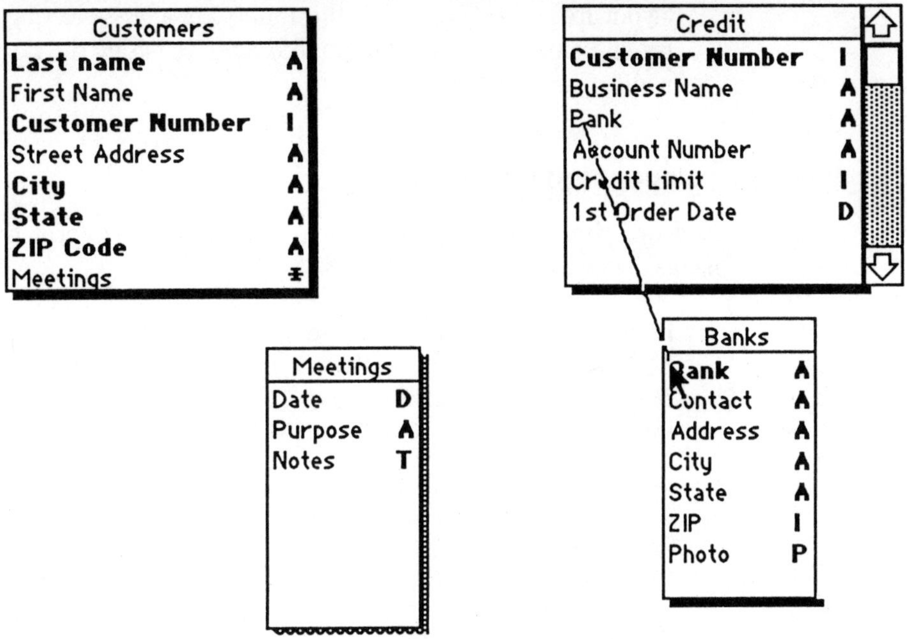

FIGURE 5-15. Move the ZIP Code objects up to the same line as the State objects, then move the two Phone Number objects up one line.

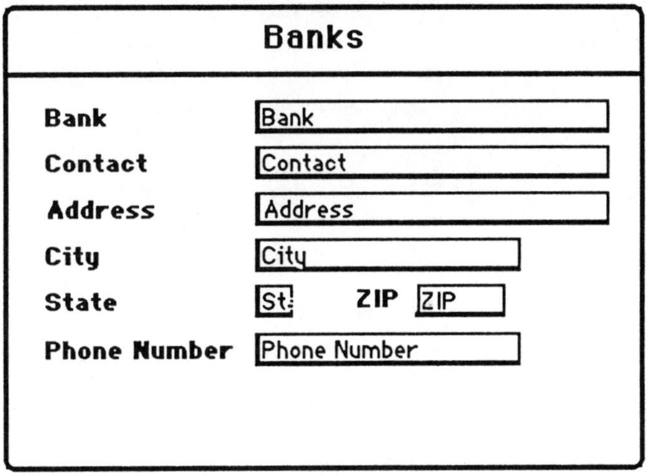

8. Return to Layout through the Design menu, then select the Bank Input layout from the list. Check the Input box after selecting the Bank Input layout name. Check the Output box after selecting the Bank Output layout name. Click the Done button.

ENTERING THE INFORMATION FOR BANKS

Now switch to the User environment to enter in the information for the seven banks. Type in the data as follows:

Bank:	Bank of America	Contact:	Maria Murphy
Address:	10 N. Main	City:	Cupertino
State:	CA	ZIP Code:	95014
Phone Number:	(408) 996-0101		

Bank:	Citibank	Contact:	Kelly Ramirez
Address:	17 University Ave.	City:	Palo Alto
State:	CA	ZIP Code:	94306
Phone Number:	(415) 323-6712		

Bank:	Fidelity Trust	Contact:	Kevin McDonald
Address:	1000 The Alameda	City:	New York
State:	NY	ZIP Code:	10021
Phone Number:	(212) 776-1111		

Bank:	First Interstate	Contact:	Liz Virden
Address:	69 Savacool Lane	City:	St. Louis
State:	MO	ZIP Code:	54996
Phone Number:	(404) 454-9888		

Bank:	Gibraltar	Contact:	Robert Moore
Address:	572 Manson Hwy.	City:	Erie
State:	PA	ZIP Code:	17219
Phone Number:	(619) 992-3344		

Bank:	Home Savings	Contact:	Ken Jochims
Address:	900 Broadway	City:	Miami
State:	FL	ZIP Code:	33625
Phone Number:	(303) 272-0758		

Bank:	Wells Fargo	Contact:	Wade LaBatt
Address:	180 Polk St.	City:	San Francisco
State:	CA	ZIP Code:	95124
Phone Number:	(415) 775-1134		

You now have three separate files and a subfile filled with data, and there are two links in the database. If any of the information for one of these banks changes, you can use the Change File/Layout command to access the Banks file and modify the information. To make the link to this file useful, however, you're going to have to modify the Credit layout.

MODIFYING THE LAYOUT FOR THE LINK

Because a link imports additional information from the linked file to the linking file, you have to create a new Credit Input layout that incorporates the information from the link. Follow these steps to create this new layout:

1. Return to the Design environment and select the Layout command. Double-click the Credit file name to reveal the layout names, and you'll see that Credit Input already exists. You want to create a new file to replace this one, so enter the new layout name Credit Input. It's all right that the name is the same. You'll recognize the new one later by the fact that the letter I is next to the existing layout's name.
2. Click New to get to the Layout dialog box. Double-click the linking field Bank [Banks] so that the list of field names in the Banks file is revealed.

   Click the 9-point font size and select the following field names in this order: Customer Number, Business Name, Bank [Banks], Contact, Phone Number, Account Number, Credit Limit, 1st Order Date. Remember that Bank [Banks] is a linking field, so you can't double-click it to select it. Instead, click it once, then click the Select button. Your screen should resemble Figure 5-16. Click the OK button when you're through.
3. Now your new layout is complete and should resemble Figure 5-17. Close the Layout box and choose the Layout command once more. Double-click the Credit file name to see the layout names and select the new Credit Input you have just created. Check the Input box, and the letter I will disappear from the old Credit Input and reappear next to the new Credit Input. Choose the old Credit Input and select Delete. When you're through removing the old layout, click the Done button.

ESTABLISHING THE LINK

Any time you input information in a layout with a link, data from the linked file is brought into the linking file's record. This is exactly what you would expect. To see how this works, switch to the User environment and use the Choose File/Layout command to get the Credit Output file in memory.

FIGURE 5-16. The field names should be selected in the order shown, and the font size should be 9 points so that everything fits in the layout.

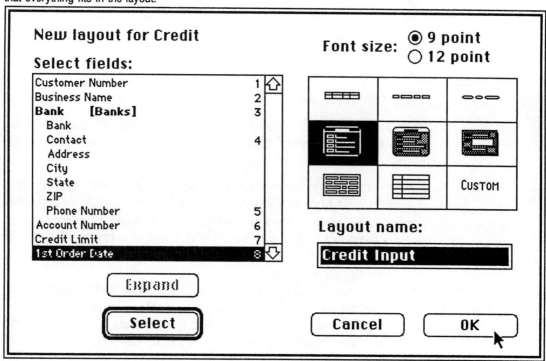

You now see a list of the seventeen records from the Credit file. Press Command-N to add a new record. You won't really be adding a new record, but you can see how choosing a bank automatically loads in the linked information. Press Tab until you get to the Bank field, then choose any of the banks. Press Tab again. The cursor moves down to the Account Number field, and both the contact name and the phone number are automatically loaded into the record.

Keep pressing the Tab key to get to the Bank field again and choose another bank. Press Tab again, and a different contact name and phone number are loaded in. You can keep doing this to see how quick and easy it is to enter the bank name and have the other information loaded into memory.

Keep in mind that you are using only a couple of fields from the Bank file. You could have used every one of them, which would have made the link even more of a timesaver, assuming you wanted all that information loaded into the Credit Input record.

FIGURE 5-17.   This new Credit Input layout has two elements drawn from the Banks file: the contact name and the phone number for the bank.

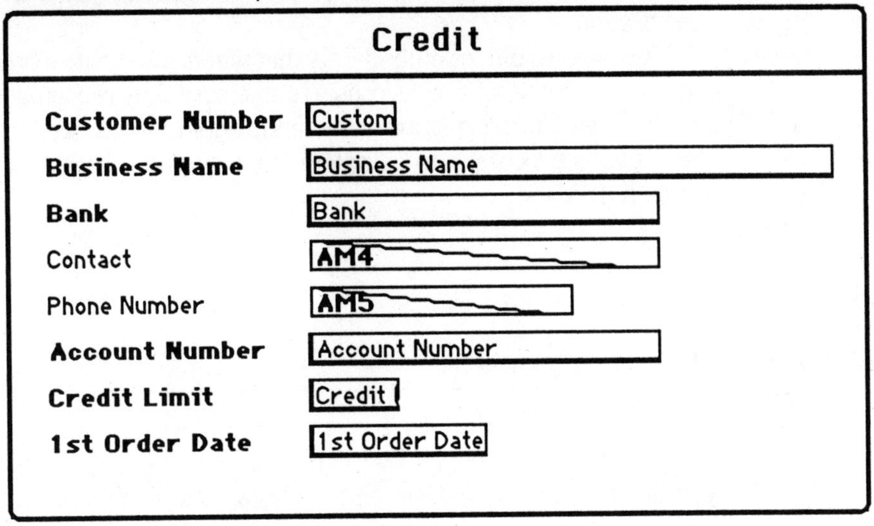

```
                        Credit

   Customer Number   [Custom]
   Business Name     [Business Name        ]
   Bank              [Bank          ]
   Contact           [AM4           ]
   Phone Number      [AM5          ]
   Account Number    [Account Number ]
   Credit Limit      [Credit (]
   1st Order Date    [1st Order Date]
```

ADDING LINKED DATA TO EXISTING RECORDS

Click the Cancel button so the sample record is not saved. Now you are going to discover something unusual. Select the first record in the list — Coffee Importers, Inc. — and press Command-M to modify the record. Notice that there is no information shown in either the Contact Name or the Phone Number fields. Even after you press Tab a few times to pass these two fields, the information is not loaded into this record.

The reason for this is that you've already entered all of those records, and when you did, no link existed between the Credit file and the Bank file (in fact, the Bank file did not exist). Therefore, 4th Dimension ignores the fact that there is a link there at all. It considers the record already complete.

There's an easy way around this situation. Return to the Bank field so that the Standard Choices list appears. The bank in the record is First Interstate. Point to the First Interstate name in the list and click the mouse button. Now press the Tab key, and the linked information is loaded into the record. By simply reentering the bank name, you make 4th Dimension bring in the necessary information.

Point to the right-pointing arrow and click the mouse button. Point to the Bank field and click the mouse button, then click the bank name that is already in the record and press the Tab key to get to the next field. Click the right arrow again to move on. Keep repeating this process of reentering the bank names. Once you are through with all seventeen records, you'll be done with this modification.

The simple rule to remember is that when you create a brand new link, you have to return to existing records to make sure they recognize the link. Do this by reentering the information in the linking field. Of course, the best way to avoid this arduous process is to complete the structure of the database before you enter all the data.

THE BIG PICTURE

As you can see, your database is starting to grow. You have to go through a few contortions to make sure all the data is linked properly, but this is only because you are building a database and entering data at the same time. The more common thing to do is to completely finish the database and its structure, then to enter all the data in the respective files.

You should be starting to see the value of links. The bigger the database gets and the more files rely on one another, the more useful links are. You may have just begun to understand links, but you've made a quantum step in understanding how powerful and useful the databases you create can be.

6

Using the Layout Toolbox

By now you probably have a pretty clear understanding of how to make layouts. Up until now, however, you haven't really used the layout toolbox, located on the left side of any Layout window. This area of the window has a variety of tools that make it easy to enhance or modify the contents of a layout. Some of the tools are for functions too complex to be addressed in this chapter, so they will be detailed later in the book. In this chapter, you will learn the basics of these tools and how to use them.

GRAPHICS TOOLS

Probably the easiest tools to understand in the Layout window are the graphics tools. You use these tools to draw lines, ovals, and rectangles, which you can then fill with a variety of patterns. Simple graphics can improve the appearance of a layout, emphasize an important part of a layout, or add color to the database if you have a Macintosh II or an Imagewriter II printer with a color ribbon.

Before you start experimenting with some of these different tools, return to the User environment and select Layout from the Design screen. Load in the Customer Input layout from the Customer file and click the Full box in the upper right corner so you can see the layout in its entirety. The toolbox on the left side is the focus of this chapter.

THE DRAW LINE TOOL

The Draw Line tool is the most fundamental graphics tool and is used to divide different parts of a layout. You can also use lines to create a small picture.

The Draw Line tool is in the upper left corner of the tool box. Click it and point anywhere in the layout. While holding down the mouse button, drag the mouse to create a line extending from the place you started to the current location of the crosshairs. You can create a line of any angle or length: when you release the mouse button, that line is formed. Also, a small black box (a "handle") appears at each end of the line. When these handles are present with any object, it means that the object is selected.

The line object is selected because you have just finished drawing it. There are two ways you can delete this line if you need to do so. Because it is selected right now, you can press the Backspace key, and the line object will be removed.

Also, as long as you have not performed any other actions after creating the line, you can select Undo from the Edit menu (or press the keyboard equivalent, Command-Z) to eliminate the line.

Before you remove this object, you need to know a couple of other things. First, lines can be of different thicknesses. To change the thickness of a line (or the lines that make up a shape), select that object and then choose a thickness from the Layout menu. The first four options in this menu are 1–Pixel Lines, 2, 3, and 4; the higher the number, the thicker the line. Currently, the line is set to be one pixel thick, although there is no checkmark or other indicator to tell you this. Select some of the other options to see the different line thicknesses.

Besides being able to change line thicknesses, you can change the pattern used to draw the line. As it is now, the line is a solid black pattern, which is especially clear to see if you have it set to be four pixels thick. From the Layout menu, choose the Fill option. A dialog box like the one in Figure 6-1 appears, showing the different patterns available. Point to any one of these (except for Black, since that is what you have already, or None, since that will make the line invisible) and click the mouse button once. The line's pattern instantly changes.

If you select the pixel width and no objects are selected, the width you select becomes the default width, unless you later change it. This means that whatever you draw is automatically set to that default pixel width, unless you purposely pull down the Layout menu and alter the pixel width of that object.

FIGURE 6-1.   Choose the fill pattern you want from the pattern dialog box.

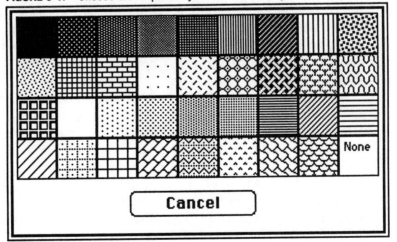

You don't need this line, so if it isn't selected already, point to it and click the mouse button to select it. Now press the Backspace key, and the line should disappear.

THE DRAW OVAL TOOL

The Draw Oval tool, located just beneath the Draw Line tool, lets you draw a circle or an oval with a variety of thicknesses, border patterns, and fill patterns. Click the Draw Oval tool and move the mouse pointer near the center of the Layout window. The crosshairs representing your current location establish a starting pointer for the oval.

Now hold down the mouse button and move the mouse around. 4th Dimension continuously shows you the oval that will be in the layout if you release the mouse button. As you move the mouse around, the oval bends and contorts in relation to your movements. There are no restrictions to where the oval can be, as long as it is within the Layout window.

When you have a fairly large oval, let go of the mouse button. The oval line will be thin since the default is one pixel thick, and the oval will be filled with white, obscuring anything behind it. As with any graphic object, you can change the fill pattern. Select the Fill option from the Layout menu and click on None. The oval is now transparent. Try a few other fill patterns, and you'll see how useful these few graphic tools can be in creating layouts that are easier to understand or that have a little more flair.

The thickness of the border also can be changed. From the Layout menu, select some of the different line thicknesses. If you choose thickness 4, you should see that despite the fill pattern you have selected, the oval's border is black, as in Figure 6-2. The reason for this is that the pattern that fills a shape and the pattern that makes up the shape's border are controlled by two different options.

To change the pattern of the border, choose the Border item from the Layout menu. A Pattern dialog box appears, and you can choose any of the patterns for the border. If the border pattern is identical to the fill pattern, there is no distinction between the border and the interior. Otherwise, the border stands out from the rest of the shape. Try selecting a few different border patterns. Black borders usually look best, but you might require a different pattern.

Once you are through experimenting with ovals, select them and press the Backspace key to delete them. Remember, you can select more than one object by holding down the Shift key while you select the objects, and then, by pressing Backspace, you can delete all of them at once.

FIGURE 6-2.   The pattern used for the border is different from the fill pattern.

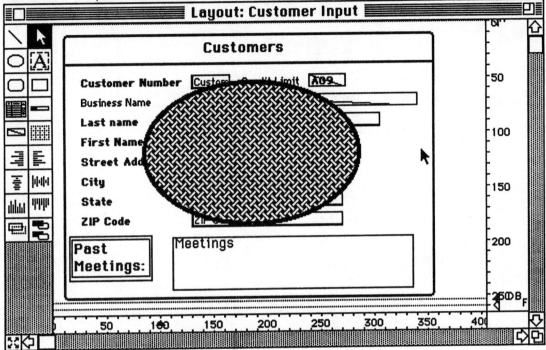

DRAWING RECTANGLES AND ROUNDED RECTANGLES

The Draw Rectangle (rounded) and Draw Rectangle (squared) tools are next to each other in the toolbox, and they perform almost exactly the same function. The only difference is that the corners of the rectangles created by these tools are rounded and squared, respectively.

Click on the Draw Rectangle (rounded) icon, then move the crosshairs into the layout. Draw a rounded rectangle around the title of this layout (Customers) to make a border around it. Because the shape is automatically filled with white, you need to specify None for its pattern. You could select the Fill option from the Layout menu; or, to access the Palette dialog box faster, just double-click on the object. Choose None, and the rounded rectangle is made transparent.

With the object still selected, pull down the Layout menu and choose 2, which means that the border will be two pixels thick. You have now created a heavy border that surrounds the title of the layout, as shown in Figure 6-3. You would make a square-corner rectangle in exactly the same way.

FIGURE 6-3. The rounded rectangle around the title of the layout has the transparent None pattern.

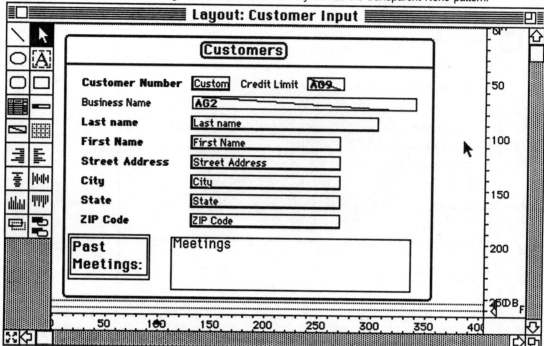

SELECTING AND MODIFYING OBJECTS

The item in the toolbox you will probably use the most is the Select tool, which is the pointing and selecting arrow located in the upper right corner. You have already used this pointer many times, and it can be used on both graphics and non-graphics objects in the layout. The Select tool is particularly useful with graphics objects, since you can reshape objects on the screen, as well as relocate them.

Selecting objects in the layout is easy: just point and click. To select more than one object (for deleting or moving several at once), hold down the Shift key as you select each object. It is also simple to move an object. Just point at the selected object (but *not* at one of its handles) and drag the mouse while you hold down the mouse button. Once you release the mouse button, the object moves to its new position.

To resize or reshape an object, point to one of the handles and, while holding down the mouse button, alter the object to your liking. For instance, select the thick, rounded rectangle you have just created, and do the following:

1. Point to any of the four handles. You will know you are pointing exactly at a handle when the pointer becomes a four-directional arrow.
2. Hold down the mouse button and drag the handle anywhere in the layout. The handle will be dragged wherever you drag the mouse, and the object is resized accordingly.
3. Notice that as you are moving the mouse around the shape of the object changes. Release the mouse button at some point to see how the object has been changed.
4. To undo this change, press Command-Z.
5. Now suppose you want the border to be wider. You could do this two ways. One way would be to drag one of the right handles a bit to the right and one of the left handles a bit to the left. The other way would be to drag one of the handles horizontally and then drag the rounded rectangle so that it is aligned with the title again. The second way is faster, so give it a try.
6. Point to one of the handles on the right side. While holding down the mouse button, stretch the rectangle so it is about an inch wider.
7. Point anywhere in the object except the handles and drag the rectangle to the left so that it is again centered with the title.

Using the handles, you can change any graphics object. You can make shapes bigger or smaller, taller or shorter, and wider or narrower. You can also change the angles and lengths of lines. If you make a mistake in repositioning or reshaping an object, use the Undo command.

DUPLICATION AND PRIORITIES

None of the objects in this layout is particularly difficult to recreate. Sometimes, however, you will probably work on an object (such as an included layout, a button, or some other variable) that takes a long time to make. Should you want one or more copies of this object, there is a menu option (and a corresponding icon in the toolbox) that duplicates whatever object or objects you have selected.

The Duplicate icon is located on the bottom of the left side of the layout toolbox, and the menu item (which does precisely the same thing as clicking the icon) is in the Layout menu. Try selecting a few items in the layout, then issue a Duplicate command. Exact replicas of these objects will be produced and selected, as shown in Figure 6-4.

FIGURE 6-4. Duplicate creates exact copies of the one or more objects that you select.

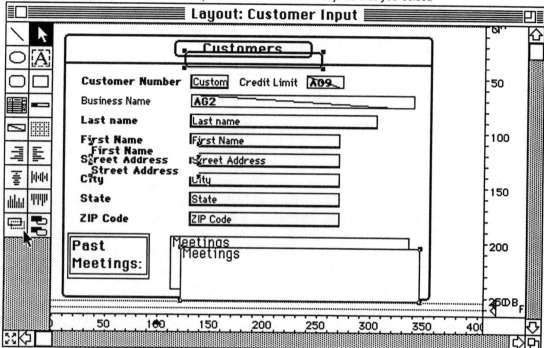

Remove duplicated objects by pressing Backspace. Now assume you want to put the customer number (with a rectangle behind it) at the top of the layout to make the customer number prominent. In fact, you want the number displayed on the left and the right side of the layout title.

You already have the customer number field, along with the rectangle, in the layout. Carefully point to the rectangle lying beneath the customer number field and click the mouse button. Now point to the field, hold down the Shift key, and click the mouse button again. The two objects should be selected.

You want to make two copies of what you have selected, so click the Duplicate icon twice to make the copies. The two selected objects have been duplicated exactly. Now point to one of those two pairs of objects and drag it to the left of the layout title. Next, drag the other pair of objects to the right of the layout title. Your layout should resemble Figure 6-5, with the duplicated object pairs flanking the title of the layout.

Duplicating objects is most useful when it would be more time consuming to create the objects from scratch or when it is important that the new object be exactly the same size as the one that already exists.

FIGURE 6-5.   The two duplicates have been moved to both the left and right sides of the layout title.

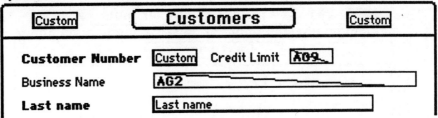

Another command that can be accessed through either the toolbox or the Layout menu is Move to Back. The icon for this command is next to the Duplicate icon (right side, bottom row of the layout toolbox). Its purpose is simple: to move the selected object behind other objects. The following procedure is a good example of how the Move to Back command gives an object lowest priority in the layout:

1. Select the Draw Rectangle (rounded) icon.
2. Draw the rectangle so it fills the visible part of the Layout window, totally obscuring everything else in the layout.
3. Double-click this new object and choose an interesting fill pattern.
4. Issue the Move to Back command by pressing Command-B, by selecting Move to Back from the Layout menu, or by clicking the Move to Back icon.
5. Your layout should look something like Figure 6-6. The large graphic you have created is behind everything else on the screen, forming an interesting background. Remove it now by making sure it's selected and then pressing Backspace.

The Move to Back command is useful for creating graphics effects or for giving an object lower priority than the surrounding objects. There is no Move to Front command, so if you want to bring an object to the front, you have to select the objects in its area and give them the Move to Back command.

USING COLORS

With the exception of the Macintosh II, Macintosh computers cannot display color, so the color feature in 4th Dimension may seem of dubious value. However, if you own an Imagewriter II printer or a Macintosh II, adding color to your database can be helpful. With a Macintosh II, you can change and see the colors on the screen, making your database easier to use and understand. With an Imagewriter II, you can print information in the color of your choice.

FIGURE 6-6. The Move to Back command puts the selected object behind everything else in the layout.

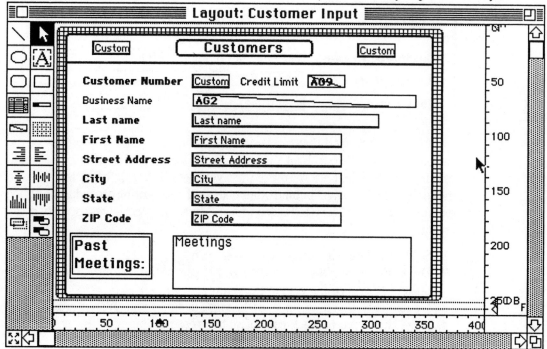

The Color menu, shown in Figure 6-7, lets you give an object a certain color. Objects displayed on the screen and on the printer are made up of a series of on pixels (black on the screen and black on the printer output at this point) and off pixels (white on the screen and white on the printer output at this point). You can change the colors of these on and off pixels for an object, giving you access to hundreds of color combinations.

The top part of the Color menu controls the color of off pixels, while the bottom part controls the color of on pixels. If you select an object and then change the color settings, the object is given that color combination. If no objects are selected, the default colors for the entire layout will be the colors you designate. You can tell which colors are being used by the check marks next to the two colors in the Color menu. There is no need to try the Color menu now, but you should understand how it works.

THE TEXT TOOL

Although the text in a layout has little to do with graphics, the text icon is a vital part of the layout toolbox. With it, you can add text of any style, font, or color to

The Text Tool   117

FIGURE 6-7.   The color menu controls the colors used for the on and off pixels, both on the screen and on the printer.

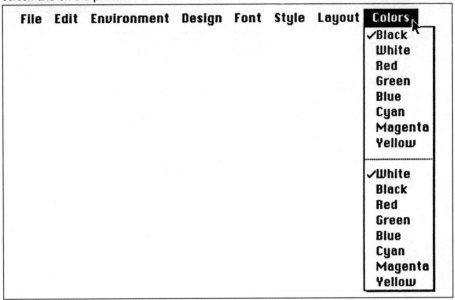

the layout. The Text tool does not create text fields. Instead, it creates permanent additions to the layout that are as constant as the graphics. You can move, delete, and reshape text objects exactly the same way you do graphics objects, and you can modify the text in a text object while in the Design mode.

Scroll down the Layout window to give yourself room to create an example text area. Take the following steps to add text:

1. Select the Text tool and move the crosshairs into the Layout window.
2. Below the existing layout, draw a rectangle that is about the length of the layout and tall enough to display a single line of text.
3. Type in the sentence, `This is a test of the Text tool, which is extremely easy to use`. There won't be enough room for the whole sentence, as shown in Figure 6-8, so only the first part will be visible.
4. Even though you can't see the whole sentence, it is there. Choose the Select tool so you can select the text object. Point to one of the lower handles and drag it down to show another line of text. As you can see, the entire sentence is in memory.
5. This text area acts as a miniature word processor. It word-wraps, which means it fits as many whole words on each line as it can. Drag one of the handles so that the text area is only about an inch wide and an inch tall, as shown in Figure 6-9. The words are adjusted so that they fit within the area.

FIGURE 6-8.   The text area isn't big enough to hold the entire sentence.

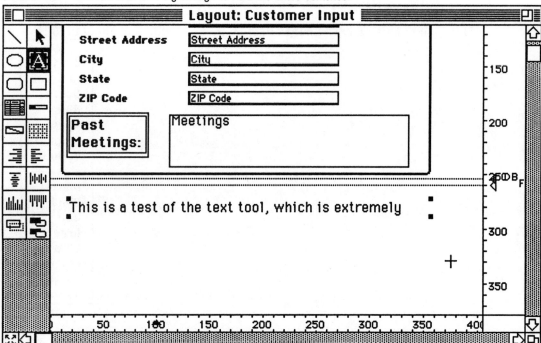

FIGURE 6-9.   The words will be adjusted to fit the width of the text area.

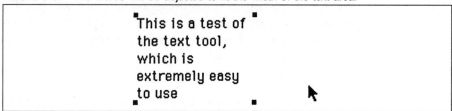

You need to keep in mind a few basic guidelines about putting text in the layout:

- Before you begin entering text, draw the area where the text will be. Try your best to estimate how much room you will need and what area you want the object to use, but if you make a mistake, it's easy to resize or reposition the object.
- To resize or move the text object, choose the Select tool first, then go to the object you want to work with.

- To enter or modify text within a text area, select the Text tool; you can then perform any text functions you want. You can modify text, delete or add text, or cut and paste text.

The Font and Style menus give your text more versatility, since you can change the font, style, alignment, and font size of any selected text with these menus. The Font menu has the names of the fonts that are installed on your system; after you select text, you change its font by selecting any of the choices on this menu.

The Style menu gives you access to six styles: plain, bold, italic, underline, outline, and shadow (you can combine the last five in any way). It also lets you make the text flush left, centered, or flush right and change the text size to 9, 10, 12, 14, 18, 24, or 36 points.

Choose the Text icon and select all the text in the text area. Now choose Times from the Font menu and 24 Point from the Style menu. Your text should resemble that in Figure 6-10, with the text still selected (white on black instead of black on white).

Text areas can have up to 32,767 characters in them, but it's unlikely they will ever need to be more than ten or twenty characters long. Most text in layouts is used for labeling or to emphasize certain instructions, but 4th Dimension gives you a lot of flexibility in how your text looks. Select the text area you have created and delete it, then scroll back up the Layout window to return to the existing parts of the Customer Input layout.

THE GRID

The grid is an invisible helper in layout design that can make creating or modifying a layout much easier. When the grid is turned off, you can move or resize

FIGURE 6-10.   Selected text can be modified in any way, such as this text, which is now 24-point Times.

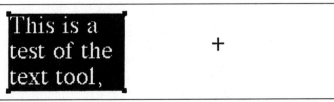

any element by one-pixel increments, thus making any changes minute and very smooth. But that same advantage also makes it difficult to line up objects in the layout or to get a perfect circle or square, since you're given so much freedom.

Turning the grid on restricts the amount of fluidity you have and makes the task of creating or modifying a layout much easier. There are two ways to turn the grid on and off: you can choose the Grid On/Off icon, which is the fifth icon down on the right side of the toolbox, or you can select Grid On from the Layout menu (which toggles to Grid Off if the grid is on). When the grid is off, the icon is lightly colored, and the command in the Layout menu is Grid On. When the grid is on, the icon is solid and dark, and the command in the Layout menu is Grid Off. As you can see, both alternatives toggle with the status of the grid.

To see how the grid can affect using the Layout window, select the thick rounded rectangle that surrounds the layout title. Move it around the screen and notice how easily it moves. You can position it anywhere on the screen with single-pixel accuracy. Reposition the rectangle as accurately as you can around the layout title.

Now turn the grid on and try moving the object around again. The motion is much more jerky, and you can't position the object as accurately as you could before. The advantage is that all the objects have to obey this grid, and it would be much easier to align a series of them or make them a certain size with the grid turned on. Type Command-Z to return the object to its original position.

Currently, the grid is set to be 10 pixels by 10 pixels, which means you can either move or shape an object ten pixels at a time in either direction (with the grid turned off, your "grid" is one pixel by one pixel, the smallest possible). You can change the size of the grid by selecting the Define Grid command from the Layout menu. When you do, the dialog box in Figure 6-11 appears, in which you can enter the number of pixel steps that you want movement allowed in the x-axis (horizontal direction) or the y-axis (vertical direction).

You could make the grid rather fine (such as a 5-by-4 or a 2-by-3 grid) or extremely restrictive (such as a 20-by-30 grid). Try a few different grid types to see how they affect the graphic fluidity in either direction. Do the following to get a better understanding of what the grid does:

- Try different grid types and move the rounded rectangle around. Try positioning the rectangle around the layout title.
- Using different grids, draw a few different shapes, such as ovals and rectangles. Notice how easy it is to make perfect squares and circles with a restrictive grid and how these grids affect your drawing of an object.
- When you are through experimenting with the grid, select all the "garbage" (random objects you have drawn while experimenting) and delete them from

FIGURE 6-11.   The Define Grid dialog box lets you set the number of pixel steps you want permitted in either direction.

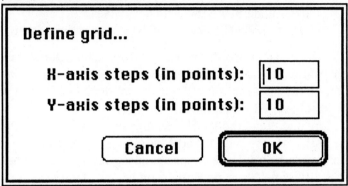

the layout. Be sure to bring the rounded rectangle back to its original spot surrounding the layout title.

The grid makes aligning objects easy, but sometimes you will already have drawn objects without the aid of the grid, objects that you now want aligned. To "snap" these objects to the grid, select the ones you want aligned, then choose the Align to Grid command from the Layout menu (or press Command-G).

You are not guaranteed that the objects will line up in a row, but they will be aligned to the grid line nearest to them. If the objects are relatively close to the same grid line, they will line up perfectly. The best thing to do is to get them as closely aligned as possible before you issue the Align to Grid command.

ALIGNMENT TOOLS

There are six icons available that do what Align to Grid does, except in a more detailed fashion. Those tools, which occupy the sixth, seventh, and eighth rows of the layout toolbox, are the Align Right, Align Left, Align Center/Vertical, Align Center/Horizontal, Align Bottom, and Align Top icons.

The names of these icons should give you a good idea of what their purpose is, but to clarify, each icon aligns the selected objects in a certain way. If you select several objects and click the Align Center/Vertical icon, the objects are vertically centered relative to each other. If you click Align Right, the same objects are given a flush-right alignment. Try the following:

1. Select seven of the field variable objects, from AG2 down to ZIP Code. Remember to hold the Shift key down to select multiple objects.

2. Click the Align Right icon. All the objects will be aligned on the right side, as shown in Figure 6-12. The rectangles you see on the left are the graphic rectangles underneath these field variables.
3. Now click the Align Left icon, and the objects return to their original positions.

There are two important reasons for proper alignment. First of all, it makes the layout look good. With objects evenly aligned horizontally, vertically, or centered, the appearance of the layout is much better than if the objects are haphazardly placed within the layout.

More important, though, 4th Dimension "reads" field variables from left to right and from top to bottom, and if any of these fields is misaligned, it might jump to an incorrect field. For example, suppose you have three fields on a line: the first and third fields are vertically aligned, but the middle one is a single pixel higher than the other two, but you can't see this tiny difference. Whoever uses the database would first have to enter the middle field, then the first one, and then the third, which certainly is an unusual way of doing it. By selecting the three objects and (in this case) clicking the Align Top icon, you eliminate this potential problem.

FIGURE 6-12.   Click Align Right, and the selected objects shift to the right.

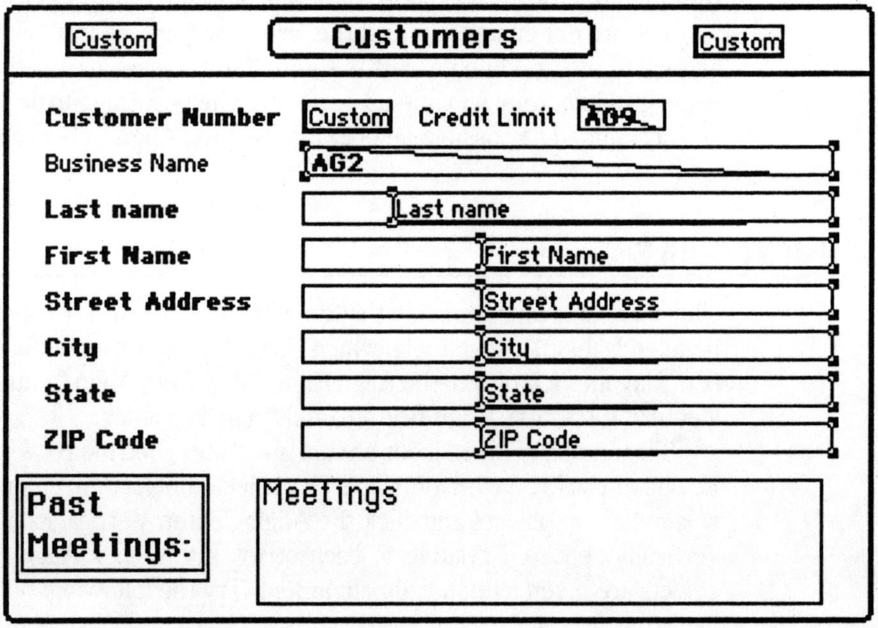

OBJECT MAKERS

A few other icons in the toolbox and a couple of other menu elements are important in the context of this chapter. The icon on the fourth row, left side of the toolbox is Include Layout, which you have used already. Using this icon, you can define an area in the layout where another layout can be displayed. Included layouts are useful for data where there is an unpredictable number of entries, and the data in the included layout can be from a linked file, a subfile, or another file in the database.

The Add Field icon, which is next to the Include Layout icon, is for adding a field to the layout from the file. This icon is useful for creating custom layouts or displaying a field more than once in a layout. Currently, you can select all the fields you need in the process of creating the layout, so this tool is detailed in later chapters.

Probably the most flexible tool of all is Create Variable, which is the icon on the left side of the fifth row. Variables can be buttons, graphs, scrollable lists, or data from linked files (like the AG2 and AG9 variables already in your layout), among many other things. The possibilities of the Create Variable tool will be a major part of the rest of this book.

Finally, there are a couple of menu items that affect the rulers displayed on the bottom and right side of the Layout window. The Define Units command in the Layout menu, whose dialog box is shown in Figure 6-13, dictates which units are used on the ruler. The units can be points, centimeters, or inches; the default setting is points. Whatever unit you choose does not affect the grid, but it does affect what measurement is displayed on the rulers.

FIGURE 6-13.   The Define Units dialog box lets you select what unit of measurement the rulers will use.

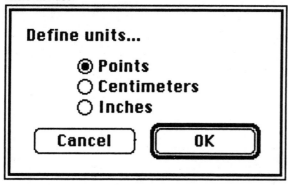

Hide Rulers in the Layout menu (which can also be accessed with Command-R) does just that: it hides the rulers. If you want to bring them back, choose Show Rulers or just press Command-R again.

LAYOUTS AND THE TOOLBOX

As you work more with layouts and need to improve their appearance and functionality, the icons and commands you've learned about in this chapter will become more helpful. Some of the items in the toolbox, such as Add Field and Create Variable, have been glossed over purposely since they are important parts of 4th Dimension that require detailed discussion. The more basic elements that you've learned about in this chapter, which are mostly for text and graphics creation, are still vitally important and should make designing and improving 4th Dimension databases far easier for you.

Components of the Layout

This chapter discusses how important the components of the layout window are to programming in 4th Dimension. You probably already know that 4th Dimension has its own very powerful programming language, which is essential to sophisticated database development. Although you won't learn how to program procedures in that language until later in this book, it is important that you understand now how the various parts of the layout interact with the procedures.

You'll learn about other layout components in this chapter, starting with the Format command, which directly alters the form of an object in a layout. To start, have the Customers database open and open the Credit Input layout.

FORMAT COMMAND

You can use the Format command to change the format of a numeric, a picture, or a date field and to change the field displayed in a particular object. There are two ways to access this command and format a field: you can double-click the field or you can click it once and select the Format command from the Layout menu (the keyboard equivalent is Command-F).

Begin by formatting the Credit Limit field. Point to it and either double-click it or click it once and select the Format command. A dialog box like the one in Figure 7-1 appears.

Underneath the words Format of field . . . are the various fields available in this layout, and the Credit Limit field is selected since you chose it. If you selected one of the other field names and clicked OK, the Credit Limit field would be replaced by the field you selected. For instance, if you clicked the Customer Number field and clicked OK, the Credit Limit field would now be Customer Number, and there would be two Customer Number fields in the layout. That would be a mistake in this case, of course, but if you ever do want to quickly replace one field with another in the layout, use the Format command.

The more important purpose of the Format command is to tell 4th Dimension how to display that particular field. Of the three field types you can format — numeric, date, and picture — the Credit Limit field is numeric, and 4th Dimension gives you a lot of flexibility in how you can format that field. For any numeric field, there are a variety of symbols you can use to construct the format:

.   Use the decimal point to place the decimal point between digits. If you expect the numbers of the field to be followed by two decimal places, your format might be ####.##. If you want the field always to be displayed with two digits after the decimal place (even if the digits are

FIGURE 7-1.   The field format dialog box lets you give the field you select special formatting characteristics.

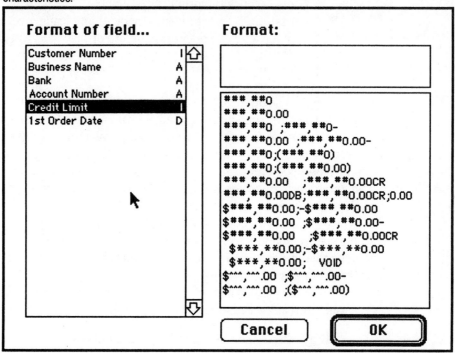

zero), you can force this by preceding the decimal place with a zero. For example, the format ####0.## would display the number 65 as 65.00.

0   A zero can represent any digit; if the digit is zero, the field displays a 0. If the number in a field is 45.10 and the format is 00.00, the number displayed is 45.10.

\#   The pound sign can represent any digit; if the digit is zero, nothing is displayed. If the format is ####.###, then 45 is printed as 45, 7200 as 7200, and 5.860 as 5.86. The zeros are not printed, except in cases when leaving out the zero would change the value of the number (5.860 and 5.86 are the same, so the zero is left out; 7200 and 72 are very different, so the two zeros remain).

^   The caret can represent any digit; it follows the same rules as the pound sign, except that when a leading zero or a trailing zero after the decimal point exists, the caret displays a space instead of nothing. For example, if the format is ^^^^.^^^^, then 1.200 is shown as 1.2

followed by two blank spaces. If you used # instead, 1.2 would be displayed with nothing after it.

*   An asterisk can represent any digit; any leading zeros or any trailing zeros after the decimal point are displayed as asterisks. A format of *****.*** applied to the number 72.5 would be displayed as ***72.5**.

You can use other alphanumeric symbols in the format as well. For instance, you can precede the numbers in a field with a dollar sign ($), put commas in the format (###,###0.00), represent negative numbers by enclosing them in parentheses, or follow each number with CR to represent a credit.

When you enter the format for a numeric field, you can enter up to three different formats to control the display of positive, negative, and zero numbers. Separate these formats with semicolons. You don't have to enter all three format types (in fact, you don't have to enter any formatting at all, since using the Format command is an option in itself). If you want to have total control over how a number is displayed, no matter what its value is, you'll probably want to enter three formats.

For example, suppose you have a numeric field that contains the current balance in a bank account. You would probably want it to have these characteristics:

- always display cents, even for round numbers
- be preceded by a dollar sign
- be surrounded by parentheses if negative
- have commas for figures for $999.99

For these formats, you would click the box underneath the word Format and enter $##,###0.##;($##,###0.##);$0.00, then click OK. The formats are for positive, negative, and zero values, respectively.

An easier way to choose a set of formats is to click one of the premade ones beneath the Format Entry box. When you do, the format instantly appears in the Format box. Try this with Credit Limit right now by clicking the fifth format from the top. Add dollar signs to precede each format, as shown in Figure 7-2. Now that you have made this format change to the field, click the Enter button.

Double-click the 1st Order Date field so you can examine the different ways to format date fields. No matter which format a date field uses to display its value, entering the date is always done in the mm/dd/yy format (such as 1/4/89 for January 4, 1989). The three different types of date formats you can use are as follows:

FIGURE 7-2.   Click the fifth prepared format and add dollar signs to it.

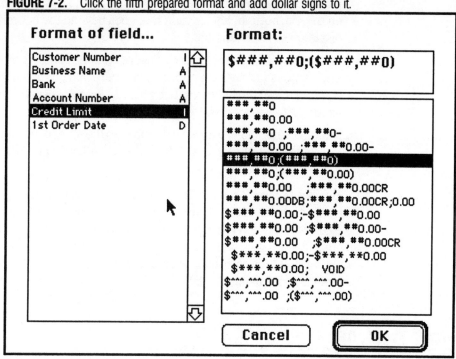

Short. This is the briefest way to display a date, since it displays the date in the same mm/dd/yy format in which it was entered. 11/12/90 would be displayed as 11/12/90.

Abbreviated. This shortens month and day names and also displays the day of the week. 1/9/88 would be Sat, Jan 1, 1988.

Long. This is the most lengthy and complete way to display a date. 1/9/88 would be displayed on the output layout as Saturday, January 9, 1988.

There is no need to change the format of the date field you have on the screen, so click the Cancel button.

Although you haven't had any experience yet with the picture field, you should be aware of the three different formats you can assign a field of that type. To format a picture field, you can select any of the following three possibilities:

Truncated. This is just a different way of saying "cut," which means that the part of the picture that does not fit within the field area is not displayed. The picture is centered so that as much of it as possible is displayed, but anything on the top, bottom, left, or right that goes beyond the boundaries of the field display area is not shown.

Scaled to Fit. This format setting ensures that the entire graphic is displayed. 4th Dimension shrinks the graphic vertically, horizontally, or both to squeeze it into the field area. If the picture is compressed one way more than another, it appears distorted.

On Background. This places the graphic on the screen without any clipping or distortion and allows the graphic to be dragged around. Of course, the graphic might block something else on the layout.

Besides being able to modify the formats of existing fields, you can also use the Format command to set the format of a field you've just put onto a layout. Use the Add Field tool (on the right side of the toolbox, fourth one down) to place a field in a layout; after you draw the area where the field should be located, the Format of Field dialog box appears automatically. Later in this chapter, you'll learn more about using the Add Field tool when you create a custom layout.

EIGHT TYPES OF LAYOUTS

Although not specifically an element within the layout window, the nine different layout choices available are important to understand when you are creating layouts for a database. Select the Layout command from the Design menu and do the following:

1. Make sure the Customers file is selected, then enter the layout name New Layout. Click the New button.
2. Select the 9-point font size and the layout type in the upper left corner, as shown in Figure 7-3.
3. Click OK, and the layout appears on the screen. Click the zoom box in the upper right corner so that the layout fills the screen.

The following paragraphs describe the eight different layouts that are available to you and the cases where they might be appropriate. You don't have to follow along by creating layouts of your own, but you can certainly do so just to see what they look like on your own screen. Whatever you do, delete these experimental layouts once you're through so they don't clutter up your database.

Layout style 1, shown in Figure 7-4, is generally used for output. It is in the upper left corner of the layout choices box, and it lists the field names at the top of the screen and has all of the corresponding field values beneath. The presence

FIGURE 7-3.   Note the nine different types of layouts available, including the Custom layout, which you create from scratch.

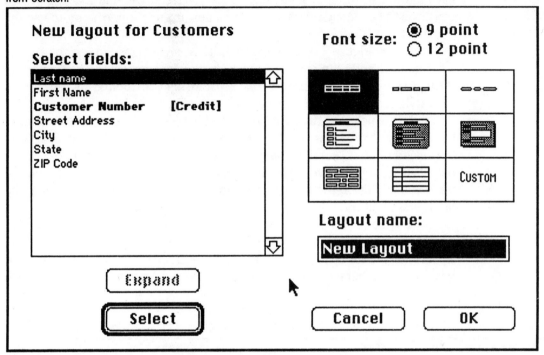

FIGURE 7-4.   Layout style 1 used as an output layout.

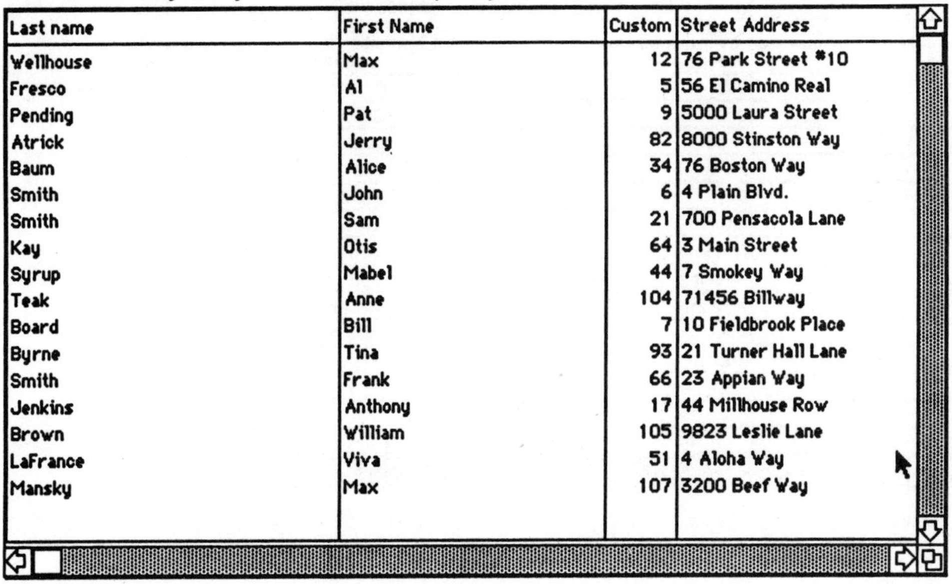

Last name	First Name	Custom	Street Address
Wellhouse	Max	12	76 Park Street #10
Fresco	Al	5	56 El Camino Real
Pending	Pat	9	5000 Laura Street
Atrick	Jerry	82	8000 Stinston Way
Baum	Alice	34	76 Boston Way
Smith	John	6	4 Plain Blvd.
Smith	Sam	21	700 Pensacola Lane
Kay	Otis	64	3 Main Street
Syrup	Mabel	44	7 Smokey Way
Teak	Anne	104	71456 Billway
Board	Bill	7	10 Fieldbrook Place
Byrne	Tina	93	21 Turner Hall Lane
Smith	Frank	66	23 Appian Way
Jenkins	Anthony	17	44 Millhouse Row
Brown	William	105	9823 Leslie Lane
LaFrance	Viva	51	4 Aloha Way
Mansky	Max	107	3200 Beef Way

of the field names makes it easy to refer to the meaning of each field, but if you have more than three or four fields in a layout, you will find that the screen usually isn't big enough to hold all the values, making it necessary to use the horizontal scroll bar.

Style 2 in Figure 7-5, which is the middle style choice in the top row, is different from style 1 in only two minor ways: it does not list the field names at the top of the screen, and the lines that separate fields are dotted instead of solid. Like style 1, this one is best for output.

Style 3, which is on the right side of the top row of choices, is best for output if you have just one or two fields to display. It draws a rounded rectangle around the fields and looks best if the fields fit entirely on the screen. Figure 7-6 shows output using style 3; even though the rounded rectangles can't surround the fields and still fit on the screen, you can view the whole output by using the horizontal scroll bar.

Style 4, located on the left side of the middle row of choices, is the one you've been using for input for most of this book. It is the most basic and easy-to-use layout for input. (Keep in mind that any of these automatic layouts can be used for input or output, but most of them are best for one or the other.) If you used style

FIGURE 7-5.   Style 2 is usually for output, and it does not list field names at the top of the screen.

Wellhouse	Max	12	76 Park Street #10
Fresco	Al	5	56 El Camino Real
Pending	Pat	9	5000 Laura Street
Atrick	Jerry	82	8000 Stinston Way
Baum	Alice	34	76 Boston Way
Smith	John	6	4 Plain Blvd.
Smith	Sam	21	700 Pensacola Lane
Kay	Otis	64	3 Main Street
Syrup	Mabel	44	7 Smokey Way
Teak	Anne	104	71456 Billway
Board	Bill	7	10 Fieldbrook Place
Byrne	Tina	93	21 Turner Hall Lane
Smith	Frank	66	23 Appian Way
Jenkins	Anthony	17	44 Millhouse Row
Brown	William	105	9823 Leslie Lane
LaFrance	Viva	51	4 Aloha Way
Mansky	Max	107	3200 Beef Way

FIGURE 7-6.   Rounded rectangles surround each line in the layout, and no field headings are displayed.

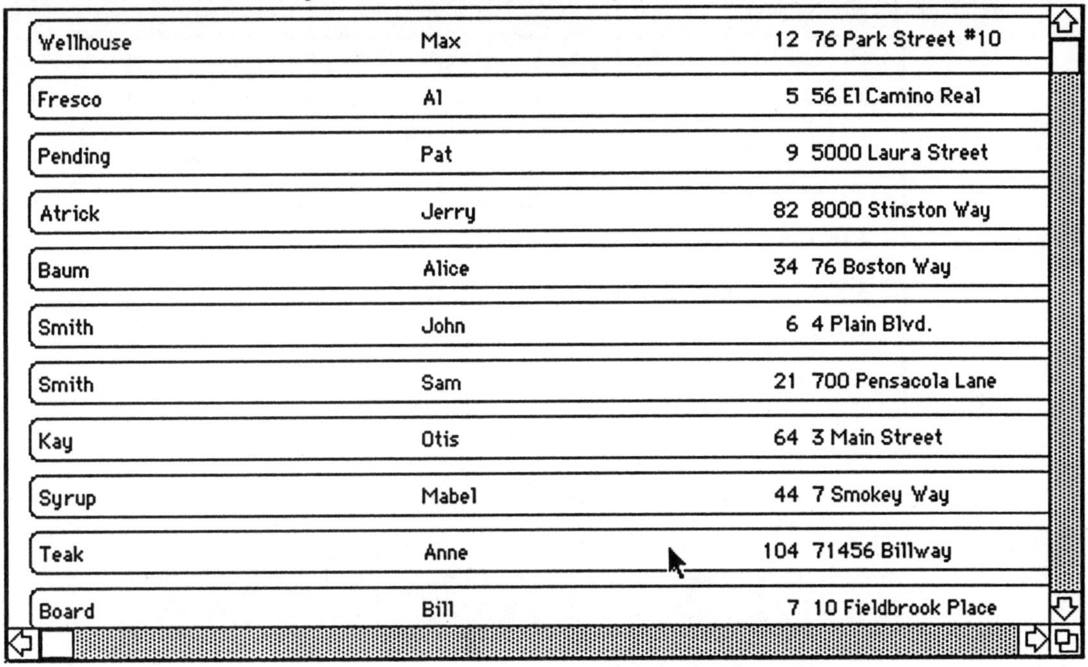

Wellhouse	Max	12 76 Park Street #10
Fresco	Al	5 56 El Camino Real
Pending	Pat	9 5000 Laura Street
Atrick	Jerry	82 8000 Stinston Way
Baum	Alice	34 76 Boston Way
Smith	John	6 4 Plain Blvd.
Smith	Sam	21 700 Pensacola Lane
Kay	Otis	64 3 Main Street
Syrup	Mabel	44 7 Smokey Way
Teak	Anne	104 71456 Billway
Board	Bill	7 10 Fieldbrook Place

4 for output, it would take up a lot of space on the screen or on the printed page. But, as you can see in Figure 7-7, it is excellent for input.

Style 5, the middle choice in the middle row of styles, is almost identical to style 4: it has field names, line-by-line entry, and is surrounded by a rounded rectangle. The only difference is that the objects (like the surrounding rectangle and the field names) have been filled with a certain color. You may prefer this style, shown in Figure 7-8, and of course you can alter *any* layout with filled colors or other alterations that you like. Style 4 could be made to look like style 5 in less than a minute, for example.

A simpler input layout is style 6, which has the names of each field, but which lacks the title at the top of the layout. It is located on the right side of the middle row of choices in the new Layout dialog box. This layout, shown in Figure 7-9, takes up less room and is therefore a possible choice for an output layout as well, if you want each field preceded by its field name.

Automatic layout style 7, the left choice on the bottom row of choices, is probably a type that you will not use often since it isn't very effective as an input or an output layout. It lacks field names, which would make it difficult to use for input, and it is so bulky that it wouldn't be very efficient as an output layout either. Figure 7-10 shows this type of style as an output layout.

FIGURE 7-7. Any automatic layout can be used for input or output, but types like style 4 are best for input.

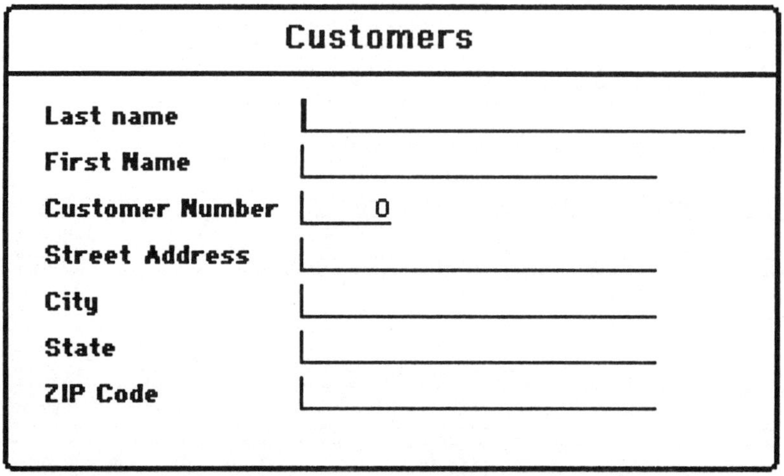

FIGURE 7-8. Style 5 has filled-in objects, but otherwise is identical to style 4.

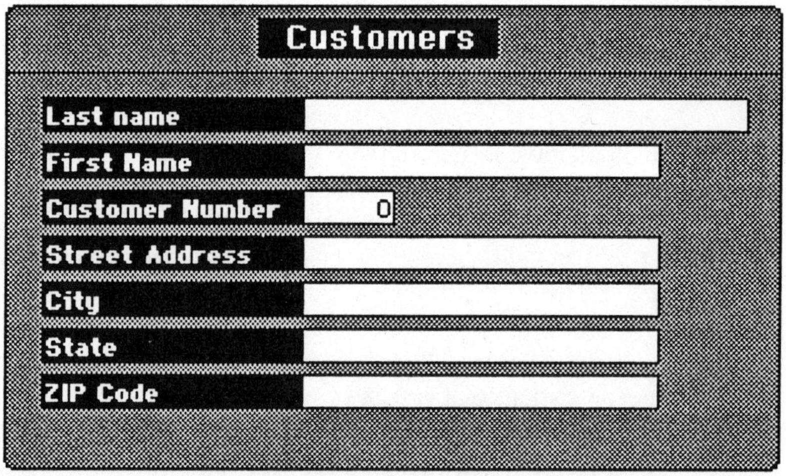

Finally, style 8, which is the middle choice on the bottom row, is fine for either input or output. Figure 7-11 shows it being used for an output layout, but because it is compact and lists all of the field names, it would be a good choice for either purpose.

As you probably know already, any layout used for input is displayed by itself on the screen, since only one record can be entered at a time. If a layout is used for output, however, as many records as possible are shown on the screen, and you scroll down the list of records with the vertical scroll bar.

FIGURE 7-9.   Automatic layout style 6 is shown here as an input layout, but it is small enough to be used for an output layout as well.

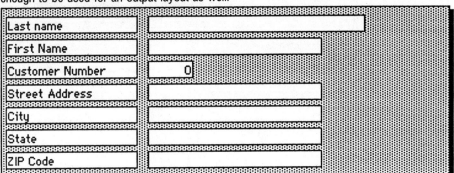

MAKING A CUSTOM LAYOUT

Another style choice, style 9, is located on the right side of the bottom row of choices. This is a somewhat different choice from the other eight in that it lets you build your own custom layout (hence the word Custom within the choice box). Building a custom layout from scratch instead of using an automatic one gives you tremendous flexibility, but it also is a lot more work. You have to put in all the graphics, fields, field names, and any other objects in the layout that you need.

Delete any experimental layouts you have created, then select the Layout command from the Design menu. Now do the following:

1. Select the Credit file name.
2. Type in the name of the new layout, Custom Input, and click the New button.
3. Choose the 9-point font size, then select the Custom layout style. Click OK.
4. Click the zoom box so that the custom layout fills the screen.

As shown in Figure 7-12, you now have a completely blank layout. The only thing showing on the layout itself are the four dotted lines you're accustomed to seeing on *every* layout, and they will be explained in this chapter.

You are going to make a rather unusual input layout in this example. Start by selecting the Draw Oval tool and draw a large oval that fits between the top line (denoted by an H, for header, on the right side of the screen) and the second line (D, which stands for detail). It should be a large oval, as shown in Figure 7-13. This object is filled with white, although you can't tell that right now. Double-click on the object to get to the Fill dialog box and select None as the fill color. You don't want this object obscuring others once you're through.

FIGURE 7-10. Style 7 isn't particularly effective for either input or output.

Wellhouse	Max	12
76 Park Street #10	Baton Rouge	
LA	70815	

Fresco	Al	5
56 El Camino Real	Sunnyvale	
CA	95423	

Pending	Pat	9
5000 Laura Street	Minneapolis	
MN	45623	

Atrick	Jerry	82

9000 Stincton Way   Dales Verdes

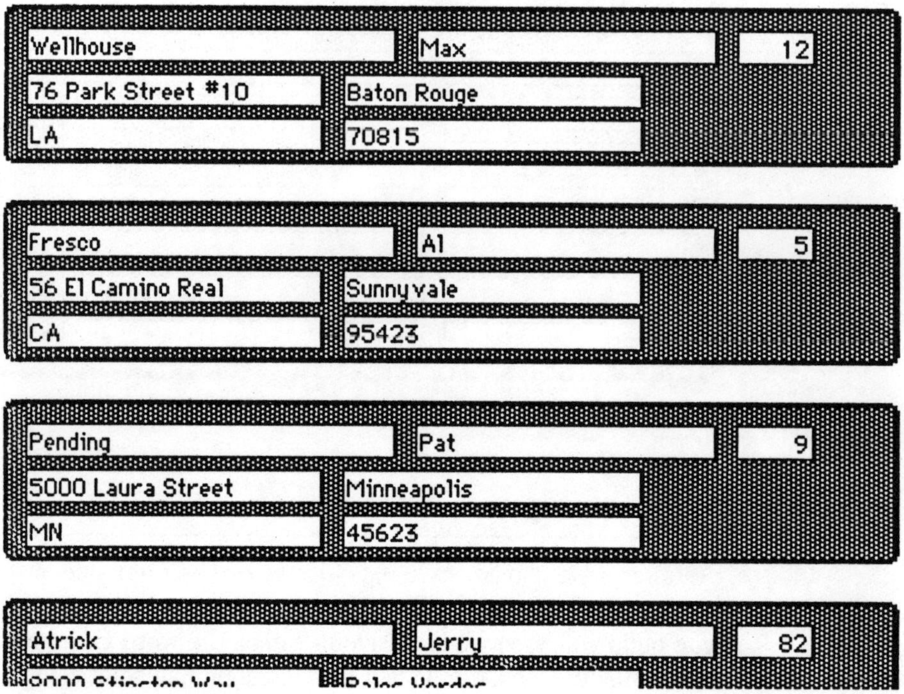

FIGURE 7-11. Style 8 is compact and understandable enough to be used for either input or output.

Last name	
First Name	
Customer Number	0
Street Address	
City	
State	
ZIP Code	

To make placing the graphics easier, turn on the grid either by clicking the Grid On/Off graphic in the toolbox or by selecting Turn Grid On from the Layout menu. Follow these instructions to put the customized input layout together:

1. Select the Text tool and draw a rectangle for the text near the top center within the oval.

FIGURE 7-12.   The layout window is completely blank, except for the four lines marked H, D, B, and F.

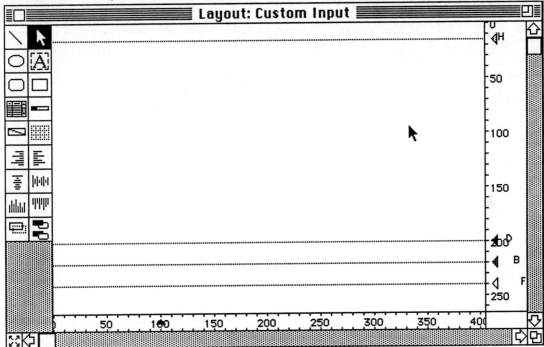

2. Select the Times font from the Font menu (if you don't have this font installed, it will make only a cosmetic difference if you use a different font).
3. Select the 18 Point, Center, and Outline choices from the Style menu.
4. Type in the word Customers. Your layout should resemble Figure 7-14. Reposition the text object if it is not placed properly.
5. Using the crosshairs of the Text tool once again, draw a rectangle below and to the left of the title. Type in the word Name.
6. Select the Add Field tool, which is the fourth one down on the right side of the toolbox. Just to the right of the word Name, draw a rectangle, as shown in Figure 7-15.
7. From the dialog box, you can select any of the fields in this file. Double-click on the first name, since you want that field to be placed in the area you have just designated.
8. Use Add Field again to draw a rectangle right next to First Name, then double-click the Last Name field when the dialog box appears on the screen. Remember, if you are not satisfied with how an object is positioned, either

FIGURE 7-13. Draw a large oval that fits between the first and second lines. This will be the border surrounding the input layout.

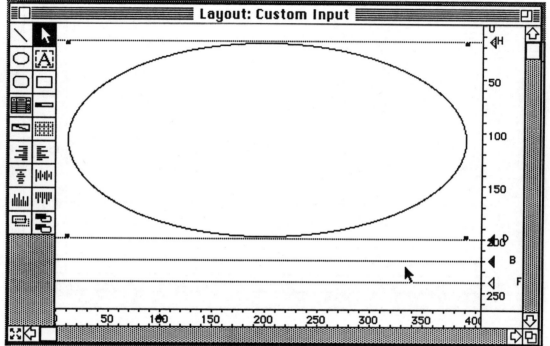

drag it to the place you want it or use the alignment tools. You can turn the grid off temporarily if you want to "fine-tune" the positions.

9. To make sure the large oval doesn't get in the way of your trying to drag or alter any of the objects, select the oval and click the Move to Back tool on the bottom of the right side of the toolbox. This places the graphics object in the back, where it belongs. It's just there for cosmetic purposes.

10. Now select the Name text object and the First Name field. Click on the Duplicate tool, and your layout should resemble Figure 7-16.

11. Drag the two items below so they can serve as the address line. Drag the field object to the right about half an inch.

12. Select the text tool and double-click on the word Name in the second line. Type in the correct field name Address. Notice that the word Address does not fit entirely within the object space, so drag one of the right handles to the right so the whole word shows. Your layout should look like Figure 7-17.

FIGURE 7-14.   The title Customers should be in large type and centered at the top of the oval.

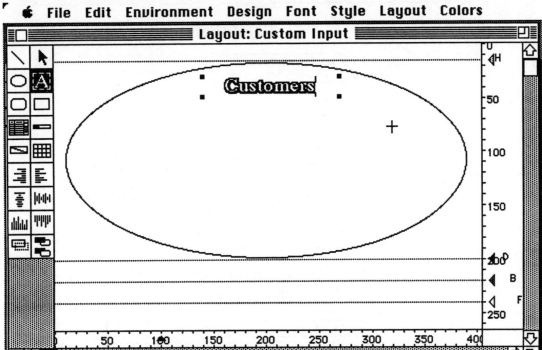

FIGURE 7-15.   Use the Add Field tool to draw the rectangle where the variable should be positioned.

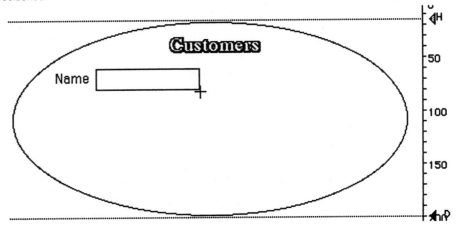

FIGURE 7-16. Choose the text object and the field object, then click Duplicate.

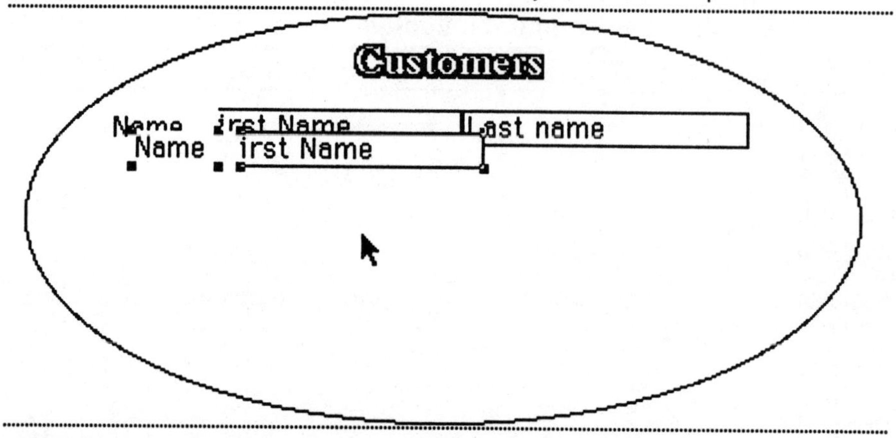

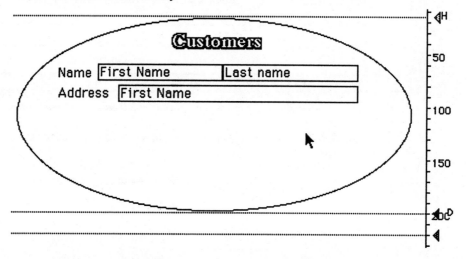

FIGURE 7-17. Change the text within the text object and make sure the objects are aligned so you can see all of them clearly.

13. Now double-click the field on the second line and change the field contents from First Name to Street Address. You duplicated these two objects to save a little time. However, make sure that if you use Duplicate you change the duplicated objects so they match your needs, as you have done here.
14. Double-click the Name and the First Name objects on the first line again and click the Duplicate tool three times. Move the first pair of objects onto the third left on the left side (City). Move the second pair to the third line on the right side (State). Move the third pair to the fourth line on the right side (ZIP Code).

15. Change the text objects so they read City, State, and ZIP. Adjust the sizes of the text and field objects appropriately, as shown in Figure 7-18.

16. Now you have to alter the field names as well. Change the first field name on the third line to City, the second field name on the third line to State, and the field name on the fourth line to ZIP Code.

17. Duplicate a text object and a field object once again and place them to the left of the ZIP Code information. Change the text object to read Cust. No. and the field object to be the Customer Number field. Everything should be lined up properly on four lines.

18. For a little graphic embellishment, put a rounded rectangle around the Customers title. Make the rectangle two pixels thick (use the Layout menu to change the thickness) and give it None for its fill color so you can still see the Customers name.

19. You might even want to add a little picture to this layout. If you have clipped a small picture from your Scrapbook, you can paste it to the layout. Figure 7-19 shows the completed layout. The picture is unnecessary; it just makes the layout more interesting.

There is nothing particularly special about choosing the Custom style. You can alter objects, delete or add fields, add graphics, and do anything else you have done here with any of the automatic layouts. The only advantage of Custom is that it gives you a blank slate to start with, in case you want to create a layout completely from scratch. Go ahead and close this layout in case you want to examine it or use it later. It won't be used as the default input layout, since Customer Input is already checked off for that purpose.

FIGURE 7-18.   Position the three pairs of duplicated objects, change the text, and adjust their sizes.

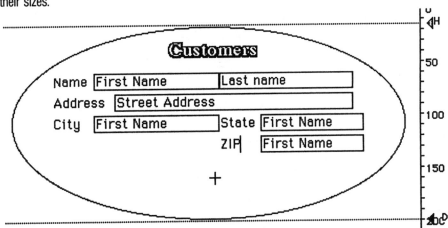

FIGURE 7-19. Here is the completed custom layout. Graphics are easy to add to the layout, as you can see.

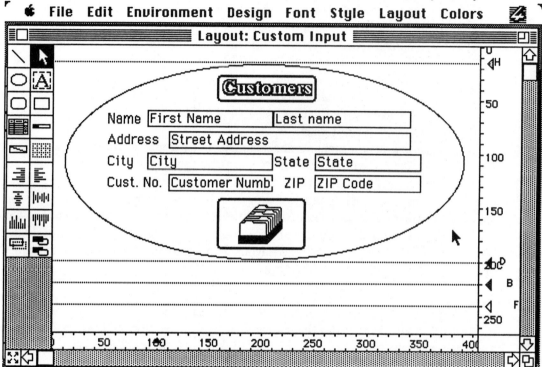

To complete your exploration of layouts, you are now going to learn about the meaning of those lines in all the layouts you've been creating.

THE EXECUTION CYCLE

Later in this book, you are going to learn how to write procedures, which are short programs that instruct 4th Dimension to carry out a particular function. For instance, if you create a customized menu that has the option Print Records on it, you have to write a corresponding procedure that prints the records whenever that option is used.

Even though you won't be learning about writing procedures for a while, you should understand now that layouts and procedures are intricately linked. This takes several forms, but one of the most important is the layout procedure. The layout procedure is a set of instructions to 4th Dimension for actions the program should take before, during, and after a particular layout is displayed.

Layout procedures are important to understand. Remember these three basic facts:

- A layout can have one and only one layout procedure (if it has a procedure at all). The layouts you have created so far don't have any layout procedures, and they still work perfectly. However, you can create a layout procedure for any of the layouts, and any layout can have only one procedure of its own.
- The layout procedure is used every time the corresponding layout is active.
- Before the layout comes on the screen, the *before* instructions are executed. While the layout is on the screen, the *during* instructions are executed. When the user presses Enter and the layout disappears from the screen, the *after* instructions are executed.

Because of all these executions, this whole concept is called the execution cycle. Following are descriptions of the three parts of the cycle and why instructions for each part might be useful:

Before. The before condition is TRUE (in other words, activated) before 4th Dimension displays a layout. Instructions here might be used for linking one file to another, setting variables to a certain value, or clearing variables. These all take place before the layout appears.

During. This condition is TRUE while the layout is being displayed, and consequently it is true while the user is entering data. Instructions during this part of the execution cycle can validate input or keep running totals of data.

After. Once the user presses Enter (or performs whatever other function that signifies completion of record entry), the after condition is set to TRUE. After the layout is entered, you might want 4th Dimension to create a graphic based on the entry within the record or perform some other function that requires that the whole record be finished.

These three conditions—before, during, and after—are only half of the execution cycle, and they pertain mostly to input layouts. The four other parts of the execution cycle—in header, in detail, in break, and in footer—pertain more to printing than to the video screen. Another difference is that while before, during, and after relate to when the layout is displayed, the other four parts of the execution cycle relate more to what is put in various sections of printed output. These four parts of the execution cycle are described in the following paragraphs.

In header. Instructions in this part of the procedure control what is printed at the top of the page (if you are using it to modify screen output, it controls what is printed at the top of the screen). Only one header appears at the top of each page.

In detail. The bulk of the layout is usually where all of the fields are located and where no special calculations are made. The in detail part of the execution cycle is located between *in header* and *in break*, and it holds the body of the layout.

In break. Sometimes you will want to compute totals of certain fields in a database. You can create subtotals and totals of sorted fields, and the in break part of the execution cycle controls where the subtotals are displayed on the printed page.

In footer. As with *in header*, there can be only one footer per page with this instruction. It controls processing at the bottom of each page, so you could have computations of certain columns printed at the bottom, for example.

These are the seven different parts of the execution cycle in a layout procedure. There are also file procedures, which are similar to layout procedures except that they execute whenever *any* layout from a particular file is used. Layout procedures provide special instructions when a particular layout is used, whereas file procedures give instructions whenever any layout from an entire file is used.

CONTROL LINES

You have probably noticed the four dotted horizontal lines on your layouts. These are called control lines, and they set up the header, detail, break, and footer areas of a layout. The vertical ruler of a layout controls the four triangles that you drag to move any of these lines. The triangles are marked H, D, B, and F, which stand for header, detail, break, and footer, respectively.

Everything above the H line is considered the header. Header material prints once at the top of each page, and it can appear on both input and output screens. You might use the header to display a title, the page number, or the date.

The contents between the header control line (H) and the detail control line (D) is the detail area, which is the bulk of the layout. This material prints once for each record.

Beneath the D line and above the break control line (B) is the break area. If you put a sorted variable within the break area that contains the total of the values in a sorted selection, that variable's value will be printed. This is mostly used to display running subtotals as each page is printed; the grand total is printed on the last page.

Finally, everything between the B line and the footer control line (F) is the footer, which can be used for page numbers, titles, or totals.

If you want to move any of these lines, simply point to the triangle of the line you want to move and drag it. If you want 4th Dimension to ignore a line, drag it to the top of the screen where the 0 is located on the vertical ruler. Don't put the lines out of their proper HDBF order, however, since 4th Dimension will ignore any out-of-order lines.

Another item on the layout screen is the small triangle on the horizontal ruler. This is the label width triangle, which you can drag to any position to indicate how wide you want your mailing labels to be, if you are using a layout to print mailing labels. When 4th Dimension actually prints the mailing labels, it fits as many across on a page as possible and scales the layout up or down so that it matches the width you've provided. Unless you are printing mailing labels and have loaded in a specific layout for that purpose, don't alter the position of the label width triangle.

In the next chapter, you're going to learn about variables, which are also essential to procedure programming. Variables can take many forms, including numbers, words, buttons, and even graphs. You'll learn how they work both within the layout and as independent storage areas.

Variables and Operators

Using the knowledge you have about 4th Dimension up to this point, you can create some fairly sophisticated databases. You can create files, subfiles, and linked files, and you understand how to create and arrange fields to store and modify just about any type of information. There are, however, limitations on what you can do in the User mode using just the tools that are immediately available. To create stand-alone databases that have the customized commands that a user will need (and that don't have any unnecessary commands), you have to write procedures.

You won't get heavily involved with writing procedures for a few more chapters, but you do need to build up a base of knowledge so that you can better understand how to write procedures. In this chapter, you're going to learn about variables, which serve not only as storage areas for procedures, but also as buttons and graph areas within layouts. There won't be a lot of actual hands-on use of 4th Dimension in this chapter, since its main purpose is to explain what variables are and how they can be used in layouts and procedures.

PROCEDURES AND VARIABLES

If you have never programmed a computer before, you might not understand what procedures and variables are. A procedure is a collection of instructions that can be given to 4th Dimension to carry out. The instructions are carried out in their given order, and these instructions could tell the database to delete a record, get a new record, show a picture on the screen, or do anything else possible within a 4th Dimension database.

The instructions that make up procedures aren't hard to learn, but they must follow a specific format. All of the commas, spaces, colons, and other special characters must be in exactly the right place and the right order. The *Command Reference* provided in the 4th Dimension packages describes in detail the dozens of commands available in the program. You'll learn about most of them in this book, but use the *Command Reference* for a comprehensive outline of commands.

As you write the procedures that are used in a database, you'll find that your work gets easier, because you can make the procedures modular. That is, you can write some procedures that carry out basic functions, and you can call these procedures from separate procedures. For example, let's say you write a procedure called *Deleterec*, which first confirms that you want to delete some records and then actually deletes those records if you confirm the request. While working on the database some more, you might need a new procedure that searches for records based on a certain criterion, asks if you want to delete them, and then proceeds with the deletion when it receives your OK. You already have a procedure that performs the second two actions, so the new procedure has to consist only of the commands to search for the records. After that, you can include the name *Deleterec* to access the existing procedure.

The basic thing to remember is that procedures can act as building blocks. One procedure might execute (that is, run) several other procedures. It saves you time and effort to rely on existing procedures if they do the job.

Variables, on the other hand, hold information and are provided names so you can get that information. Information can be in the form of a graphic, an integer, someone's name, an address, or even an indicator that tells if a button is clicked (1) or not (0). Think of variables as 4th Dimension's memory. It's a fragmented memory, but if you give the variables logical names, it will be easy for you to use them.

Variables are flexible entities. They can be deleted, altered, strung together, compared with other variables, and subjected to any other legal devices in 4th Dimension. As you learn more about procedures, you will quickly discover how variables are so central to any logical decisions made in the database you create. That is why it is important to fully understand them after you're through with this chapter.

VARIABLE OPERATORS

To create a variable, you first need to give it a name. You have to follow a few rules when providing a name:

- A variable that is available throughout the database, no matter what procedure is being used, is called a global variable. If you are using a variable just within a certain procedure, and you might be using that same variable name in other procedures, the variable is local.
- Both global and local variables can have names up to eleven characters long. Local variable names always begin with a dollar sign. For example, a global variable might be named Button, while a local variable might be named $Total.
- The first character of the name must be a letter in the alphabet, but the characters that follow it can be numbers, letters, the space character, an underscore, or the period. Don't use the colon, plus sign, or any of the other symbols. To avoid confusion, it's usually best just to use alphabetic characters and to occasionally use numbers when you need to define more clearly the contents of each variable.

Say you want to create a variable named States, and you want that variable to have a value of 50. You might suspect that typing States = 50 in the procedure editor would accomplish this. Instead, 4th Dimension would compare the values of States (which is not even defined yet) to the value 50 and return the answer False. When you use just the equals sign, you are making a logical comparison.

What you want to make is an *assignment*. You want to assign a certain value to a variable name. You do this by first typing a colon and then typing the equal sign. Some examples of variables that are assigned certain values follow:

States: = 50

Operator: = Timo Bruck

$Name: = Firstname + + Lastname

In the third example, the variable being assigned a value ($Name) was given the combined values of $Firstname, a blank space, and $Lastname. You can use variables on either side of the assignment, as long as you are assigning the value to the variable on the left side of the : = expression. In this case, if Firstname is John and Lastname contains the name Smith, then the local variable $Name is assigned the value John Smith.

The plus sign, which adds the values of two variables, is one of the operators in 4th Dimension. Operators are symbols that perform certain operations on variables, numbers, and other objects. The following sections describe the various operators and how they might be used.

NUMERIC OPERATORS

Numeric operators are usually used for actual numbers or numeric variables. These basic math functions can be used on any combination of numbers or variables, and they follow left-to-right precedence. To override precedence, use parentheses. For example, instead of typing 10 + 60*20/30, you would type 10 + 60*(20/30) so that the 20/30 calculation is computed first and then multiplied by the sum 10 + 60.

Also remember the : = assignment if you are assigning values to variables based on numeric results. If Total1 equals 25 and Total2 equals 35, then Total3: = Total1 + Total2 gives Total3 a value of 60.

Addition. Use the + sign. 10 + 5 would return 15.

Subtraction. Use the – sign. 10 – 5 would return 5.

Multiplication. Use the * sign. 10*5 would return 50.

Division. Use the / sign. 10/2 would return 5.

Exponentiation. Use the ^ sign. 10^2 would return 100.

STRING OPERATORS

A string is a series of characters that can range from one character long to thousands of characters long. If a variable contains the word *database*, for example, the word *database* is considered a string (as opposed to a number). There are two operators that can affect strings:

Concantenation. Use the + sign. Concantenation is just a different way of saying "stringing together." If the variable Firstname is equal to the string *Tom* and the variable Lastname is *Jones*, then Firstname + Lastname would yield *TomJones*. Notice that there is no space between the two words. They are simply connected together.

Repetition. Use the * sign, followed by the number of times you want the string to be repeated. If you want a string to be concantenated with itself a number of times, use the repetition symbol. If the variable Message contains the string *Alert!*, for instance, then typing **Message*5** would return the string *Alert! Alert! Alert! Alert! Alert!* The string is repeated five times.

DATE OPERATORS

Dates in 4th Dimension procedures are in the format !mm/dd/yyyy!, which means the month, date, and year are separated by slashes and surrounded by exclamation marks. January 16, 1992, would be entered as !01/16/1992!. There are a couple of operators in 4th Dimension that make working with dates easier:

Addition. Use the + sign. To find out a date that is a certain number of days after a particular day, type in the date, the plus sign, then the number of days in the future. Typing in !01/16/1992! + 9 would return !01/25/1992! since January 25, 1992, is nine days after January 16, 1992. Because dates are so difficult to work with numerically, this function is useful if you want to compute large figures, such as 1,000 days ahead.

Difference. Use the – sign. This computes the number of days between the two dates you provide. If you enter !05/01/1989!–!05/13/1989!, 4th Dimension returns 12, indicating a twelve-day difference between those two dates. Again, the number of days between two dates is difficult to compute without this function.

LOGICAL OPERATORS

As important as all the operators already mentioned are, the logical operators are used more than any of them. The logical operators let 4th Dimension decide what relationship a certain variable or number has with another, which is critical information in a procedure.

Equality. Use the = symbol. This returns a TRUE if the first expression is equal to the second or a FALSE if the expressions are not exactly equal. 123 = 123 would return TRUE, Scott = Scott would return TRUE, while Scott = SCOTT would return FALSE, because the two expressions are not exactly the same.

Inequality. Use the # symbol. This does exactly the opposite of the = symbol, since it returns TRUE if the two expressions are not equal and FALSE if the two expressions are equal. California # Texas would return a TRUE, since the two expressions are not equal to one another.

Greater than. Use the > symbol. If the first expression is greater than the second, a TRUE is returned. If not, you get a FALSE. 50 > 49 would return a TRUE, while Moon > Zoo would return FALSE, since Moon comes earlier in the alphabet than Zoo (later letters are considered "greater" than earlier letters).

Less than. Use the < symbol. If the first expression is less than the second, a TRUE is returned. If not, you get a FALSE. 40 < 120 would return a TRUE, while Cheese < Ape would return FALSE.

Greater than or equal to. Use the two symbols > = . If the first expression is greater than or equal to the second (such as 4 > = 5 or 4 > = 4), a TRUE is returned, otherwise a FALSE is returned.

Less than or equal to. Use the two symbols < = . If the first expression is less than or equal to the second, a TRUE is returned, otherwise a FALSE is returned. Tree < = Tree and Computer < = Personal would both return TRUE.

AND. Use the & symbol. This is a conjunction that connects one logical expression with another, with the individual expressions enclosed in parentheses. If the logical expressions connected by & are all true, then a TRUE is returned. If just one of them is not true, a FALSE is returned. The expression (Yardstick = Yardstick) & (1000 = 1000) & (Football = Basketball) would return a FALSE, since the last expression is not true.

AND is helpful when you want only a TRUE given a series of true logical circumstances. For instance, if (First Name = Ronald)&(Last

Name = Reagan), then you might want the database to print *You were a U.S. President!*

OR. Use the | symbol (which is at the lower right portion of the keyboard). This returns a TRUE if either the expression preceding the | or the expression following the | is true, but a FALSE is returned if both are false. The logical expression $(20 < 10)|(100 > 20)|(\text{Jake} < = \text{Abby})$ returns TRUE, because even though the first and third expressions are false, the second expression is true. The fact that anything within this expression is true makes the result of this composite statement true.

An important fact to remember is that you can mix the AND (&) and OR (|) expressions in any way that is appropriate. For that matter, you can mix any logical expressions. Fortunately, it isn't often that you have to type in anything too logically complicated. If you do, it's a good idea to break the problem into several logical steps, so you are less likely to make a mistake and so the problem is easier to understand if you have to debug (fix) a problem in the procedure.

IDENTIFIERS IN PROCEDURES

Even though this chapter is about variables, you have to understand some of the fundamental components of a procedure in order to use those variables. In a procedure, there are many other objects besides variables, including file names, layout names, and fields. Each of them is identified by 4th Dimension by a unique format. For instance, a variable's format is that it simply stands by itself. The variable Grand Total is referred to as Grand Total within a procedure. On the other hand, a layout called Credit Input would have to be surrounded by quotation marks, so it would be typed into the procedure as "Credit Input". The various formats necessary for the different parts of a procedure are described in the following paragraphs.

CONSTANTS

There are several types of constants. First is the numeric constant, which you enter directly. You would enter the number 1,250 as 1250 and the number 50.567 as 50.567. Do not include commas in the numbers you enter, but you can include a minus sign for negative numbers.

The alphanumeric constant, which can consist of letters, symbols, numbers, or anything else on the keyboard, should be surrounded by double quotation marks. It can be up to eighty characters long. Some examples are "Please enter the search string" and "There are over 100 records in this file! Please back up the disk."

Finally, there is the date constant. As mentioned earlier, the date constant consists of an exclamation mark, two digits for the month, a slash, two digits for the day, a slash, four digits for the year, and an exclamation mark. November 30, 1966, would be entered as !11/30/1966!

FIELD NAMES

A field name, which can be up to fifteen characters long, is addressed by first typing the name of that field's file within brackets and then following the file name with the field name. To address the Address field that is in the Customers file, you would type [Customers]Address. To check if the contents of a ZIP code field contained in the Customers file is less than or equal to 50000, you would type [Customers]ZIP Code < = 50000

FILE NAMES

File names, as stated in the previous paragraph, should be enclosed in square brackets. File names can be up to fifteen characters long. Examples include [Customers], [Credit], and [Banks], which are three file names from the Customers database you've been constructing.

LAYOUT NAMES

A layout name, which is also limited to fifteen characters, is contained in quotes within a procedure. Some examples include "Customer Input", "Bank Output", and "Credit Input". Because the name is a string expression, it is possible to address a layout with a string expression. For instance, suppose you have three layouts called "Layout1", "Layout2", and "Layout3". You can address any one of them by entering the layout name as "Layout" + Value, with the variable Value being equal to either 1, 2, or 3.

PROCEDURES

You can access procedures you have created in 4th Dimension by just typing in their names. Suppose you have a procedure called Print Customers. To use that procedure from another procedure, all you have to do is enter the words Print

Customers within the text of that procedure in the desired place. 4th Dimension makes it easy for you to recognize your own procedure names within procedures since it puts them in italicized text, as you'll discover later.

SETS

A set, which you'll learn more about in coming chapters, is addressed by using double quotation marks. Some examples of set names in a procedure are "Records to Print" and "Monthly Sales Reports".

SUBFIELDS

To address a field in a subfile, you need to include the name of the subfile between the name of the parent file and the name of the subfield, and you need to separate the subfile and the subfield with an apostrophe. In the Customers database, for example, there is a subfield named Purpose in the subfile Meetings, whose parent file is Customers. To address the Purpose subfield, you would type `[Customers]Meetings'Purpose`. The brackets around the file and the apostrophe between the subfile and the subfield are both required.

LAYOUT VARIABLES

The first type of variable you'll learn how to put to use is the layout variable. Layout variables contain values of items in a layout (check boxes, radio buttons, OK buttons, Cancel Buttons, et cetera) or values that can be used to display graphs, show a scrollable list, or call an external procedure for use in the layout. In general, layout variables are directly connected with a particular layout and are used in a type of procedure called a layout procedure, which is associated with a certain layout.

To make use of a layout variable, you first have to define a variable area in the layout. After you do, 4th Dimension displays a dialog box requesting the variable name, the type of variable, and its format. Follow these steps:

1. Use the horizontal scroll bar to move the contents of the layout somewhat to the left. You should have about an inch and a half of white space on the right portion of the window.
2. Select the Create Variable icon from the toolbox, which is the fifth tool down on the left side.
3. Using the crosshairs, draw a rectangle on the right side of the layout window like the one shown in Figure 8-1.

FIGURE 8-1. Draw a rectangle where the variable will be placed.

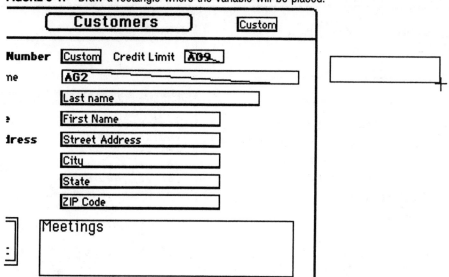

You have just defined the area in this layout where the layout variable will be placed. A dialog box like the one in Figure 8-2 appears on the screen, which has a place for the variable name to be entered, a series of ten radio buttons to choose the type of variable you want, and an area devoted to the format of the variable.

Before going any further, you should have a general understanding of what each variable choice means. As each layout variable is described, click the corresponding radio button so that any needed changes in the dialog box will take place.

Enterable variable. Don't let this name deceive you. An enterable variable isn't always enterable. It is enterable only in dialog boxes, where it takes on the appearance of a field. In a dialog box, you could use an enterable variable to get some kind of input. The dialog box might state, "You didn't give me the first name. Please enter it." The user could then type the information within the enterable variable that is in the dialog box. While entering this information, the user can backspace or perform any of the other text functions available within a field. After entering the information, the user would click the OK button. Remember that in layouts other than dialog boxes, enterable variables are not enterable at all. They can be displayed only if you put them there.

Nonenterable variables. These variables cannot be entered under any circumstances. Like fields, they can hold information, but their contents can

FIGURE 8-2.   The variable dialog box lets you enter the characteristics of the variable you are creating.

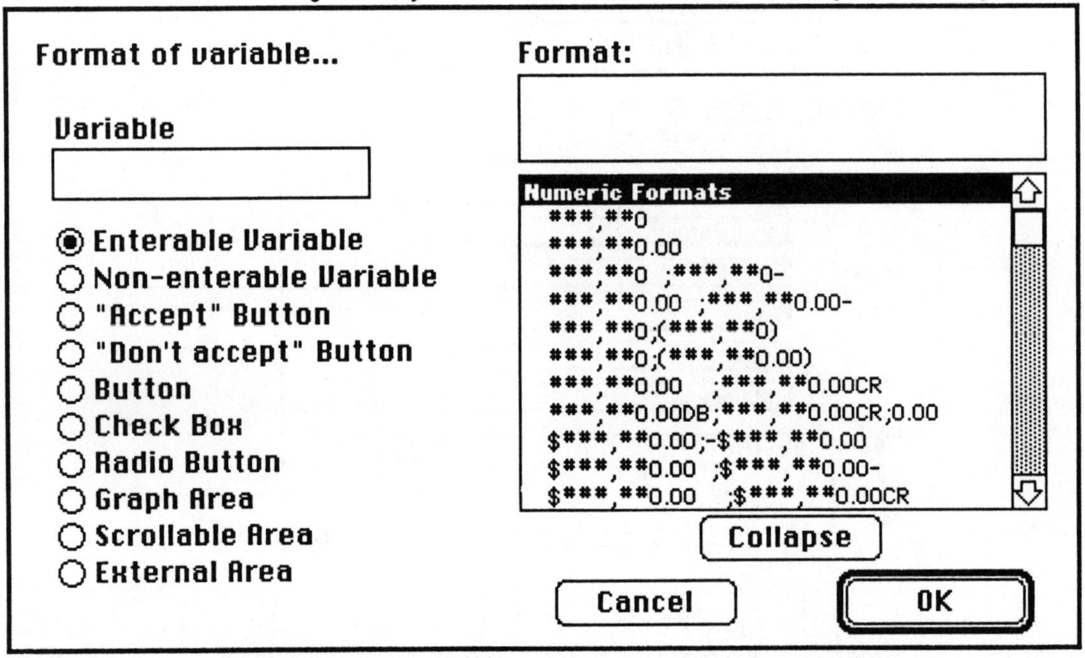

```
Format of variable...           Format:
                                 ┌──────────────────────────────┐
Variable                         │                              │
┌───────────────────────┐        └──────────────────────────────┘
│                       │        ┌──────────────────────────────┐
└───────────────────────┘        │ Numeric Formats            ⇧ │
                                 │ ###,##0                      │
 ◉ Enterable Variable            │ ###,##0.00                   │
 ○ Non-enterable Variable        │ ###,##0 ;###,##0-            │
 ○ "Accept" Button               │ ###,##0.00 ;###,##0.00-      │
 ○ "Don't accept" Button         │ ###,##0;(###,##0)            │
 ○ Button                        │ ###,##0;(###,##0.00)         │
 ○ Check Box                     │ ###,##0.00  ;###,##0.00CR    │
 ○ Radio Button                  │ ###,##0.00DB;###,##0.00CR;0.00│
 ○ Graph Area                    │ $###,##0.00;-$###,##0.00     │
 ○ Scrollable Area               │ $###,##0.00 ;$###,##0.00-    │
 ○ External Area                 │ $###,##0.00   ;$###,##0.00CR⇩│
                                 └──────────────────────────────┘
                                        ┌──────────────┐
                                        │   Collapse   │
                                        └──────────────┘
                                  ┌──────────────┐  ┌──────────────┐
                                  │   Cancel     │  │     OK       │
                                  └──────────────┘  └──────────────┘
```

only be displayed. Notice that with both enterable and nonenterable variables, you have a whole range of formats from which to choose. The contents
of this format listing will not change for any of the radio buttons you select.
You can refer to the meaning of any of these formats in the previous chapter,
and you can enter your own customized format in the format box if none of
them meets your needs.

The next four variable descriptions are about buttons. You should understand a number of important rules before you use any button variables:

Disabling of button panel.   When you put any button in a layout, the button
panel that 4th Dimension provides disappears. The button panel consists of
the left-pointing arrow, the #1 record icon, the right-pointing arrow, and the
Enter and Cancel buttons. If you place one or more buttons of your own in
the layout, these other buttons vanish. Therefore, you need to provide a
button for all the functions that your database requires (entering records,
moving through records, and so on).

Value of buttons.   A button can have a value of 0 or 1. When a button variable
either equals or is set to 0, this indicates some kind of "off" condition, such

as the radio button is off, the check box is empty, or the button has not been clicked. If the button variable equals or is set to 1, this indicates an "on" condition, such as the radio button has been turned on, the check box is checked, or the button has been clicked.

Button status. When 4th Dimension first calls a layout procedure or displays a layout, all button values are set to 0. If you want certain buttons to be set to 1, you should establish those assignments at the beginning of the layout procedure.

Naming buttons. Each button is given some kind of variable name, and it is helpful if the name suggests the function. Also, the text displayed within the button does not have to correspond to the variable name. A button variable might be named Save OK, whereas the text inside the button might read Save the Records?. When you select one of the button types from the variable dialog box, the word Format: above the format box changes to Button Text:, and you can enter the button text there.

- **Accept button.** This button usually indicates an OK. In fact, there is a 4th Dimension system variable called OK, which changes to 1 if this button is clicked. This button is usually for some kind of confirmation or go-ahead, such as saving or entering a record.
- **Don't Accept button.** This is typically the Cancel button, and the 4th Dimension system variable OK is changed to 0 when this button is clicked. This button is usually used to leave the current layout without using any of the changes made.
- **Button.** This general-purpose button does not affect the OK variable. You might put a function like Load Record, List Customers, or Print Record on a button like this.
- **Check Box.** A check box can be either on (1) or off (0), and clicking a check box toggles it from an on to an off condition and vice versa. You can have as many check boxes in a layout as you like. Unlike the previous three types of buttons, the button text for a check box is displayed to the right of the check box instead of inside a button, so be sure to provide enough room for the text when you draw the Create Variable rectangle. You can change the shape of the variable area later if it's not the right size.
- **Radio Button.** Radio buttons exist in groups of choices where only one choice at a time is acceptable. The dialog box on your screen is a good example, since only one button type can be selected; when you click one button, the dark circle in the previously selected button disappears.

For instance, you might have credit rating possibilities of Excellent, Good, Fair, and Poor. Only one of these can be selected, so you would need four radio buttons in this group. The names of the radio buttons have to have the same first letter, so you might call them Credit1, Credit2, Credit3, and Credit4.

You can have as many groups of radio buttons in a layout as you want, but each group is considered an independent entity where only one of the buttons can be selected. Also, button text is printed to the right of the button, so allocate enough room for this text when you draw the Create Variable rectangle.

- **Graph Area.** 4th Dimension can display a graph within the area you define based on the data you provide. You'll learn how to create graphs later in the book.
- **Scrollable Area.** When you have a list of data that you would like to show, draw a scrollable area for it to be displayed. You'll learn more about this later in the book.
- **External Area.** The external area is not covered in this book. When an external area is accessed, 4th Dimension uses a routine outside the database and turns over complete control to that routine. This is beyond the scope of this book, but if you are interested in learning more, read pages 237–248 of the *Command Reference*.

PUTTING LAYOUT VARIABLES TO WORK

To complete this chapter, you are going to create a few layout variables of your own in the Credit Input layout. The Create Variable dialog box is already on the screen, so follow these instructions to provide the layout with some buttons:

1. Type in the name of the first button variable, which will be OK.
2. Select the type of button you want, which in this case is the Accept button.
3. Type in the button text, which is **Enter Record**. The dialog box on your screen should look like Figure 8-3.
4. Click the OK button. A button with the words Enter Record appears in the layout.
5. You could create the two other buttons in the same way, but to save time, just click the Duplicate icon (on the bottom of the left side of the layout toolbox) a couple of times. You now have three buttons, as shown in Figure 8-4.

FIGURE 8-3. Enter the variable name, the type of button, and the button text for every button you add to the layout.

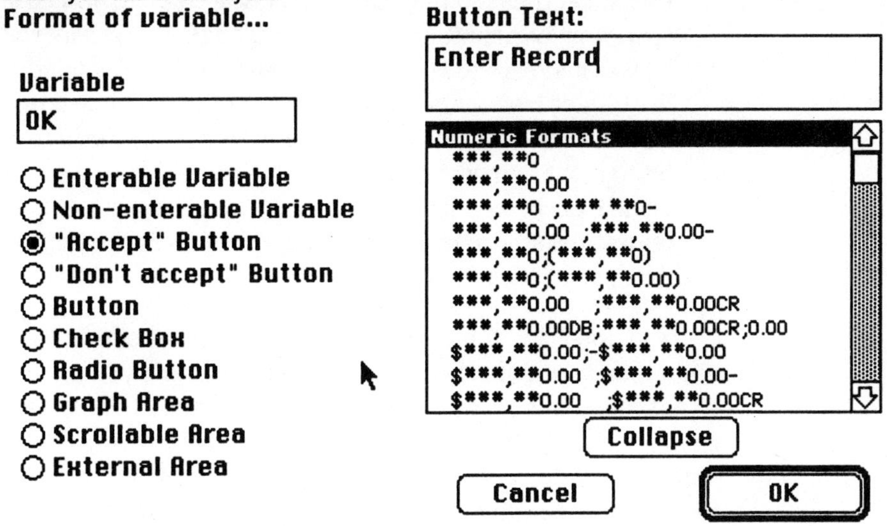

Format of variable...

Variable

`OK`

○ **Enterable Variable**
○ **Non-enterable Variable**
◉ **"Accept" Button**
○ **"Don't accept" Button**
○ **Button**
○ **Check Box**
○ **Radio Button**
○ **Graph Area**
○ **Scrollable Area**
○ **External Area**

Button Text:

`Enter Record`

Numeric Formats
```
***,**0
***,**0.00
***,**0  ;***,**0-
***,**0.00  ;***,**0.00-
***,**0;(***,**0)
***,**0;(***,**0.00)
***,**0.00   ;***,**0.00CR
***,**0.00DB;***,**0.00CR;0.00
$***,**0.00;-$***,**0.00
$***,**0.00  ;$***,**0.00-
$***,**0.00   ;$***,**0.00CR
```

[**Collapse**]

[**Cancel**]   [**OK**]

FIGURE 8-4. Duplicate can make identical buttons quickly.

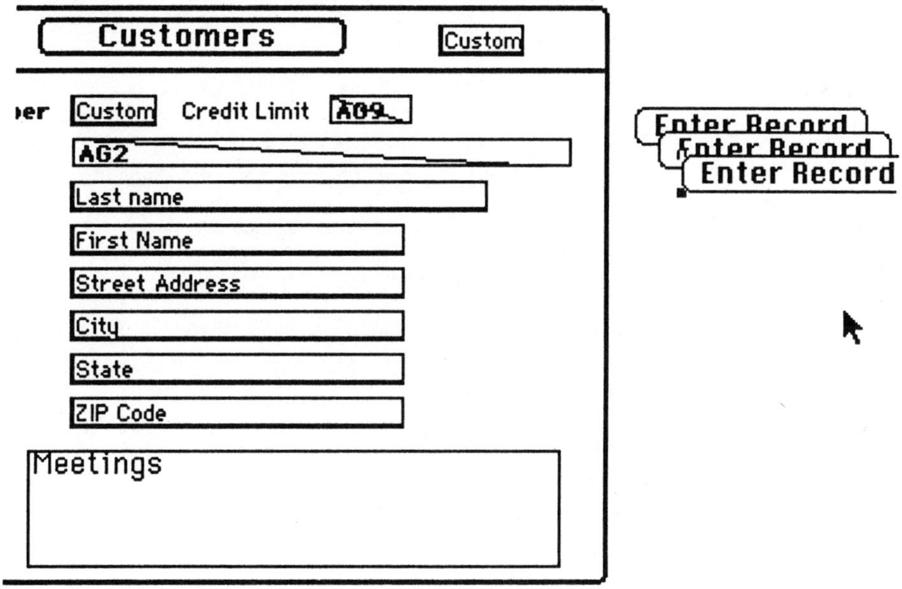

6. You don't want the other two buttons to be the same, of course. First, reposition them so they are in a vertical column, spaced about half an inch apart from one another. You can position them any way you like, actually, as long as it looks good. To align them perfectly, select all three and then click the Center Horizontally alignment icon (seventh one down on the left side).
7. Double-click the second button, and change its name to Next. Change the button text to read Enter and Next. Click OK.
8. Double-click the third button and change its name to Cancel. Alter the button text so it reads Cancel Entry. Finally, change the button type to Don't Accept and click the OK button.

You now have three buttons in this layout, as shown in Figure 8-5. These buttons are immediately usable, as you'll discover if you go to User mode and try to enter another record. Because the functions of these layout variables are already defined, they don't necessarily need a procedure. If you wanted these buttons to perform more complex functions, or if you were using check boxes, radio buttons, or one of the other layout variables, you would have to write an accompanying layout procedure.

You won't learn how to write procedures until the next chapter, but for now you can add some more buttons for practice. Follow these steps:

FIGURE 8-5. The three buttons have been placed in the Credit Input layout and are ready to be used.

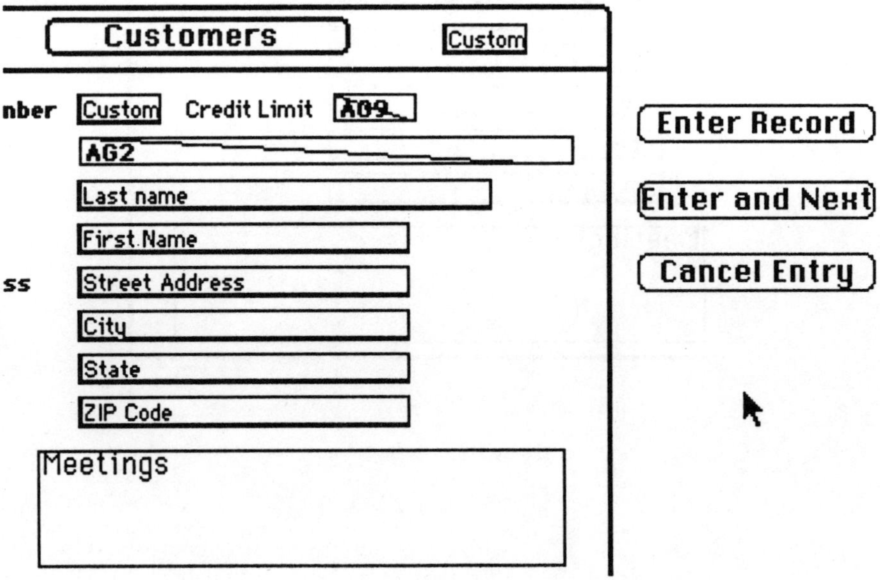

1. After you've closed the Customer Input layout window, open up the Credit Input layout.
2. Suppose this company has two types of credit accounts: net 30 days and net 60 days. A customer can have only one type of account, so this calls for a pair of radio buttons, one called Net 30 and another called Net 60.
3. Use the Create Variable crosshairs to draw a rectangle to the right of the Credit Limit field. Put it far enough to the right so it doesn't clutter the look of the layout.
4. You need to type in a variable name, so enter Credit30. Click Radio Button as the button choice, then enter the button text Net 30. Click OK to complete the entry of this button variable.
5. Now click the duplicate icon so there are two radio buttons.
6. Double-click the second button you've just created and enter the new variable name as Credit60. Change the button text to Net 60. Press the OK key. You now have the two radio buttons you need, and they'll be grouped together since their names begin with the same letter of the alphabet.
7. Position the Net 60 button beneath the Net 30 button. Use the alignment icons to straighten these radio buttons out.
8. Draw a rounded rectangle around these buttons to set them off from the rest of the layout (this is strictly a cosmetic change).
9. Double-click the rectangle to change the fill pattern to None, then select the 2 Pixel Lines option from the Layout menu. Your completed radio buttons with the accompanying graphic around them should look like the ones in Figure 8-6.

FIGURE 8-6. The radio buttons are complete. They are offset from the other objects because they are surrounded by a graphic.

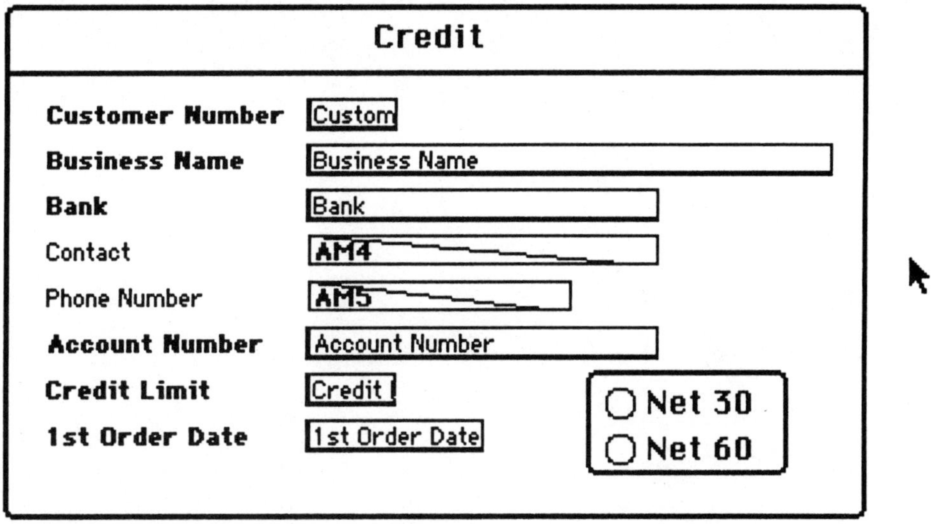

These radio buttons don't really do anything at this point. If you try using the Credit Input layout in the User mode, you'll be able to click each button, but it won't have any effect on the database. When you learn how to write procedures, you'll put these buttons to use. For now, give them a try just to see how they function in the User mode.

In the next chapter, you'll finally learn how to write procedures and how to put all variables, buttons, and formats to use. Procedures give you access to a powerful language that helps you truly fine-tune a database to have the commands and functions you need.

9

Procedures and Menus

Programming is something you may or may not have done before. If you have programmed a computer, even in a fairly simple language like BASIC, you will find that programming in 4th Dimension's procedural language is not terribly difficult. If you have never programmed, you might have to take this chapter a little slower, but the going will be easier if you remember three important concepts in programming:

1. A program follows a specific path, and its instructions are carried out in that order. Usually, the instructions in a program are carried out from top to bottom, unless the program branches to a different part of itself.

   For instance, the program might check to see if a button is pressed. The program could state that if the button is pressed, it should continue on with the next program statement, but if it is not pressed, it should return back to the beginning of the program. This is logical, but the program is not following a perfectly sequential order. The order in which the instructions are carried out is determined by the decision making that the program is performing.
2. A program makes the computer do exactly what you tell it to do. Many people are frustrated when the computer is not doing what they want it to do, but if the program contains even a small bug (like a semicolon where a colon should be), it might not work. You must be careful to avoid typographic errors and improper command formats.
3. Keep in mind that even simple programs rarely work perfectly the first time. You can always go back and debug the program or add any improvements, so unless you are performing a very complex operation, it is unlikely that you'll cause any damage to the database.

The little programs in 4th Dimension are referred to as "procedures." They are like computer programs since they consist of preset keywords and operators that tell the computer to carry out a certain task. Procedures usually depend on each other to work properly. If you think of a program as an entire body, then procedures would be the arms, the legs, the torso, and the head, all of which must work together to be useful.

Simple procedures carry out functions that are already possible in the User mode, such as finding records, sorting, searching, and modifying records. Procedures for functions like these usually require only a few lines of code. Complex procedures that are possible only in the Custom mode might perform such tasks as accepting input through buttons in a layout or making decisions based on the information in a database.

This book is not intended to be an advanced programming guide to 4th Dimension's procedural language. However, by learning the programming fundamentals in this and subsequent chapters and by using the reference guides that come with the program, you should be able to create all but the most complex procedures for your databases.

PROCEDURE EDITORS

4th Dimension provides two different editors with which you can create procedures: the Listing editor and the Flowchart editor. The Listing editor is text-based, the Flowchart editor is graphics-based; a procedure created in one format *cannot* be viewed in the other.

Although both types of editors can accomplish the same thing, the Listing editor is more commonly used, since it isn't quite as cumbersome as the single-page-oriented Flowchart editor. For this reason, you'll learn how to use the Listing editor in this book. If you want to explore the Flowchart editor, refer to pages 243–253 of the *4th Dimension User's Guide*.

Be sure you are in Design mode, then select the Procedure option from the Design menu (or press Command-P). The dialog box shown in Figure 9-1 appears, allowing you to either create a new procedure or choose an already existing procedure. No procedures exist yet, but if they did, you could see their names by double-clicking the words Global Procedures on the left side. This would reveal the names of any global procedures you had created. If you double-clicked File/Layout Procedures, you could access any of the existing procedures associated with the files and layout names listed.

There aren't any procedures yet, so click on Global Procedures and take a look at the buttons in the middle of the dialog box:

Delete. This button deletes a selected procedure. You haven't selected any procedures because none exist right now, so the Delete button is not available to use. When you do click Delete, 4th Dimension confirms that you want to eliminate that procedure from the disk.

Sort. You can use the Sort button only when one of the bold-faced procedure types (such as Global Procedures) is selected. When you click Sort, the procedures under the selected type are sorted in alphabetical order. This is handy when you have a lot of procedures and want to organize them.

FIGURE 9-1. This dialog box lets you create new procedures or load existing procedures from the disk.

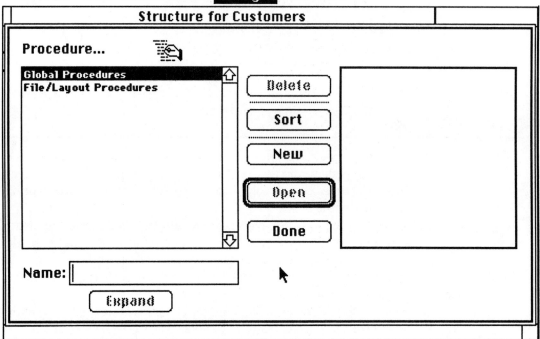

New. The New button creates a new procedure. To create a global procedure, you would click on Global Procedures, type a procedure name in the box located in the lower left, then click the New button.

Open. Clicking this button opens a selected procedure. Double-clicking the procedure name does the same thing.

Done. Click the Done button when you are through working with the dialog box and don't want to open any procedures.

Type in the name of the first procedure you are going to create: **Show All.** Now click the New button, and the dialog box shown in Figure 9-2 appears. This dialog box lets you select whether you want to use the Listing editor (the default choice) or the Flowchart editor. You will be using the Listing editor, so type in Show All again and click OK.

FIGURE 9-2.   Clicking the radio button tells 4th Dimension if you want to use the Listing editor or the Flowchart editor.

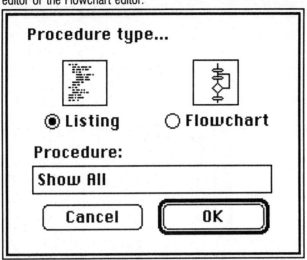

ENTERING A PROCEDURE

Your screen should now contain the Listing editor, which is shown in Figure 9-3. This editor is where you enter and edit a procedure and consists of the following parts:

Editing Area. The blank, upper half of the editor is where you actually enter and edit the procedure. The contents of the editing area include keywords, routine names, field names, alphanumerics, and other components that make up the instructions for the procedure. You can scroll this area independently to access any part of a very long procedure.

Keyword area. This scrollable list, located on the bottom left half, contains keywords like If, Case Of, and End While. You can either type in these keywords manually or click them within the keyword area. Clicking a keyword makes it appear in the editing area at the current location of the cursor.

Fields area. This area contains all the field names from the default file. If you want to switch to a different file, click either the left or the right arrow above the fields area. Again, this is a scrollable list, so if you have many field names, you can get to any of them and enter them either by clicking the name or by typing it in yourself. It's usually a good idea just to click it, since 4th Dimension automatically uses the correct format for entering the field name.

FIGURE 9-3.   The Listing editor consists of the editing, keyword, fields, and routines areas.

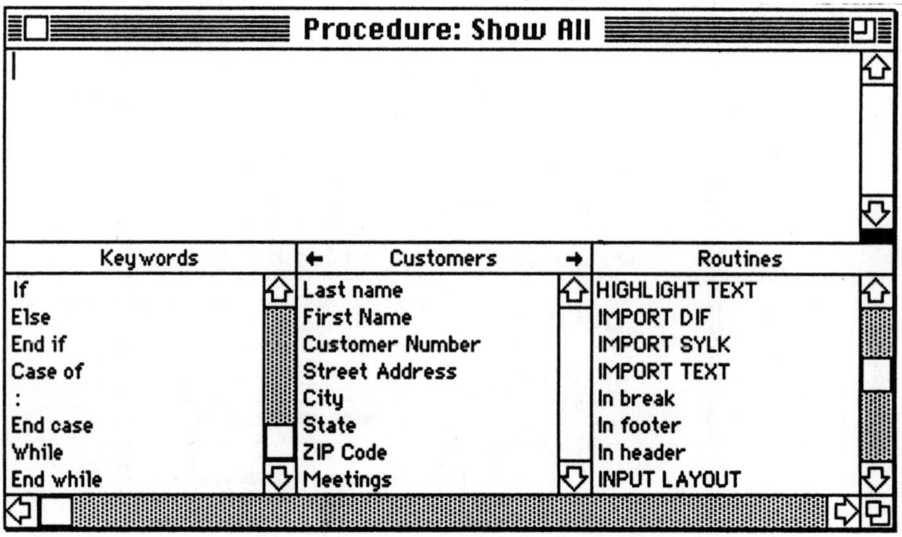

Routines area. This is a very long, scrollable list of the routines available in 4th Dimension, such as Save Record, Open Window, and Highlight Text. These routines are in alphabetical order, and you can enter a routine name by typing it in or clicking it.

As you write your own procedures, their names will be at the very bottom of the routines list. Scroll to the bottom of the list right now, and you'll see the procedure name Show All in italics. Developer-created routines are shown in italics to distinguish them from the built-in commands.

You also have several standard window features. The split-window bar located on the right side can be dragged down to hide the keyword area, the fields area, and the routines area so you can have the maximum amount of room to write code. You can drag the bar back up later if you need those areas. You can also click the zoom box to make the Listing editor fill the screen or adjust the size box to resize the window.

EDITING WITH THE LISTING EDITOR

Using the Listing editor is probably the easiest part of procedure programming. To enter a procedure, simply type it in using all the standard Macintosh editing features you know. You can backspace, add and delete text, move the cursor to any part of the document, and select text for replacement.

Although 4th Dimension does not tell you if you have made a mistake while you are typing, it does catch syntactic errors after you enter a line with the Return key. If you enter a line with incorrect syntax, 4th Dimension puts bullet characters (●) around the offending command. You must correct the command *and remove the bullet characters* before you can reenter that line successfully.

Finding and replacing text is just as easy. To find a piece of text, use the Find command from the Search menu bar, shown in Figure 9-4. You can enter the text you want to find in two different ways: you can type it in the Find dialog box, or you can select the text from the editor that you want to find before you issue the Find command. When the dialog box appears, this text is automatically put into the dialog box. This can be a timesaver if you want to find a particularly long piece of text and don't want to type it in. However you enter the text, click the OK button once it is entered.

The Replace command works in exactly the same way, except you also have to type in the new text you want in place of the old text. The dialog box for Replace, shown in Figure 9-5, can accept the contents of the Replace . . . box from either the keyboard or the Listing editor, but you have to enter the contents of the With . . . box from the keyboard. Once both items are entered, click the Replace button.

Two other commands in the Search menu — Find Next and Replace Next — let you find or replace a piece of text without having to reenter the information for the dialog box. All four of the commands have keyboard equivalents, as shown in the menu.

When you close a procedure's window, that procedure is automatically saved to disk, but you might want to save the procedure periodically as you are working on it. The Save Procedure command from the File menu saves the currently selected procedure to the disk. If you want to replace the procedure with the one most recently saved to the disk (in case you have made some changes that you

FIGURE 9-4.   Four commands are available for searching and replacing text in the Listing editor.

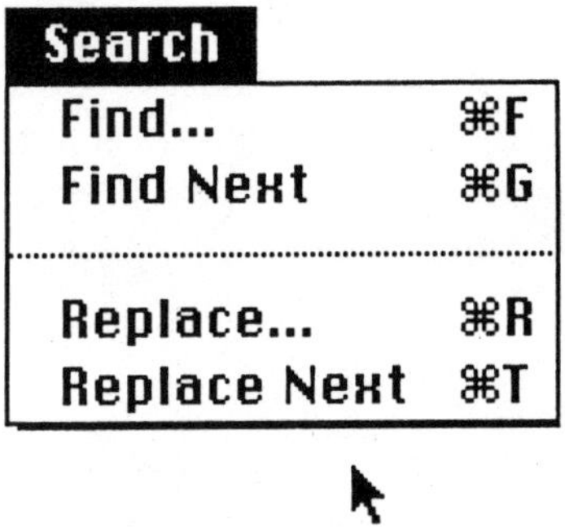

Search	
Find...	⌘F
Find Next	⌘G
Replace...	⌘R
Replace Next	⌘T

FIGURE 9-5. Enter the text you want to find in the top box; enter the text you want to replace it with in the lower box.

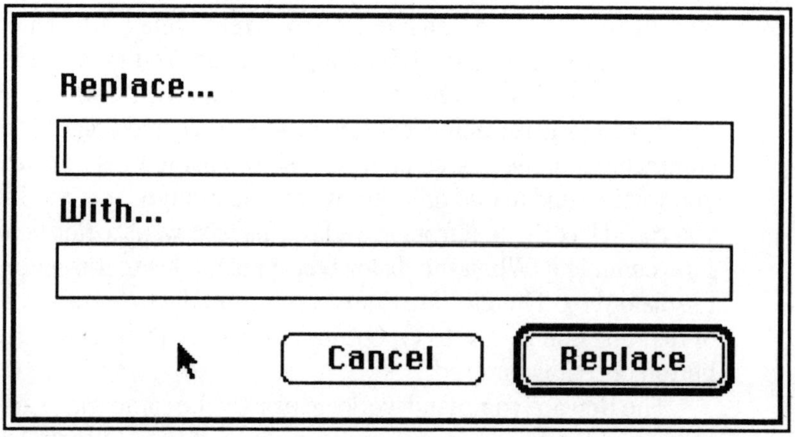

```
┌─────────────────────────────────────────────┐
│  ┌───────────────────────────────────────┐   │
│  │                                        │   │
│  │  Replace...                            │   │
│  │  ┌──────────────────────────────────┐  │   │
│  │  │                                  │  │   │
│  │  └──────────────────────────────────┘  │   │
│  │  With...                               │   │
│  │  ┌──────────────────────────────────┐  │   │
│  │  │                                  │  │   │
│  │  └──────────────────────────────────┘  │   │
│  │            ┌────────┐  ┌──────────┐    │   │
│  │        ▶   │ Cancel │  │ Replace  │    │   │
│  │            └────────┘  └──────────┘    │   │
│  └───────────────────────────────────────┘   │
└─────────────────────────────────────────────┘
```

don't want), choose the Revert to Saved command from the File menu. As long as you have not closed the window, Revert to Saved loads in the latest version of the procedure that you saved.

Before you begin learning about the individual commands, finish up with the procedure you were going to create on the screen. Type in exactly what is shown below and edit out any mistakes you might make:

```
DEFAULT FILE ([CUSTOMERS])
ALL RECORDS
DISPLAY SELECTION
```

Now point to the Close box and click the mouse button. You have now created a three-line procedure called Show All, which will load in all the records from the Customers file and display them.

COMMANDS FOR LAYOUT AND RECORD SELECTION

For most of this chapter, you will learn about individual keywords, their function, and their proper format. At the end of the chapter are several sample procedures that demonstrate how keywords and operators can work together. This section details the various commands that control selection of a layout or a record within a procedure.

Command:	**Default File**
Format:	Default File ([*file name*])
Use:	This command selects a default file (denoted by *file name*) for a procedure. It is a useful command if you don't want to bother entering the file name for every command where the file name is required. Default File is typically near the beginning of a procedure, so that 4th Dimension knows which file to work with.
Example:	To make the file called Customers the default file, type Default File ([Customers]) in the procedure. Any commands following this one will relate to the Customers file, unless another file is explicitly stated.

Command:	**Input Layout**
Format:	Input Layout ("*Layout Name*")
Use:	This command determines which layout will be used for input in the database. As long as you state the default file to be used, you have to enter only the layout name in the parentheses. If you do not state a default file or if you want to use the layout from a different file, you have to precede the layout name with the file name. For instance, to use the Credit Input layout from the Credit file, you would type Input Layout ([Credit]"Credit Input").
Example:	Suppose you are writing the procedure to get information on customers. The layout you have created is called Customer Input, and that layout is contained within the file called Customers. You would enter Input Layout ([Customers]"Customer Input"), or, if you have set Customers as the default file, you could just type in Input Layout ("Customer Input"). This layout will be used for any input in the procedure unless you change the Input Layout later in the same procedure.

Command:	**Output Layout**
Format:	Output Layout ("*Layout Name*")
Use:	Use this command to tell 4th Dimension which layout to use for output. It works in exactly the same way as the Input Layout command. It's a good idea to enter the Default File command before Output Layout, but if you don't, remember to precede the layout name with the file name, for example, Output Layout ([Credit]"Credit Output").

Example:	In a procedure where you want the layout called Customer Output to be used for output and where you have defined Customers as the default file, you would type Output Layout ("Customer Output").
Command:	**All Records**
Format:	All Records ([*file name*])
Use:	This command loads in all the records from the default file into memory. When you first open a database, none of the records is currently selected. When 4th Dimension encounters an All Records command within a procedure, all the records from the default file are loaded into memory. If you have not defined a default file or if you want to load in all the records from a different file, enter the name of the file name after the All Records command. For example, to load in all the records from the Credit file, you would type All Records ([Credit]).
Example:	If you have defined the Customers file as the default and you want all the records in the Customers file to be loaded into memory, you would enter the command All Records in the procedure at the step in the procedure when all the records should be loaded into memory. This is usually near the beginning of the procedure, although you can place the command in any logical place, depending on when you want the records to be loaded.
Command:	**First Record**
Format:	First Record ([*file name*])
Use:	This command performs somewhat the same function as the #1 icon you encountered in the User mode. That is, it makes the first record of a selection the current record. The difference is that it does not display the record, but only makes it the current record (you'll learn about the Display Record command shortly). If you have not specified a default file or if you want to load the first record from a different file, include the file name after the command. First Record ([Credit]), for example, makes the first record in the Credit file the current record.
Example:	Assume you have set Customers as the default file and you have issued the All Records command to load all the records into memory. Typing First Record makes the first record in Customers the current record. A Display Record command shows that record on the screen.

Command:	**Last Record**
Format:	Last Record ([*file name*])
Use:	This command is similar in function to First Record, except that it makes the last record of the current selection the current record. Again, specify the file name if you have not done so with Default File or if you want to use a different file.
Example:	Typing Last Record within a procedure takes the last record from the current selection in memory and makes it the current record.

Command:	**Next Record**
Format:	Next Record ([*file name*])
Use:	When you move through the records in a current selection, a record pointer determines the current record. In the case of First Record and Last Record, the record pointer moves to the first or the last record in a selection, respectively. The Next Record command moves the record pointer to the next record in the current selection and loads it into memory. The record is not displayed until Display Record is encountered in the procedure, and entering the file name after the command is optional.
	One special note about Next Record and Previous Record is that a special variable called End Selection determines whether you have reached the end of a selection. As long as there is another record after the current one, Next Record will retrieve it and End Selection's value will remain FALSE. If, however, there aren't any more records succeeding the current one, Next Record will not load any record into memory, and the value of End Selection will be TRUE, telling you that there is no next record.
Example:	The following procedure loads all the records from the Customers file into memory, goes to the first record, and then loads in the second record and displays it.

```
Default File ([Customers])
All Records
First Record
Next Record
Display Record
```

Command:	**Previous Record**
Format:	Previous Record ([*file name*])
Use:	This command works just like Next Record, except that it goes in the opposite direction. Previous Record loads into memory the

record previous to the current record. The End Selection variable returns a FALSE as long as there is a previous record to be loaded. If there are no more records (that is, the current record is the first one), End Selection returns a value of TRUE.

Example:

The following procedure loads in all the records from the Credit file and moves to the second to last record in the selection. It also displays that current record.

```
Default File ([Credit])
All Records
Last Record
Previous Record
Previous Record
Display Record
```

Command: **Display Record**

Format: Display Record ([*file name*])

Use: This command displays the current record in memory, using the current input layout for display. It may seem strange that the input layout would be used for output, but this makes sense since only one record is being shown, and you want to show as much information as possible (input layouts usually contain more information than output layouts, as you've seen).

Example: Several of the examples already provided show Display Record being used. Just enter Display Record in the procedure at the point where you want the current record shown.

Commands: **Records in File**
Records in Selection

Format: Records in File ([*file name*])
Records in Selection ([*file name*])

Use: As with all the other commands in this section, you can enter either of these commands with or without a file name following it, depending on your needs. In any case, Records in File returns the number of the records contained in a file, whereas Records in Selection returns only the number of the records in a file's current selection. Naturally, Records in Selection is always less than or equal to the number of Records in File.

Example: Suppose you want to assign a variable called TotSel the value of the number of records selected in the Credit file. You would enter this in the procedure:

```
TotSel:=Records in Selection([Credit])
```

WORKING WITH RECORDS

A database has to give the user some way of entering, saving, and deleting individual records. 4th Dimension has a number of fundamental commands that are crucial to even the most basic programming. Although some of them seem to do the same thing, they have subtle differences. This section covers the commands that allow the user to create, modify, save, and delete single records.

Command: **Add Record**

Format: Add Record (*file name*;*)

Use: This is somewhat of a "do it all" command, since it lets the user create and save a new record for the database, as long as the layout contains some kind of Accept button. The Accept button is typically labeled OK or Add Record, and when creating the button in the layout, it should be the Accept button type.

When you issue the Add Record command in a procedure, 4th Dimension creates a blank record, makes that the currently selected record, and displays the input layout to get the information. The record is added to the default file, unless you specify a different file name in parentheses. You can also add an asterisk if you don't want the input layout to have scroll bars or the zoom box. You need the parentheses only if you include a different file name or the asterisk.

An important thing to remember about Add Record is that it can accept data only through fields, not through variables. If you have a layout that contains input variables, use the Create Record command instead of Add Record.

Example: The following line allows the user to input a new record into the file called Sales History using the current input layout from this file. Because an asterisk is included, the input layout will not contain scroll bars or the zoom box.

```
Add Record ("Sales History";*)
```

Command: **Create Record**

Format: `Create Record ([`*file name*`])`

Use: Create Record allows for more flexibility in getting records, but, unlike Add Record, it does not save the record. Create Record can accept information through input variables in a dialog box. When you issue this command, 4th Dimension creates a new blank record to store the input. The blank record is the current record, and the input is obtained from the dialog box you specify with the Dialog command.

                The Dialog command, which you'll learn more about later, puts a dialog layout on the screen. A dialog layout is just like any other layout, except that it uses layout variables instead of field variables for input. Naturally, you have to create the dialog layout in advance, but as long as it is available in the file, typing `Dialog` (*"file name"*) brings it to the screen for use.

Example: The following short procedure accepts a new record for a file called Personal using the dialog layout called Birthdate. The procedure does not save the information until a Save Record command is issued, which you'll learn about next.

```
Default File ([Personal])
All Records
Dialog ("Birthdate")
Create Record
```

Command: **Save Record**

Format: `Save Record ([`*file name*`])`

Use: This command saves the current record, usually from a Create Record command, to the current file. In the event you want to save the record to a file other than the default file, include the file name after Save Record.

                When a user clicks the Accept button in the dialog box, a system variable in 4th Dimension called OK is set to 1. This indicates that the user has entered the information and wants 4th Dimension to save the record. A simple If . . . Endif statement tests to see if OK is set to 1 (you'll learn more about this logical test near the end of this chapter).

Example: The following routine is the same as the one for Create Record,
               except that it waits until the Accept button (whatever it might be
               called) is clicked before it saves the record.

```
Default File ([Personal])
All Records
Dialog ("Birthdate")
Create Record
If (OK=1)
      Save Record
End if
```

Command: **Modify Record**
Format: Modify Record ([*file name*];*)
Use: This command loads in the data from the current record and
               displays it on the screen using the input layout. As the com-
               mand's name suggests, the main purpose of Modify Record is to
               change the contents of a record that already exists. If the Accept
               button in the input layout is clicked (that is, the system variable
               OK is equal to 1), then whatever changes are made will be saved.
                   The file name and the asterisk are optional. Include the
               asterisk if you don't want the input layout to have scroll bars or a
               zoom box.

Command: **Delete Record**
Format: Delete Record ([*file name*])
Use: To delete the current record in memory, use the Delete Record
               command. This is a somewhat dangerous command if the proce-
               dure isn't perfected, since it will delete the current record per-
               manently without verifying with the user that the deletion
               should be made. Of course, if there is no current record, this
               command has no effect.

SELECTION COMMANDS

Entering, modifying, and saving individual records are important, but for a database to really be practical, it has to work with groups of records as well. The

current selection, which can be everything in a file (after an All Records command is issued) or a certain portion (after a Search command, for instance), can be addressed as a whole in a 4th Dimension procedure.

Command:	**Display Selection**
Format:	`Display Selection ([`*file name*`];*)`
Use:	This command displays the current selection on the screen using the output layout, unless there is only one record in the current selection, in which case the input layout is used to display the record. If you prefer that the output layout be used even if there is only one record in the current selection, include the asterisk in parentheses following the command.

Once the current selection is displayed, the user can view any record by double-clicking that record. The single record is then displayed using the input layout, so more data can be seen. As you can see in Figure 9-6, there is a Done button on the output screen, which the User can click after looking at the selection. This display can also be scrolled if all the records don't fit on the screen at once.

Example:	The following procedure loads in all the records, then displays the current selection (which is everything) on the screen.

```
Default File ([Customers])
Input Layout ("Customer Input")
Output Layout ("Customer Output")
All Records
Display Selection
```

Command:	**Modify Selection**
Format:	`Modify Selection ([`*file name*`];*)`
Use:	This command acts very much like Display Selection in that its format is the same, it displays the current selection using the output layout, and the user can double-click any record to see it in the input layout. The difference is that in Display Selection none of the data can be changed, whereas in Modify Selection any of the fields can be altered.

Say a user scrolls through an entire list to find a particular record that has to be changed. After the user double-clicks the record, that record is displayed in the input layout and can be modified in the same way as it was first entered. The existing information is still there, but the user can move to any field and

FIGURE 9-6.   Double-click any record to see it displayed in the input layout; click Done to return to the previous screen.

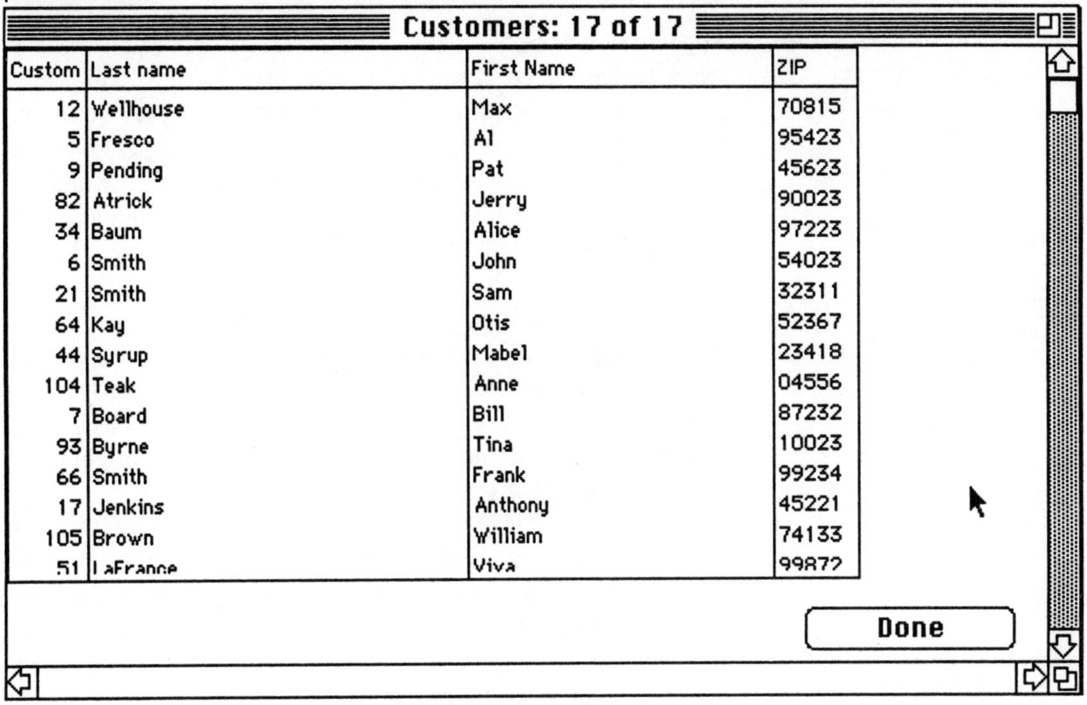

```
┌──────────────────────────────────────────────────────────────────────────┐
│ ▦▦▦▦▦▦▦▦▦▦▦▦▦▦▦▦▦ Customers: 17 of 17 ▦▦▦▦▦▦▦▦▦▦▦▦▦▦▦▦▦        ▣▤ │
├────────┬──────────────────────┬────────────────────┬──────────┬──────────┤
│ Custom │ Last name            │ First Name         │ ZIP      │       ⇧  │
│     12 │ Wellhouse            │ Max                │ 70815    │          │
│      5 │ Fresco               │ Al                 │ 95423    │          │
│      9 │ Pending              │ Pat                │ 45623    │          │
│     82 │ Atrick               │ Jerry              │ 90023    │          │
│     34 │ Baum                 │ Alice              │ 97223    │          │
│      6 │ Smith                │ John               │ 54023    │          │
│     21 │ Smith                │ Sam                │ 32311    │          │
│     64 │ Kay                  │ Otis               │ 52367    │          │
│     44 │ Syrup                │ Mabel              │ 23418    │          │
│    104 │ Teak                 │ Anne               │ 04556    │          │
│      7 │ Board                │ Bill               │ 87232    │          │
│     93 │ Byrne                │ Tina               │ 10023    │          │
│     66 │ Smith                │ Frank              │ 99234    │          │
│     17 │ Jenkins              │ Anthony            │ 45221    │   ▶      │
│    105 │ Brown                │ William            │ 74133    │          │
│     51 │ LaFrance             │ Viva               │ 99872    │          │
│        │                      │                    │          │          │
│        │                      │          ┌──────────────────┐ │      ⇩  │
│        │                      │          │      Done        │ │         │
└────────┴──────────────────────┴──────────└──────────────────┘─┴──────────┘
```

alter the information. After modifying the record, the user can click either the OK button to enter the modified record or the Cancel button so that 4th Dimension ignores the changes.

Example: The following procedure displays all the records and lets the user modify any of them by double-clicking:

```
Default File ([Customers])
Input Layout ("Customer Input")
Output Layout ("Customer Output")
All Records
Display Selection
```

Command: **Delete Selection**

Format: Delete Selection ([*file name*])

Use: This command deletes the entire current selection from the default file or from the file within the parentheses. You must be even more careful with this command than you are with Delete

Record, since Delete Selection can wipe out an entire file if all the records are selected.

Command: **Apply to Selection**

Format: Apply to Selection ([*file name*];*statement*)

Use: This *very* useful and powerful command lets you apply a one-line statement or procedure to an entire selection. Apply to Selection works on a record-by-record basis, which means that whatever you are doing with selected records, 4th Dimension loads each one in progressively until all have been accessed.

What you do with Apply to Selection depends on the file you are working with. If you want to add up all the credit you have outstanding, you might use Apply to Selection to add up all the Credit Limit fields (as in the following example). In another procedure, you might use this command to change all Last Name fields to all capital letters. In another procedure, you might mark all prices down 10% to reflect a sale.

In any case, Apply to Selection is a powerful but potentially time-consuming command. As 4th Dimension is doing its work, a thermometer (indicating what percentage of the task has been done) is displayed on the screen so the user has a constant progress report of the work. To cancel the operation, the user can click the Cancel button, in which case the system variable OK changes from a 1 to a 0. As with anything else in programming, you would have to include some lines in the procedure to monitor the value of OK so 4th Dimension acts accordingly. Very little is done for you in the Custom mode.

Example: Here is a procedure that would take all the values in the field Credit Limit and add them up in a variable called AllCredit. This would be a useful routine, since the user could find out his or her credit liability.

```
AllCredit:=0
Default File([Credit])
All Records
Apply to Selection (AllCredit:=AllCredit+[Credit]Credit
    Limit)
```

SEARCHING AND SORTING

Most standalone databases should have the power to select a group of records based on specific criteria. For instance, a user might want to find all customers with credit limits greater than $5,000 or those who live in a certain city. Three commands — Search, Search by Index, and Search by Selection — all can be used to create a new selection in a file based on whatever rules you establish in the procedure.

Command:	**Search**
Format:	Search ([*file name*];*expression*)
Use:	In its simplest form, the Search command displays the search window like the one shown in Figure 9-7. The user can create any sort of search function, load in one from the disk, or save the one on the screen.

When the Search command is followed by an expression in parentheses, it requires a logical statement. This statement typically compares a field name with some sort of value, and you can link together logical expressions with the AND (&) symbol or the OR (|) symbol. You can separate logical expressions with parentheses. Long logical statements are prone to errors, so use parentheses generously.

As an example, you might enter the line **Search ((|Credit| Credit Limit > 5000)&(|Customer Number| < =50))** to find

FIGURE 9-7.   You can use the Search Window to create logical search expressions.

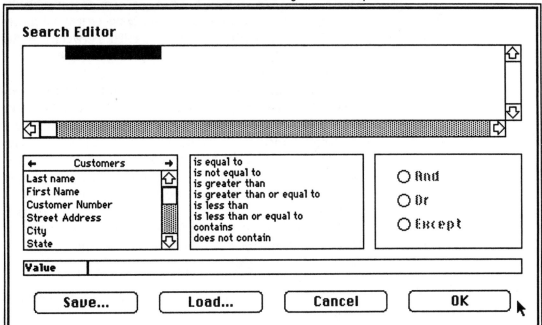

all the customers who have a credit limit over $5,000 and have a customer number less than or equal to 50. The parentheses separate the two logical expressions, and the & sign logically guarantees that only records that meet both the first *and* the last criteria are selected.

Example: The following procedure loads in all the records in the Customers file and displays all the records with ZIP codes less than 30000 or greater than 70000.

```
Default File ([Customers])
All Records
Search ((([Customers]ZIP Code<30000)|([Customers]
    ZIP Code>70000))
Display Selection
```

Command: **Search by Index**

Format: Search by Index (*field operator expression*;*)

Use: This command searches much faster than the Search command, but it works only on indexed fields. Like Search, it makes the records that meet the criterion the current selection, and it makes the first record in that selection the current record.

Unlike Search, Search by Index uses only two operators: equal (=) and between (±). The equal sign checks alphanumeric, numeric, and date equalities; the between symbol checks to see if a value falls within a certain range. The between operator can be used only *once* in a logical expression, and if it is used, it must be the last part of the expression.

Search by Index uses the semicolon (;) to link logical expressions instead of & and |. The colon is an AND operator. Another character you can use with alphanumeric expressions in Search or Search by Index is the wildcard, represented by the at sign (@). The @ symbol can be attached to the end of an alphanumeric expression so that only the characters preceding the @ sign have to match with another expression to be a match. For example, the expression Jo@ would match Jones, Johnson, Joelle, or any other alphanumeric expression beginning with Jo.

Examples: This line finds the records with the last name Smith:

```
Search by Index ([Customers]Last Name="Smith")
```

The following line gets all customers numbered between 25 and 50:

```
Search by Index ([Credit]Customer Number ± 25;50)
```

The next line retrieves all customers with first names between George and any name beginning with Ma:

```
Search by Index ([Customers]First Name ± "George";
    "Ma@")
```

Command:	**Search Selection**
Format:	`Search Selection ([`*file name*`];`*expression*`)`
Use:	This command works in exactly the same way as the Search command, except that it searches only through the current selection. The expression is a single logical expression or a group of them linked together by AND (&) or OR (|) symbols. Both Search and Search Selection are slow compared to Search by Index, but the logical expressions they accept can be more versatile.
Example:	The following procedure first gets the customer records with last names greater than Kni@ (with @ as the wildcard). It then searches that selection for the customers whose first order date was before January 1, 1980, and displays those records.

```
Search by Index ([Customers]Last Name>"Kni@")
Search Selection ([Credit]First Order Date<!01/01/1980!)
Display Selection
```

Command:	**Sort by Index**
Format:	`Sort by Index (`*field name*`;`*operator*`)`
Use:	This is the fastest way to sort records in 4th Dimension's procedural language. To sort the current selection in the default file, type `Sort by Index`, followed by the field name that will be the basis for sorting. Then type either the > operator (for ascending sort) or the < operator (for descending sort). Of course, the field you use *must* be indexed to be usable by the Sort by Index command.
Example:	Suppose you have seven records in the Customers file that contain a field called Last Name. The last names in the records are Jones, Smith, Brown, Harris, and Greenberg. If you issue the command `Sort by Index (Last Name;<)`, the records are sorted so that Smith's name is the first and current record, followed by the rest of the new current selection, Jones, Harris, Greenberg, and Brown. This is a descending sort, so the alphabetization is backward.

Command: **Sort Selection**

Format: Sort Selection (*field name;operator*)

Use: Used by itself without any field name or operator, Sort Selection displays the Sort dialog box, which you've already seen. This dialog box lets the user enter the field names that should be used as the basis of the sort and whether those fields should be sorted in ascending or descending order.

When used with a field name and an operator, Sort Selection can sort based on one or more fields in ascending (>) or descending (<) order. If you want to link more than one sort operator, use the semicolon. For instance, if you want to sort the Customers file in ascending order based primarily on ZIP Code and secondarily on Last Name, you would type Sort Selection ([Customers]ZIP Code;>; [Customers]Last Name;>).

Example: The following procedure loads in all the records from the Credit file and sorts them ascendingly based on their account number.

```
Default File ([Credit])
All Records
Sort Selection ([Credit]Account Number;>)
Display Selection
```

VARIABLES

When a variable is created in a database; it resides only in memory. When the user quits the database, the values of all the variables are gone forever unless they are saved to disk. Fortunately, saving and loading variables is easy in 4th Dimension, as long as you structure your procedures so that variables are saved and loaded in the appropriate places where changes in their values might be made by the user.

Command: **Save Variable**

Format: Save Variable (*document;variables*)

Use: To save a variable or variables to the disk, you have to list only two things in the parentheses following the command: the name of the document you want to give the variable holder and the list of variables you want saved in that document. If you have more than one variable to be saved to a document, separate each variable name with a semicolon.

Example: The following routine adds up all the credit limits from the Credit file and saves this value to disk under the name TotalLimit.

```
AllCredit:=0
Default File([Credit])
All Records
Apply to Selection (AllCredit:=AllCredit+[Credit]Credit
    Limit)
Save Variable ("TotalLimit";AllCredit)
```

Command: | **Load Variable**
Format: | Load Variable (*document*;*variables*)
Use: | The format for this command is the same as the one for Save Variable. The document name should be one that already exists on the disk and contains variables, and the variable names should be separated by semicolons, if there is more than one variable to load.
Example: | Suppose you want to load in the value of AllCredit, which you saved earlier in the document called TotalLimit. You would type Load Variable ("TotalLimit";AllCredit). The value of AllCredit is now in memory, ready for your use.

Command: | **Clear Variable**
Format: | Clear Variable (*string*)
Use: | To erase one or more variables from memory, use the Clear Variable command. The string within the parentheses should contain an alphanumeric expression that is the name of the variable you want to erase. 4th Dimension erases the value of the variables in memory with that name or that begin with that name.

For instance, Clear Variable ("Var") erases all variables that begin with the letters Var, including Var10, Var, Variable-Total, and Varsity. If you don't type any string, that is, Clear Variable (""), then all the variables in memory, including the system variables, are erased. This command does not affect any variable values stored on the disk.

Command: | **Undefined**
Format: | Undefined (*variable*)
Use: | This command checks to see whether the variable you name has any value in memory. If the variable you name has an assigned value, then Undefined returns TRUE. If the variable does not have a value, Undefined returns FALSE. The values TRUE and FALSE are useful in execution statements such as If . . . Then, since 4th Dimension can take one action if there is a value

present or another action if there is not a value present. You will see in the examples at the end of this chapter how Undefined can be used.

SYSTEM VARIABLES

A number of special reserved variables in 4th Dimension contain values that you might find helpful. Some system variables, such as OK, can be used all the time to see if the User has pressed a certain key or if some action has taken place. Other system variables, like RcdDelimit, are not used as often.

You cannot assign your own values to these system variables. They are intended for your information only, and when used within procedures, they are invaluable. A list of the system variables and their respective functions follows.

Document. This variable contains the name of the document most recently created or loaded. A document can be created or loaded with any of the following commands: EXPORT DIF, EXPORT SYLK, EXPORT TEXT, IMPORT DIF, IMPORT SYLK, IMPORT TEXT, LOAD SET, LOAD VARIABLE, SAVE SET, SAVE VARIABLE, SET CHANNEL, USE ASCII MAP. You are familiar only with the LOAD VARIABLE and SAVE VARIABLE commands right now, but Document might still be a useful variable to reference.

Error. This variable contains the 4th Dimension error message based on the most recent procedural error. Refer to Appendix H in the *Command Reference* for a complete list of the error codes.

KeyCode. This variable contains the ASCII code of the key that was most recently typed. This works only in ON EVENT CALL functions.

Modifiers. This variable is the companion variable to KeyCode, since its value indicates the last modifier key that was typed. The values can be 1 for the Command key, 2 for the Shift key, 4 for CapsLock, and 8 for the Option key. If any of these keys are pressed in combination, the value is the sum of the corresponding numbers. For example, if Shift and Option are pressed, Modifiers would equal 10, since the value of Shift is 2 and the value of Option is 8. Added together, these equal 10.

MouseDown. As with KeyCode and Modifiers, this variable works only in procedures with the ON EVENT CALL command. If the mouse button is pressed down, MouseDown equals 1. If the mouse button is not pressed down, MouseDown equals 0.

OK. This is the most frequently used system variable. It is typically used to check whether an Accept button has been clicked, in which case it equals 1. Otherwise, it equals 0. When a Delete button is pressed, it contains the value 2. OK has many other uses; its values based on certain command actions follow:

Add Record:	1 if user validates, 0 if not
Add Subrecord:	1 if user validates, 0 if not
Apply to Selection:	1 if operation is through, 0 if user clicks Cancel
Confirm	1 if user clicks OK, 0 if not
Dialog	1 if user validates, 0 if not
Export DIF	1 if operation is through, 0 if user clicks Cancel
Export SYLK	1 if operation is through, 0 if user clicks Cancel
Export Text	1 if operation is through, 0 if user clicks Cancel
Import DIF	1 if operation is through, 0 if user clicks Cancel
Import SYLK	1 if operation is through, 0 if user clicks Cancel
Import Text	1 if operation is through, 0 if user clicks Cancel
Modify Record	1 if user validates, 0 if not
Modify Subrecord	1 if user validates, 0 if not
Print Dialog	1 if printing through, 0 if user clicks Cancel
Print Label	1 if printing through, 0 if user clicks Cancel
Print Selection	1 if printing through, 0 if user clicks Cancel
Print Settings	1 if user clicks OK in both print dialog boxes, 0 if not
Report	1 if printing through, 0 if user clicks Cancel
Request	1 if user clicks OK, 0 if not
Search	1 if operation through, 0 if not
Search by Index	1 if user OKs Search, 0 if not
Sort by Index	1 if sorting complete, 0 if user clicks Cancel button
Sort Selection	1 if sorting complete, 0 if user clicks Cancel button
Set Channel	1 if user clicks Open or Save, 0 if not

PROGRAM EXECUTION

Procedures rarely follow a perfectly linear path. In other words, if you have thirty lines in a procedure, it is not likely that the procedure will be executed from lines one to thirty without any interruption. Procedures make decisions, branch to different parts of themselves, and "loop" in some places, just like programs.

Branching and looping are simple concepts to understand. Branching is basically the act of taking one action given a certain circumstance and taking another action if that circumstance does not exist. It is like coming to a stop light:

you either go (if the light is green) or stop (if the light is red). Likewise, a procedure might add some value or display some message if something is true and do something entirely different (or nothing at all) if it is not true. Branching is just making a decision and acting on it.

Looping is the repetition of a line or lines. If you want the procedure to do something twenty times, it is not efficient to type in the same line for that action twenty times in a row. It makes a lot more sense to loop that single function twenty times, thus saving both time and memory.

This section introduces you to three functions related to the execution of a procedure: If ... Else ... Endif, Case of ... Else ... End case, and While ... End While. The first two are branching statements, the third is a looping statement. All three are important, timesaving commands.

Probably the easiest of these functions to understand is If . . . Else . . . Endif. Its format is

```
If (expression)
action
Else
action
End If
```

4th Dimension evaluates the logical expression contained in parentheses. If the expression returns a value of TRUE, then the first action is taken. If the expression returns a value of FALSE, then the second action is taken. The Else and the second action are optional, so if they are not there, 4th Dimension goes to the point after the End If to continue with the rest of the procedure.

You can use the logical expressions you already know about with If . . . Else . . . Endif, and the actions taken can be more than one statement long. You might have numerous lines of code written to be used only when a TRUE value is returned, and even more lines of code in case a FALSE is returned. For example, the short routine that follows checks to see if the ZIP Code field equals 95050. If it does, a message is displayed.

```
If ([Customers]ZIP Code="95050")
MESSAGE ("You live in Santa Clara, California")
Else
MESSAGE ("You do not live in Santa Clara, California")
End if
```

Ending the statement with End if is important, so 4th Dimension knows where the logical test finishes.

The Case of . . . Else . . . End case function analyzes a list of logical expressions and finds the first one that is true. When it finds the first true statement, it performs whatever action is underneath that statement in the procedure. If none of the expressions is true, the statement either does nothing or does whatever is listed under the Else keyword. Else is optional, since you might not want to program an alternative action.

The format of this statement for three logical expressions is

```
Case of
    :  expression1
    action1
    :  expression2
    action2
    :  expression3
    action  3
    Else
    action  4
End case
```

There are a few important things to note here. First, each logical expression is preceded by a colon, which denotes it as a logical expression. Second, 4th Dimension recognizes *only* the first true expression, if any, and takes that action. It *does not* take the actions of all the true statements. Finally, End case closes the expression so the procedure knows where the logical test ends.

Case of is helpful when you want to evaluate a set of possibilities and take only one action, based on the value of the first TRUE logical expression found. For instance, suppose you want to print a special message based on the age and the sex of a person. A person can be only one age and one sex, so Case of would be an appropriate way to find the one expression with a TRUE value. The following routine finds the correct expression and prints a message based on it:

```
Case of
    :  (Age<=20) & (Sex="Male")
    Message ("Hello, young man")
    :  (Age<=20) & (Sex="Female")
    Message ("Hello, young lady")
    :  (Age>20) & (Sex="Male")
    Message ("Hi, Guy")
    :  (Age>20) & (Sex="Female")
    Message ("Hi, Gal")
    Else
    Message ("What are you, anyway?")
End Case
```

The looping expression While . . . End While continues to perform certain functions until a logical expression is no longer true. Its format is

```
While (expression)
action
End While
```

The expression can be any logical condition, and you can link conditions together with the AND (&) or OR (|) symbol. End While tells 4th Dimension to loop back to the beginning of the While ... End While statement to keep performing whatever action is listed as long as the expression returns a value of TRUE. For instance, the little routine that follows keeps accepting new records until the Cancel button is pressed. As long as OK is equal to 1 (that is, the Accept button has been pressed), new records are accepted.

```
Default File ([Customers])
Input Layout ("Customer Input")
Output Layout ("Customer Output")
OK:=1
All Records
While (OK=1)
    Add Record
End While
```

BUILDING SOME SAMPLE PROCEDURES

You've read a lot about different keywords and techniques. Now it is time to put together some sample procedures to actually use in your Customers database. For each of the following four procedures, open a new procedure window and give it the name listed on the first line. Be very careful to type in the procedures exactly as they are shown and to close each window as you finish a procedure (they will be saved automatically).

One other thing to note is the comment lines. You can include comments in your procedures by typing the reverse apostrophe (') located in the upper left portion of the keyboard. Comment lines should either be on their own lines or *follow* the statements on a shared line. Anything following a reverse apostrophe on its line is ignored, which means you can type letters, symbols, and words. These comments are helpful tools later when you try to figure out what you did and why.

```
Add Customer
'Add Customers to Database until Cancel is clicked
    Default File ([Customers])
    Input Layout ("Customer Input")
    Output Layout ("Customer Output")
    All Records
```

```
While (OK=1)
    Add Record
End While
```

Show All
```
'Show All: You've typed this one in already/it displays all the
    records
Default File ([Customers])
All Records
Display Selection
```

Sort by Last
```
'Sort Customers by indexed Last Name and display current selection
Default File ([Customers])
Output Layout ("Customer Output")
All Records
Sort by Index ([Customers]Last Name;>)
Display Selection
```

Total Credit
```
'Add Total Outstanding Credit and display that figure briefly
Default File ([Credit])
TotCredit:=0
All Records
Apply to Selection (TotCredit:=TotCredit+[Credit]CreditLimit)
Save Variable ("TotCredit";TotCredit)
Message ("Total credit outstanding is "+String (TotCredit))
While (I<2000)
    I:=I+1
End While
```

CREATING MENUS

You have now written four procedures for your database, and you will write
plenty more. However, the user of your customized database needs some way to
request these procedures. On the Macintosh, this is done through menus. 4th
Dimension comes with a menu editor so you can create customized menus that
access your individual procedures.

Right now, only the structure of the database should be on your screen, since
all the procedure windows should be closed. Select the Menu . . . option from the
Design menu, and a dialog box appears. If your database already had one or more
existing menu bars, they would be listed here, and you could open or delete
any of them. No menus exist yet, so point to the New button and click the
mouse button.

The menu editor, shown in Figure 9-8, is now on the screen. The menu editor lets you create menu titles, items underneath those menus, and the associated procedures that are accessed given a certain item choice. The menu editor also lets you give menu items special attributes, such as keyboard-equivalent characters, separation lines, and special font styles.

The various parts of the menu editor are as follows:

Menus. This lists the different menus that will be displayed in the bar. Currently, File is the only one listed. The Apple menu and the File menu, which will appear in any menu bar you create, cannot be altered. Therefore, they are not shown in the menu editor. To add an item to this list, just point to the white space below existing menu titles and double-click the mouse button (or select Append Menu from the Menu menu).

Items. When you select one of the menus from the left side of the menu editor, all the items that will be listed under that menu are shown. To add a new item, double-click in the white space under Items or select Append Item from the Menu menu).

Procedures. This is where you enter procedure names. When you enter an item, type in the corresponding procedure name to its immediate right. If no procedure is listed, 4th Dimension automatically quits. If you are in Custom

FIGURE 9-8. The menu editor provides you with every feature you might want when you are creating database menus.

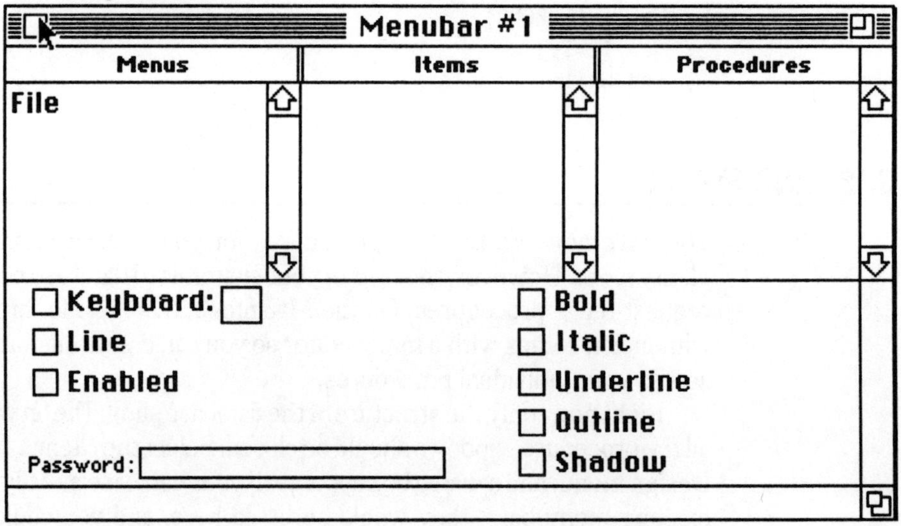

mode, 4th Dimension quits to the Design mode. If you are using 4D Runtime with a standalone database, 4th Dimension quits to the Macintosh Finder.

Keyboard. When you select an item, you can also enter a keyboard-equivalent character. For instance, if you select the item called Quit, you might type in the letter Q in the Keyboard box. In the database, pressing Command-Q therefore does the same thing as selecting Quit from the menu.

To properly enter a keyboard-equivalent character, you need to check the check box and enter a character that (a) is not being used elsewhere in the menu and (b) makes logical sense. The letter Q is perfect for the Quit command, whereas the letter H would not make any sense.

There are a few characters you *cannot* use because they are reserved by the system. These are C (for Copy), V (for Paste), X (for Cut), Z (for Undo), and the period (for Cancel).

Line. Check the Line box if you want a dividing line place in the menu. To get a dividing line, create a blank item and select that item. Next, check the Line box. There won't be any item there, but a dotted line will be in its place on the menu.

Enabled. Check the Enabled box if you want the menu item to be immediately available to the user. Typically, you'll want every item to be enabled, but if not, remove the check from this box after you have selected the item you want disabled.

Font Styles. You can add a variety of styles to menu items, including bold, italic, underline, outline, and shadow. Use these styles with great discretion, if at all. Most good databases don't have unnecessary styles in their menus. Alter the style of a menu item only if it seems appropriate or helpful to the user.

As you develop each menu item, a sample menu appears in the upper right corner. You can examine this sample menu by pointing to the title and holding down the mouse button, but you cannot access any of the commands. This just gives you a cosmetic view of how the menu is developing.

To see the sample menu, select the word File underneath Menus. There is only one item here—Quit. If you pull down the File menu in the upper right corner, you will see Quit. Select the Quit item and give it the keyboard-equivalent character Q. Now pull down the menu again, and you'll see the Command-Q symbol next to the Quit item. Quit does not have a corresponding procedure, which means that it will quit from the database (which is appropriate in this case).

Pull down the Menu menu and notice the items there:

Append Menu adds a menu title at the bottom of the Menus list. If the menu list gets long, it is scrollable.

Insert Menu inserts a menu title above the currently selected menu.

Delete Menu deletes the currently selected menu.

Append Item adds a menu item to the bottom of the Items list. This is a scrollable list, and you should provide a corresponding procedure for every item (except Quit).

Insert Item inserts a menu item above the currently selected item.

Delete Item removes the currently selected item.

Show Custom Menus gives you a sneak preview of what your completed database screen will look like. You can look at the contents of any of the menus, and you can add a "splash screen" (background graphics) to the database. Choose this item now, and you'll see a giant 4th Dimension logo in the background. You can add graphics of your own, simply by cutting them from somewhere else (like the Scrapbook or a painting program) and pasting them here. To get out of Custom Menus, click anywhere on the screen.

Take the following steps to begin constructing the menu bar for your database. Since you have only four procedures, this won't take long.

1. Append a new menu called Customers.
2. Enter the following items with the corresponding procedures and keyboard equivalents:

Item	Procedure	Keyboard equivalent
New Customer	Add Customer	N
Show All Customers	Show All	A

Check the Line box for this

Sort by Last Name	Sort by Last	L

3. Append a new menu called Credit.
4. Enter this item with the corresponding procedure and keyboard equivalent:

Item	Procedure	Keyboard equivalent
Total Outstanding	Total Credit	T

5. Find a graphic in the Scrapbook that you like, then press Command-C to copy it.
6. Select the Show Custom Menus item from the Menu menu and press Command-V to paste your graphic.

Figure 9-9 shows a sample splash screen, complete with the menu bar that has just been created. Now you can close the menu editor. This menu will be available for editing and additions later.

FIGURE 9-9.   The splash screen is a custom graphic you can add as the background for a database.

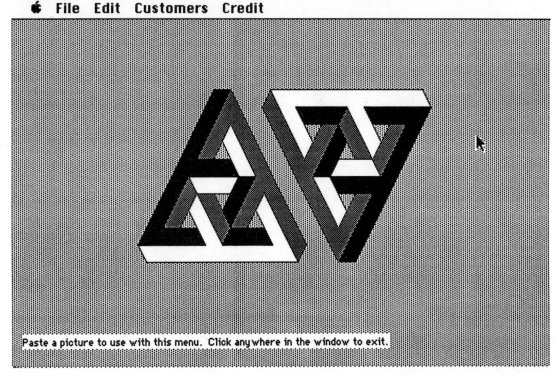

In this chapter, you have learned how to write some basic procedures and how to make them accessible to the user. Feel free to go to the Custom mode right now to test your menus and the procedures they can access. When you are through experimenting, select the Quit command to return to the User mode in 4th Dimension. Before you begin the next chapter, return to Design mode so you can learn how to use more commands and techniques.

PART 3

Beyond the Fourth Dimension

or Creating a Standalone Application from Start to Finish

10

Graphics and the User Interface

Even though many of the graphics that appear in a 4th Dimension database are automatic, you have a lot of control over the layouts, the graphics themselves, and the appearance of the user interface. By using procedures, you can control everything from the menus to the windows to the dialog boxes, and most of the graphics and user interface commands are extremely easy to use. In this chapter, you'll explore various aspects of the user interface as well as the graphics potential of 4th Dimension.

MENU COMMANDS

In the last chapter, you learned how to use the menu editor to create menu bars that provide access to procedures. 4th Dimension automatically created a menu bar called Menubar #1; had you created different sets of menu bars, they would have been named Menubar #2, Menubar #3, and so on. A menu bar is one of the few things in 4th Dimension that you can't name yourself.

Several commands control what menu bar is available and how individual menu items appear.

Command: **Menu Bar**
Format: Menu Bar (*integer*)
Use: Sometimes a database may be so complex that you have to build two or more different menu bars for it. When you have several different menu bars (Menubar #1, Menubar #2, and so on), you can make any of them the current menu bar by typing Menu Bar, followed by the number of the menu bar in parentheses. When the database is first started, the first menu bar appears by default.

         There is a complementary function to Menu Bar called Menu Selected, which returns a four-byte integer indicating which menu is being used (the higher integer number) and which menu item number has been selected (the lower integer number). If no menu is selected, Menu Selected returns 0.

         Otherwise, you need to do a simple conversion to make the value returned usable. To find the menu being used, divide Menu Selected by 65,536 and take the integer of that number. For instance, to assign the menu number to a variable called Which-Menu, you would type

```
WhichMenu:=Int(Menu Selected/65536)
```

Determining the menu item number requires taking the modulo of Menu Selected with the modulus 65,536. For instance, to assign the item number to a variable called WhichItem, you would type

```
WhichItem:=Mod(Menu Selected;65536)
```

A final note on how the menus are counted: you might expect the Apple menu to be 1, the File menu to be 2, the Edit menu to be 3, and your menus to be 4, 5, 6, and so on. However, the Apple and Edit menus are *not* counted, so the File menu is menu number 1, and your own custom menus are menus 2, 3, 4, and so on.

Example: The following routine uses Menubar #3 and loads the values of the menu and the menu item selected into variables once a menu has been selected.

```
Menu Bar (3)
While (Menu Selected=0)
Wend
MenuNo:=Int(Menu Selected/65536)
ItemNo:=Mod(Menu Selected;65536)
```

Command: **Disable Item**

Format: `Disable Item` (*menu number*;*item number*)

Use: There are two ways to disable a menu or an item within a menu: you can use the custom menu editor to make a menu or menu item disabled by default, or you can use the Disable Item command. If you want to disable a specific item, type `Disable Item`, followed by the number of the menu and the number of the item in that menu. Both numbers should be in the parentheses and separated by a semicolon. If you want to disable a menu and all its items, make the item number 0.

Again, the Apple and Edit menus are not counted in the menu number system. The File menu is number 1, and your custom menus are numbered from left to right as 2, 3, 4, and so on. Menu items are counted 1, 2, 3, and so on, from the top down. If you want to restore all the default settings for a particular menu bar, just issue the Menu Bar command with the appropriate menu bar number.

You'll want to disable menus or items when the user should not be given access to something. For example, suppose you create a database with several different access levels. On one security level, you might want to disable commands like Delete Record and Display Budget, since those are confidential, whereas on another level (which might be accessed with a password), those items could be enabled.

Example: The following command disables the entire third menu and the fifth item in the second menu.

```
Disable Item (3;0)
```

Command: **Enable Item**

Format: Enable Item (*menu number;item number*)

Use: This command enables (or "turns back on") a menu or menu item that was disabled either in the User environment (when you created the custom menu) or with the Disable item command. Enable Item is followed by two numbers enclosed in parentheses: the number of the menu and the number of the item in that menu. If you want to enable the menu and leave the items in the menu in their current state, enter the item number as 0.

Example: The first of the following two commands enables the third item in the File menu; the second command enables the fourth menu but does not affect any of the items.

```
Enable Item (1;3)
Enable Item (4)
```

Command: **Check Item**

Format: Check Item (*menu number;item number;string*)

Use: A check mark beside a menu item indicates that that item has been selected. In word processing programs, you'll often see check marks next to font types and sizes, since that is the easiest way to show which items in the menu bar are currently chosen (with a command like Save, it would be senseless to put a check mark next to it, since that would have no meaning).

You can place a check mark next to an item with the Check Item command. In the parentheses that follow the command, put first the number of the menu, then the number of the item, and then the string representing what you want next to the menu. To erase that check mark, use " " for the string.

Example: The following line puts a check mark next to the third item in the second menu.

Check Item (1;3;Char (18))

WINDOWS AND THE SCREEN

You can create custom windows on the screen to hold input layouts, messages, dialog boxes, and other objects. Windows are a familiar sight to most Macintosh users, and you can make your database more attractive by using customized windows and the custom fonts and font styles available in 4th Dimension. You can have only one custom window on the screen at a time, but it will be placed over the contents of the current 4th Dimension output.

Command: **Open Window**
Format: Open Window *(x1;y1;x2;y2;type;title)*
Use: This is the most versatile of the window commands because it lets you open any one of seven different types of windows of any size and title. The most important thing to understand is the contents of the parentheses that follow the command. *x1* and *y1* are integers that represent the upper left corner of the window. *x1* is the distance (measured in pixels) from the upper left corner to the left edge of the screen. *y1* is the distance from the upper left corner to the top of the screen. *x2* and *y2* represent the distance in pixels from the lower left corner to the right edge of the screen and to the bottom of the screen, respectively. The fifth argument is the window type. The type of window you specify can be any one of the following seven. If you don't enter a number for the window type, 4th Dimension uses the Alert box (type 1) by default.

Window type	Number
Standard document window	0
Alert box/dialog box	1
Plain box	2
Plain box with shadow	3
Document window without zoom box	4
Document window with zoom box	8
Rounded corner window	16

The sixth argument, which is also optional, is the window title. You can give the window a title, which will appear centered on the top portion of the window, but the title is a string expression, so be sure to enclose it in quotation marks. When the window is displayed, anything that would normally appear on the screen (layouts, messages, and so on) appears inside the window.

Example: The following example lets you enter the number of a window type, then it displays that window with a brief message. Try out this procedure—you can test it in the User environment by selecting Execute Procedure from the Special menu. Execute Procedure lists all the available procedures; double-click on the name of this one to see it work, as shown in Figure 10-1.

```
OK:=1
While (OK=1)
 If (OK=1)
 type:=Num (Request ("Enter the window type"))
 End if
 Close Window
 Open Window (50;200;350;300;type;"Window Test")
 Message ("Hello there. I'm a window. What do you think  of
me?")
End while
```

Command: **Set Window Title**

Format: Set Window Title (*"title"*)

Use: You can change or set the title of the current window with this command. The current window can be either the custom window on the screen or the 4th Dimension window (if no custom window is displayed).

FIGURE 10-1.   This short procedure lets you enter window types; it then displays that type of window on the screen.

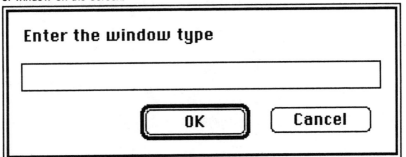

Example: Suppose a custom window is on the screen, and you want to change its name to Data Input. Your procedure needs the line Set Window Title ("Data Input"). When this line in the procedure is encountered, the window title is changed immediately.

Command: **Close Window**
Format: Close Window
Use: Getting rid of a window is a lot easier than creating it. To remove a custom window from the screen, include the Close Window command within the procedure. This command removes only the custom window you have created, not the 4th Dimension window. Therefore, if no custom window is on the screen, the Close Window command has no effect.

Command: **Erase Window**
Format: Erase Window
Use: If you want some fast "window washing," use this command to eliminate the contents of the custom window. The Erase Window command eliminates anything within the window and returns the text cursor to the default position of 0,0 (the upper left corner of the window).

Command: **Go to XY**
Format: Go to XY (*x*,*y*)
Use: When a custom window first appears on the screen, a text cursor is placed in the upper left corner at position 0,0. The first number is the horizontal (x-axis) position, and the second number is the vertical (y-axis) position.
Example: The following procedure puts two lines of text inside the window. The "I'm up here!" text begins at the default location of 0,0; the "I'm down here!" text begins at the 3,4 location, as determined by the Go to XY command.

```
Open Window(120;50;250;150;4;"Text Window")
Message("I'm up here!")
Go to XY(3;4)
Message("And I'm down here!")
While (i<30000)
i:=i+1
End while
Close Window
```

Command: **Screen Height** and **Screen Width**
Format: Screen Height and Screen Width
Use: Because of all the different sizes of monitors appearing on the market for the Macintosh, you can't be sure when you create a database that the screen that will be used will be the standard Macintosh display. It might be a much larger screen, and your windows and other information would all be confined to the upper left portion instead of placed on the screen as you originally intended.

There is a way around this. Using the Screen Height and Screen Width commands, you can find the height of the screen (from the top of the menu bar to the bottom of the screen) and the width of the screen, both measured in pixels. You can then use this information to make sure that custom windows are displayed correctly, such as in a centered format; or to determine the size of a large screen, if you have one.

Example: The following routine loads the height and the width of the screen into the variables SH and SW, respectively.

```
SH:=Screen Height
SW:=Screen Width
```

Command: **Invert Background**
Format: Invert Background (*variable name*)
Use: Not only can you create and modify custom windows, you can fine-tune the contents of a layout with the Invert Background command. Invert Background affects the background behind the variable you name. If the background is normal, the command inverts it. If the background is already inverted, the command toggles it back to normal. If you print the record, any inverted backgrounds are also displayed like that on the printed copy as well as on the screen.

Command: **Font**
Format: Font (*variable;number or string*)
Use: You can change the fonts of layout variables with the Font command. Follow the Font command with the name of the variable that is to use the font and then either the font number or the font name you want that variable to use. The font numbers and names are as follows:

Font number	Font name	Font number	Font name
0	systemFont	9	toronto
1	applFont	11	cairo
2	newYork	12	losAngeles
3	geneva	20	times
4	monaco	21	helvetica
5	venice	22	courier
6	london	23	symbol
7	athens	24	taliesin
8	sanFran		

Using different fonts helps to emphasize certain variables or just gives variables a different style.

Example: To show the variable AG2 in the courier font, you would enter

`Font (AG2;22)` or `Font (AG2;"courier")`.

Command: **Font Size**

Format: `Font Size (`*variable;point size*`)`

Use: You can reduce or enlarge the type size of a variable value that is being displayed. The point size can range from 1 (ridiculously small) to 128 (extremely large); typical sizes are 12, 14, and 24. If you enter 0, the variable is shown in its default font size.

Example: If you want the variable AG2 to be displayed in 18-point size, you would enter `Font Size (AG2;18)`.

Command: **Font Style**

Format: `Font Style (`*variable,style*`)`

Use: There are eight different font styles in 4th Dimension: plain, bold, italic, underline, outline, shadow, condensed, and extended. When a variable is first displayed, it is in plain (style = 0) mode. You can provide a number to 4th Dimension that specifies in which style or styles a variable should be displayed. The styles and their style numbers are as follows:

Font style	Font style number	Font style	Font style number
Bold	1	Shadow	16
Italic	2	Condensed	32
Underline	4	Extended	64
Outline	8		

By adding the numbers, you can combine the styles. For instance, if you want variable Total to be shown in bold italics, you would enter Font Style (Total,3), since the number for bold (1) and the number for italic (2) equal 3.

STRINGS

You already have a pretty good idea of what a string is: a collection of letters, numbers, and/or symbols that is considered as one unit. The letter A could be a string. So could the sentence "I am using 4th Dimension today." Even %$#@@@ + ? is a string. Strings are entered into procedures within quotation marks (for example, Name:="Timothy"), unlike numbers, which are left as they are without the use of any symbols, including commas (for example, Value:=12000).

In this section, you'll learn how to work with and manipulate strings within procedures.

Command: **String**
Format: String (*expression*)
Use: There are two ways to use the String function, depending on the numeric expression enclosed in the parentheses. The first way is to include a number, a variable, or a function that returns a number (examples are 50, 120, SumTotal, Records in File). This makes the number usable as a string, which is essential when you are attaching a numeric expression to a string.

You can also use the String command to get the date value from a field containing the date. The date is in the format mm/dd/yy, so February 19, 1989, would be 02/19/89.

Example: Following are examples for the two formats:

```
Message ("The total sales for the last year according to
these records is $"+String(TotalSales) " for Western
Operations."
Message ("The first order from that account was on
"+String([Credit]1st Order Date))
```

Command: **Substring**
Format: Substring (*string;start;number*)
Use: If you want to take out a portion of a string, you can use Substring to identify which string (the first argument) you are working

with, which character in the string (*start*) to begin with, and how many characters (*number*) from that string you want to extract.

For instance, if you want to assign the variable Middle five characters from the string called Whole, beginning with the eighth character, you would enter Substring (Whole;8;5). The original string — in this case, Whole — is not affected. Substring just makes a copy of that portion and puts it in the variable Middle. Of course, you can give your variables whatever name you want.

Example: The short procedure that follows extracts the middle name from a person's whole name. This wouldn't work with just any name, because the position and the length of middle names vary. After these two lines are through, the value of MyName would be Jonathan Thomas Richards and the value of MiddleName would be Thomas.

```
MyName:=("Jonathan Thomas Richards")
MiddleName:=Substring (MyName;10;6)
```

Command: **Ascii** and **Char**

Format: Ascii (*string*) and Char (*number*)

Use: You may be familiar with the ASCII code, which is a standardized way that computers represent characters. The capital letter A, for instance, is equal to ASCII code 65 on almost all computers, and capital letter B is equal to 66. The ASCII code is helpful in determining which key on the keyboard has been pressed, if one character is equal to another, and what ASCII value a certain character or symbol holds.

The Ascii function returns the ASCII code of the first character in a string; no matter how long the string is, only the first character is considered. Lowercase and uppercase letters have different ASCII codes.

Char, which is the converse of Ascii, converts an ASCII number to the corresponding character. This is useful if you want to display in a message characters that you cannot input directly, such as carriage returns or quotation marks.

Example: The following line assigns the variable Code the ASCII value of the letter R, since that is the first letter of the string.

```
Code:=Ascii("Rolling")
```

The next line prints out a short quotation surrounded by quotation marks. This would not be possible without Char, because quotation marks typically begin and end strings.

```
MESSAGE ("And she said, "+Char(34)+"0h
My!"+Char(34))
```

Command:	**Uppercase** and **Lowercase**
Format:	Uppercase (*string*) and Lowercase (*string*)
Use:	These functions return strings in either all uppercase letters or all lowercase letters. You can print these modified strings out directly or assign different variables to them.
Example:	Uppercase ("Testing one TWO three") returns the string *TESTING ONE TWO THREE*
	Lowercase ("Testing one TWO three") returns the string *testing one two three*.

Command:	**Length**
Format:	Length (*string*)
Use:	This command returns the length of a string or a string expression, measured in total characters. This includes all characters, including spaces and symbols.
Example:	Suppose the variable MyName contains the user's name in a string. You can find out the length of that name by typing

```
NameLength:=Length (MyName)
```

DIALOGS

In any user interface, communication to the user is absolutely critical. 4th Dimension provides you with a lot of tools to give messages or information to the database user.

Command:	**Dialog**
Format:	Dialog (*string*)
Use:	It isn't always appropriate to get information strictly through fields. Sometimes you will want to collect information in the form of variables (such as radio buttons, check boxes, and other layout variables). A layout that uses variables instead of fields is called a dialog layout.
	The dialog layout itself is useless without the Dialog command. Dialog puts the dialog layout on the screen and lets the user enter information in the dialog layout. If you have included buttons in the layout, you can use those to accept the information or Cancel the input. If there are no buttons in the dialog layout, 4th Dimension provides the user with OK and Cancel buttons.

The only way to see how this works is to actually create a dialog layout and a Dialog procedure, so follow these steps to add those items to your database.

Example: First you need to create a dialog layout. You know a lot about creating layouts already, so here is the basic information: you need to create a dialog layout called Locate that contains six items.

- The first item is a text object with the word Locate in bold and rather large type.
- The second item is an enterable variable called Locate.
- The third and fourth items are radio buttons with, respectively, the variable names bLast and bCity and the button text Last Name and City.
- The fifth and sixth items should be Accept and Don't Accept buttons called, respectively, Locate and Cancel.

This is a custom layout, which you need to put together piece by piece. You can use whatever graphics or text you like, as long as the dialog layout somewhat resembles the one in Figure 10-2.

Now close the Layout window and enter the procedure named Locate shown below.

```
Default File ([Customers])
All Records
Input Layout ("Customer Input")
Output Layout ("Customer Output")
Locate:=""
If (OK=1)
     If (bLast=1)
          Search by Index ([Customers]Last
Name=Locate)
     Else
          Search by Index ([Customers]City=Locate)
     End If
End If
Display Selection
```

Try this procedure in the User mode by choosing Execute Procedure from the Special menu. The way this works is easy to understand: the user clicks either the Last Name or the City

FIGURE 10-2.   You can make this dialog box look however you like, as long as the variable names are the same.

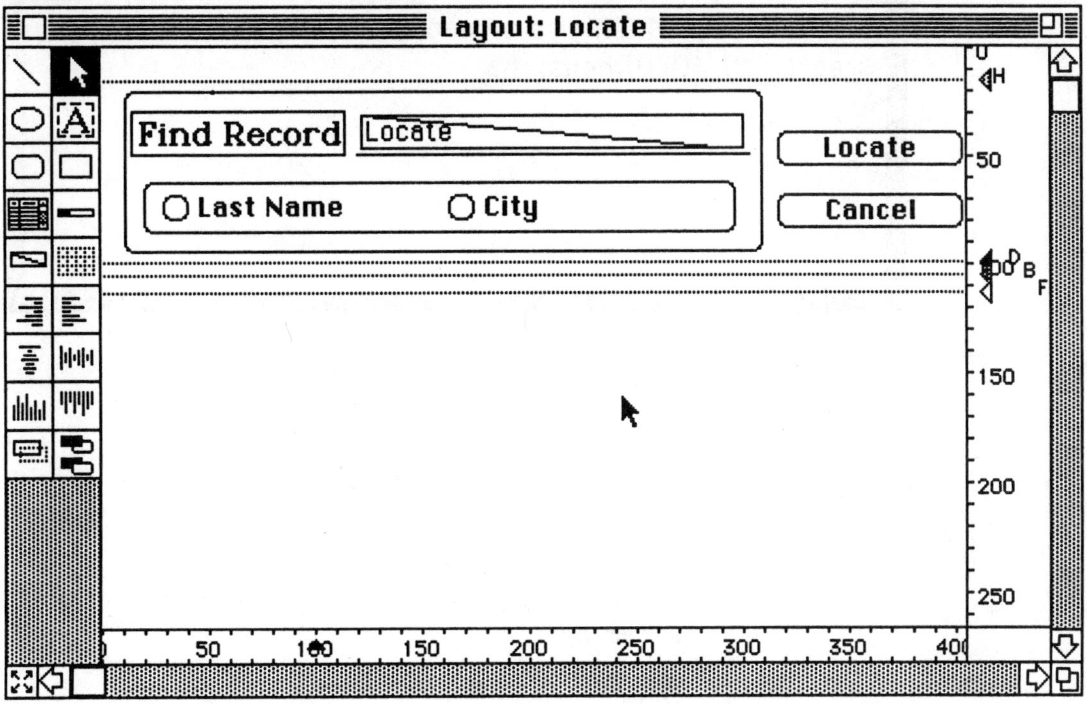

radio button to indicate how the search should be performed. Next, the user types in the last name or the city name, whichever is appropriate, and clicks the Locate key to find the cities that match. The dialog layout provides a fast, easy, customized way for the user to make a very specific search.

Command: **Message**

Format: Message (*string*)

Use: You have used this command several times already. The Message command lets you display a string or the string contents of a variable on the screen. When you use message, the string appears in a message box or, if you have opened a custom window, inside the custom window. The message remains on the screen until some other event takes place on the screen or the procedure comes to an end.

Example: The following routine puts a message in a message box, as shown in Figure 10-3. The While/End While loop makes sure

FIGURE 10-3. Because no custom window is open, the message is in a box of its own.

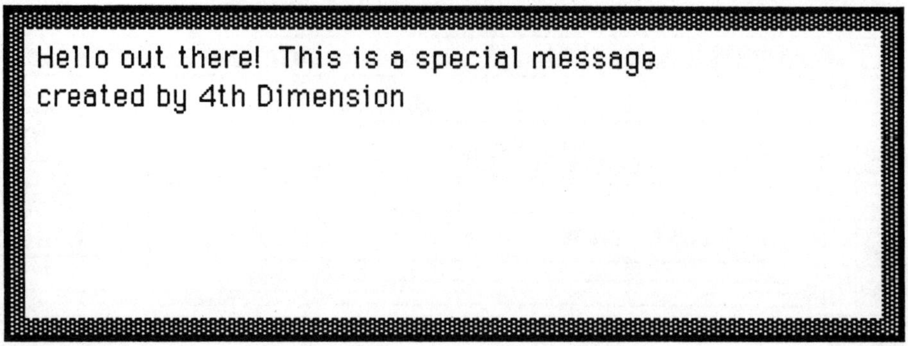

```
Hello out there! This is a special message
created by 4th Dimension
```

the message box stays on the screen long enough for you to read it. The Char(13) function puts a carriage return in the string so that words are not split onto different lines.

```
MESSAGE("Hello out there! This is a special
message"+Char(13)+ "created by 4th Dimension")
While (i#2000)
i:=i+1
End while
```

Command:	**Confirm**
Format:	Confirm (*string*)
Use:	This command is somewhat like a message box because it displays a string within a box, but it also contains OK and Cancel buttons, along with a little graphic, as shown in Figure 10-4. Use the Confirm box to make absolutely sure the user wants to go ahead with whatever command was just issued (such as deleting a record or quitting the database). The Cancel button gives the user a way out.
Example:	The result of the following line is shown in Figure 10-4.

```
Confirm ("Are you sure you want to delete this
record?")
```

Command:	**Alert**
Format:	Alert (*string*)
Use:	This command works much like the Confirm command, except that there is no Cancel key in the box. Therefore, you should use Alert just to provide information to the user. If you want to give

FIGURE 10-4.   The Confirm box contains an OK and a Cancel button.

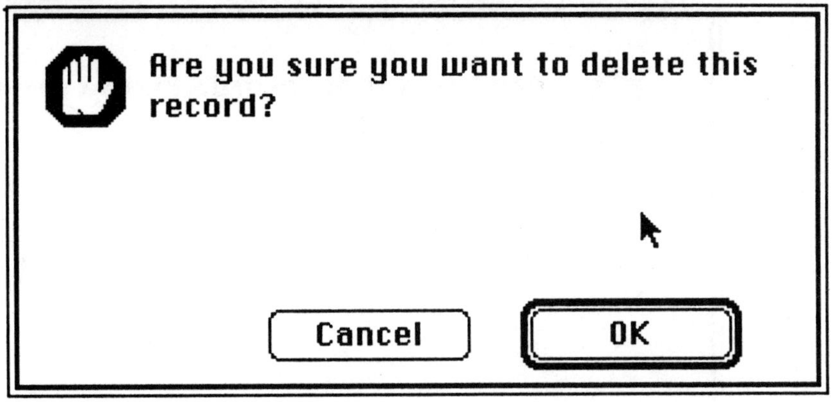

Example:	the user a way to cancel a command, use the Confirm command instead.
	Figure 10-5 shows the result of the line Alert

```
("I can't find that record. Please re-enter the search
criterion.")
```

Command:	**Request**
Format:	Request (*string;default input*)
Use:	This is a somewhat more powerful dialog box than the others since it not only provides OK and Cancel keys but also accepts input from the user. Often a user will forget to input a particular piece of information, or for some reason the database requires extra information. Request does not stand on its own; you need to assign some variable the value received from Request, as shown in the example, or use it as a function in some other way.
	The Request command displays the message (which is the string argument) and, if you want, can have a default input if that is appropriate. For a question like "What is your name?" it would probably be senseless to have a default input, whereas for a question like "Where in New York City are you?" a default input like Manhattan might be appropriate.
Example:	The following line displays the request box shown in Figure 10-6. The default input is Macintosh Plus, but the user can enter a different computer name simply by typing it. Whether the default is used or not, the user should click OK to enter the input.

```
ComptType:=REQUEST ("What computer do you own?";"Macintosh
Plus")
```

FIGURE 10-5.   The Alert box has just an OK button, so use it only to provide information.

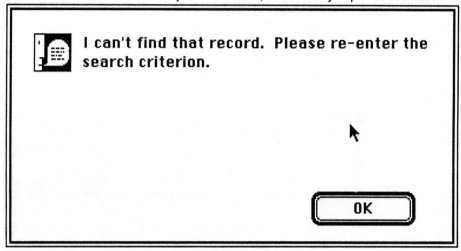

FIGURE 10-6.   You can click OK if you want to input "Macintosh Plus," or alternate input can be typed in.

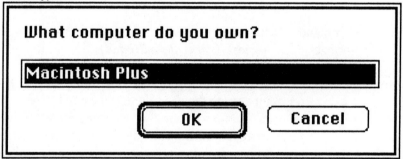

Command: **Beep**
Format: Beep (*duration*)
Use: This command makes the computer beep for a period of time equal to *duration* times 1/60 second. If you do not include an argument, Beep by itself emits a tone for .5 second.
Example: Beep (120) makes the computer beep for 2 seconds.

Command: **Messages Off** and **Messages On**
Format: Messages Off and Messages On
Use: 4th Dimension has a number of progress messages to indicate how long a search, a sort, or some other function is taking. These progress messages are usually helpful because they give the user an idea how things are going, but if functions are being

saxperformed so fast that the progress reports have no value, turn them off with the **Messages Off** command.

To turn the progress messages back on, use **Messages On**, which is the default setting for the database.

GRAPHS

The Graph File command can be used to create a graph based on data within a file. To use Graph File, you need to specify which file to use, the type number of the graph you want displayed, the alphanumeric field that will be used to label the x-axis, and the numeric field or fields that will be used to plot the y-axis.

The eight different types of graphs and their corresponding numbers are as follows:

Graph type number	Graph type	Graph type number	Graph type
1	Column graph	5	Area graph
2	Proportional column	6	Scatter graph
3	Stacked column	7	Pie graph
4	Line graph	8	Custom picture graph

Graph type 8 uses a picture of a Macintosh by default. If you want to change the picture it uses, wait until the graph appears on the screen, copy the picture you want from the Scrapbook, then choose the y-axis data series to which you want to paste the picture.

For now, create a short routine that will graph the credit limits of various companies. Type in the Graph Credit procedure as a global procedure for the Credit file as follows:

```
All Records
Default File ([Credit])
Graph File ([Credit];1;[Credit]Business Name;[Credit]Credit Limit)
```

Notice that four elements follow Graph File: first, the optional file name (credit); next, the type number of the graph (1); third, the alphanumeric field (Business Name) that will be used to label the x-axis; and finally, the numeric field (Credit Limit) that will be used to plot the y-axis.

Close this Procedure window and execute it from the User environment. Your screen should resemble Figure 10-7, with all the credit limits plotted, along with abbreviated versions of the business names.

FIGURE 10-7.   The Graph File command plots all the points from the record fields.

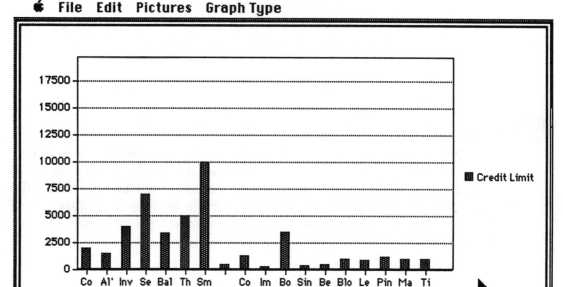

Just for fun, try using different graph types. Figure 10-8 shows what happens if you change the second argument in the previous example from 1 to 7, so that a pie chart is produced.

There's a much easier way to change graph types, however. When a graph is plotted on the screen, two special menus appear: Pictures and Graph Type. The Pictures menu lets you paste the picture currently in the Clipboard to any of the y-axes. The Graph Type menu lists all eight types of graphs so you can choose any of them directly. In addition, you can print this graph directly from the screen by selecting Print from the File menu.

As mentioned earlier, you can list more than one y-axis field so that several different fields are plotted simultaneously. This won't work in the pie chart, of course, since only one y-axis field can be shown at a time, so 4th Dimension uses the first one you list.

If you enter a Graph File command by itself without any arguments, 4th Dimension brings up the screen shown in Figure 10-9, allowing the user to select the parameters for graphing. This might be appropriate when a large number of

FIGURE 10-8.   Changing the graph type argument alters the graph.

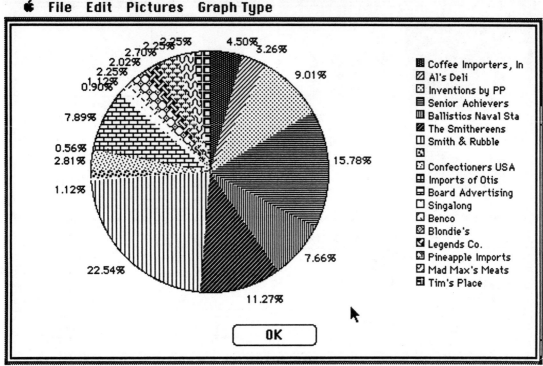

graphs are possible in a database and it is impractical to include all the possibilities within individual procedures.

BUILDING SOME SAMPLE PROCEDURES

Earlier in this chapter, you wrote the Find procedure to locate any existing record based on a customer's last name or the city field. Using what you have learned in this chapter, you can construct a few more useful procedures like the ones that follow.

The first procedure creates a pie graph showing the credit limits of all the customers. This graph will use the business names in the legend; notice that the menus are disabled before the graphing begins and are reenabled once the procedure is through running. It's a good idea to turn off menus if they should not be accessible by the user during the course of the procedure.

FIGURE 10-9. The Graph dialog box lets you enter your own parameters for building a graph.

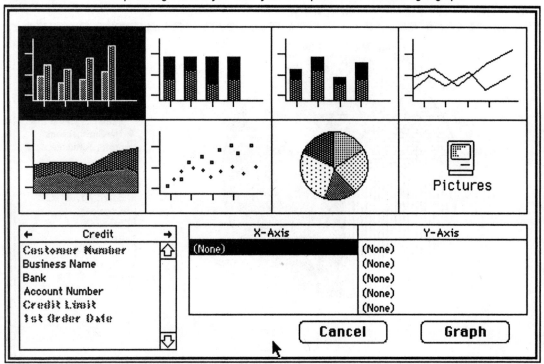

```
'Call this procedure Graph Credit
Clear Variable("") 'this clears any variable values from memory
All Records
Disable Item(1;0) 'turn off the menus
Disable Item(2;0)
Disable Item(3;0)
Disable Item(4;0)
Default File([Credit])
Graph File(7;[Credit]Business Name;[Credit]Credit Limit)
Enable Item(1;0) 'turn the menus back on
Enable Item(2;0)
Enable Item(3;0)
Enable Item(4;0)
```

Every Macintosh program and application has an "about" box, which indicates the program's name, author, and creation date. Sometimes, about boxes have help screens, lavish graphics, and even sound. The one created by the following procedure is simple. It opens up a small window and displays a few lines about this database. You might want to have more sophisticated about boxes in your creations by designing one as a layout and then displaying it with the Dialog command, but for now try this easy one.

```
'Call this procedure About
Disable Item(1;0)
Disable Item(2;0)
Disable Item(3;0)
Disable Item(4;0)
Open Window(100;100;400;220;0;"About Customers")
'Char(13) below represents a carriage return
Message("Customers Database"+Char(13)+Char(13)+"This is a simple
demonstration database"+Char(13)+" of business customers")
Message(Char(13)+Char(13)+" by Tim Knight © 1988")
'the little routine below makes the computer pause a few moments
i:=0
While (i<200)
i:=i+1
End while
Close Window
Enable Item(1;0)
Enable Item(2;0)
Enable Item(3;0)
Enable Item(4;0)
```

Because the variable *i* is being used in several procedures, it is important that its value be set to 0 for every procedure where it is used. In fact, it is not important that the values of variables be retained from procedure to procedure, so open up each procedure you have created so far and enter the command Clear Variable ("") as the first line. This clears the value of any variables in memory and ensures that there is not an unwanted value left over from another procedure.

The next procedure you are going to enter deletes a record from memory. This sounds like a simple procedure, but it is somewhat complicated, because it has to make very sure the user erases only what he or she wants to erase. Because this procedure is longer than the others, you will type it into the computer in steps.

The first part of the procedure is easy to understand. It chooses the Customers file for the default, disables the menus, and zeros out the variables in the procedure.

```
'Call this procedure Delete Customer
Default File([Customers])
Disable Item(1;0)
```

```
Disable Item(2;0)
Disable Item(3;0)
Disable Item(4;0)
bCity:=0
bLast:=0
Locate:=""
OK:=0
```

Next, the procedure selects all the records and opens up a window where the Locate dialog will be placed. You originally created Locate for the Find procedure, but you can use it here as well to find the record (or records, if more than one meets the description) to be deleted.

```
All Records
Open Window(50;50;480;200;3;"Delete Customer")
Dialog("Locate")
```

Now you are going to create several "nested" If . . . Then . . . Else statements. Follow the logic very carefully. The first logical step checks to see if the OK variable equals 1 (that is, the OK in the dialog box has been clicked). If so, the computer goes to the next line of the procedure. If not (that is, Cancel has been clicked), the computer goes to the end of the procedure where the End If is located and returns to the splash screen.

The line following If (OK = 1) checks to see if the radio button named bLast has been clicked on, indicating the search should be made through the Last Name field. If it has, the search is made. If not, then the lines following Else are used.

```
If (OK=1)
 If (bLast=1) 'is the Last button clicked on?
  Search by Index([Customers]Last name=Locate)
 Else
```

If the bLast button has not been clicked, the procedure checks to see if bCity has been clicked. If it has, the procedure searches the City field to find any matches. If not, an alert box appears stating that one of the buttons needs to be clicked. The logic here is that if the first button has not been clicked (bLast does not equal 1) and the second button has not been clicked (bCity does not equal 1), then the user has not clicked either of them and has to be told to do so. Once the user clicks the OK button in the Alert box, the procedure returns to its beginning.

```
If (bCity=1) 'is the City button clicked on?
 Search by Index([Customers]City=Locate)
Else 'neither of the buttons has been clicked
 ALERT("You need to click one of the buttons to find a record")
```

delete customer 'access this procedure again (i.e., start over)
```
      End if
   End if
```

If the procedure has gone this far, then one of the buttons has been clicked and the search has been made. Now the computer checks to see if there are any records in the selection. If there are, a confirm box appears that asks if the user really wants to remove the record denoted by the variable Locate (whether that's a last name or a city, it appears within the sentence). If there are no records in the selection, the procedure uses an Alert box to notify the user that it has not found a record that matches the criterion given. Once the user clicks OK, then procedure starts over so the user can try again with different criteria.

```
   If (Records in selection#0)
    Confirm("Are you sure you want to delete this "+Locate+"
    record?")
   Else
    Alert("I can't find that record. Please try again.")
    Clear Variable("")
```
    delete customer
```
   End if
```

Finally, if the computer has gone through all the If . . . Then . . . Else tests to this point, there is at least one record to be deleted. Once the OK button is clicked, confirming that the user wants to go ahead with the deletion, the procedure deletes the selection, selects all of the records that remain, then reenables all of the menus.

```
   If (OK=1)
      Delete Selection
    End if
   End if
  All Records
  End if
  Enable Item(1;0)
  Enable Item(2;0)
  Enable Item(3;0)
  Enable Item(4;0)
```

SOME MENU CHANGES

You have a few more procedures now, so you have to make corresponding changes to the menu bar. Open up Menubar #1 and alter it as described here:

1. Under the File menu, add a couple of other items: the first item in the list should be About Customers, which uses the procedure called About. Below this, add as an item a line to separate the Quit command from About Customers. Turn the Enable check box off for the line, since there is no reason a line should be enabled.
2. Under the Customers menu, put an item called Find Customer above Sort by Last Name, which uses the Find procedure. Make the keyboard-equivalent the F key.
3. Under the Customers menu, add an item underneath New Customer called Delete Customer, which uses the Delete Customer procedure. Make the keyboard-equivalent the D key.
4. Also under Customers, choose the line item. Notice that it is enabled. You want the lines in these menus consistently disabled, so click the Enable check box off. Notice the difference when you access the sample Customers menu and the line cannot be selected.
5. Finally, add an item called Graph Credit to the Credit menu, which uses the procedure Graph Credit. Make G the keyboard-equivalent.

CHAPTER

11

Sets, Subrecords, and the Execution Cycle

You've seen how powerful manipulation of the current selection can be in both the User environment and the Custom environment. The current selection consists of anywhere from none to all of the records of a file, and it can be searched, sorted, and subjected to a formula (with the Apply to Selection command). The concept of the current selection has its limitations, however. There can be only one current selection per file, and it can't be compared or used in conjunction with another current selection.

SET RECORDS

4th Dimension has a solution for these weaknesses in a database concept called sets. Sets are similar to current selections in that a set is a reference table that points to a group of records. A set can range from none to all of the records in a file. More important, you can have multiple sets for a single file.

Having multiple sets alone is useful. You might want to create several sets to separate records for the east, central, and western parts of a country, or you might want two sets to separate old customers from new customers. You can think of sets as multiple current selections, with the difference that one record might be in several sets. Another similarity between sets and the current selection is that both have a single current record.

The real power of sets is that they can be combined and compared to create a new set. The new set might be a combination of the two, or it might contain those records that are found in both sets. It is important to remember that a set is a part of a file, and if you are going to perform operations on sets, they must belong to the same file. A common use for this type of feature would be to find duplicate records within a set and eliminate them. If you've ever received two sets of junk mail because your name and address are listed twice in a mailing list, you can appreciate the power of this function.

Eleven commands relate to sets: Create Empty Set, Create Set, Use Set, Add to Set, Clear Set, Intersection, Union, and Difference. The Save Set and Load Set commands save and load sets from the disk, while the Records in Set command tells you how many records are in a set.

Command:	**Create Empty Set**
Format:	Create Empty Set (*string*)
Use:	This command creates an empty set with the name you specify in parentheses. You can add records to this set with the Add to Set command. If you want to use a file other than the default file,

enter the file name before the string and separate the two with a semicolon.

Example: To create a new set called Western Customers from the Customers file, you would type `Create Empty Set ("Western Customers")`. If the default file is anything except Customers, you would type `Create Empty Set ([Customers];"Western Customers")`.

Command: **Create Set**

Format: `Create Set (`*string*`)`

Use: This works like the Create Empty Set command, except that it loads the current selection into the new set. Also, if there is a current record in the current selection, that record is also made the current record in the set. If there is no current record, the first record of the current selection is made the current record.

Example: The following procedure creates a set of all customers with a ZIP code greater than 75000.

```
DEFAULT FILE ([Customers])
ALL RECORDS
SEARCH ([Customers]ZIP Code>75000)
CREATE SET ("ZIP 75000")
```

Command: **Use Set**

Format: `Use Set (`*string*`)`

Use: The Use Set command is a reversal of the Create Set command. Instead of putting the current selection into the set, it takes the set and makes it the current selection. After you are through performing operations on sets, you will often want to take the final version of the set and make it the new current selection.

Example: To make the set Duplicate Records the current selection, you would type `Use Set ("Duplicate Records")`. The current selection for the file to which Duplicate Records belongs would be altered so that it contains the same records as the set. The current record in the set would be made the current record in the current selection as well.

Command: **Add to Set** and **Records in Set**

Format: `Add to Set (`*string*`)`

              `Records in Set (`*set*`)`

Use: This command adds records, one at a time, to the set specified by the string within the parentheses. Add to Set adds the current record from the current selection to the set. There is also a system function available called Records in Set, which returns the number of records in the set you specify. For example, Records in Set ("My Set") returns the number of records in the set My Set.

Example:

The following procedure alphabetically sorts all the records in a file, then compares each name to the name previously checked to see if they are the same. If they are the same, then they are duplicate records and are added to a set. The set can be used later to delete the duplicate records. Actually type in and save this procedure in the Customers file under the name DelDups, then add the command Delete Duplicates to Menubar #1 under the Customers menu, as shown in Figure 11-1.

```
Default File ([Customers])
'Zero out the variables that will hold previous values read.
PreviousLastName:=""
PreviousFirstName:=""
All Records
'Make an empty set to hold the duplicates.
Create Empty Set ("Delete These Duplicates")
'Sort by ZIP, last name, then first name. Sorting by ZIP
'decreases likelihood that two people who really do have the
'same name will be mistaken as duplicates.
```

FIGURE 11-1.   Add the Delete Duplicates command to the custom menu.

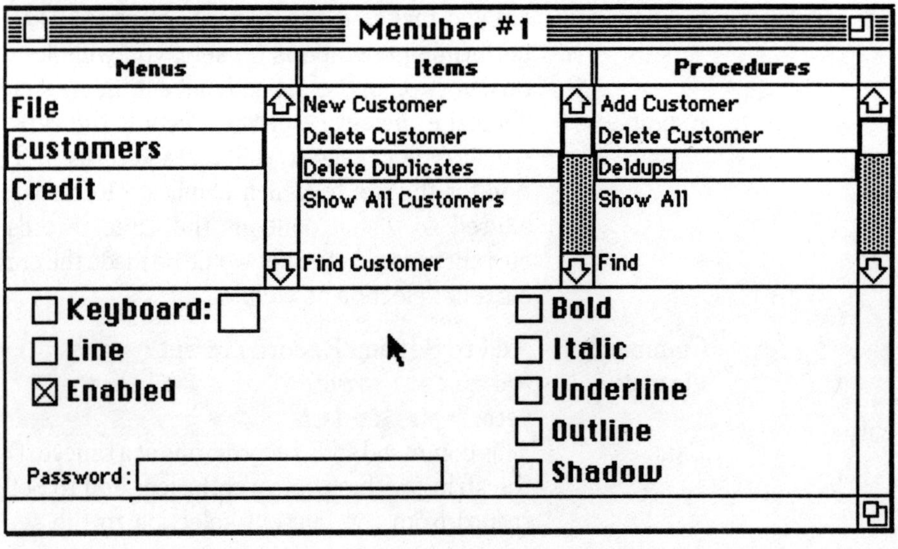

```
Sort Selection ([Customers]ZIP Code;>;[Customers]Last
  Name;>;[Customers]First Name;>)
'While loop lasts as long as there are records to read.
While (Not(End Selection))
  'Check to see if last name and first name of this record and
  'the last one read are identical. If so, add this record to
  'the set.
  If (([Customers]Last
Name=PreviousLastName)&([Customers]
  FirstName=PreviousFirstName))
  Add to Set ("Delete These Duplicates")
  End If
  'Store first and last names into variables for comparing to
next record.
  PreviousLastName:=[Customers]Last Name
  PreviousFirstName:=[Customers]First Name
  'Move on to next record.
  Next Record
End While
```

Command:	**Clear Set**
Format:	`Clear Set` (*string*)
Use:	This command eliminates the set denoted by the string name and clears all the memory formerly occupied by that set. Actually, sets take up virtually no memory, since they contain only pointers to the records, not the records themselves. Therefore, it's not a good idea to clear sets just for the sake of more memory. However, if a procedure has finished working with a set, it should be programmed to clear that set from memory.
	As with some other commands, you can use the at sign (@) as a wildcard to clear out more than one set. `Clear Set ("@")` clears out *every* set in memory, while `Clear Set ("My@")` removes all sets that begin with My (such as MyComputers, MyCustomers, and My).
Example:	To delete the set called "Delete These Duplicates" from memory, you would enter `Clear Set ("Delete These Duplicates")`.
Command:	**Intersection**
Format:	`Intersection` (*first set*; *second set*; *new set*)
Use:	The Intersection function examines the contents of the first and second sets and finds all the records that are in both sets. It takes

those records and stores them in a third set. The third set can be one of three things: (1) a totally new set that 4th Dimension creates and gives the name specified; (2) a set that already exists, in which cases 4th Dimension erases the data currently held in the set and replaces it with the data from the Intersection function (so be careful not to use names of sets that already exist in memory and whose data you don't want eliminated); or (3) the name of the first or second set, in which case that set is replaced with the new data from Intersection.

Intersection is typically used to find some kind of match between two sets. For instance, you might have a set called Macintosh Users, which lists all the people in your database who own a Macintosh, and another set called Central USA Customers. By combining these two sets with the function Intersection ("Macintosh Users"; "Central USA Customers"; "Central US Macs"), you would create a new set called Central US Macs, which has only the records of Macintosh users who are in the central part of the United States.

Example:

Suppose you have two sets called Set 1 and Set 2, and you want to create a new set, called Set 3, that contains the records found in both Set 1 and Set 2. You would enter Intersection ("Set 1";"Set 2";"Set 3"). If Set 1 contains customers 1, 2, 3, 4, 5, 6, 7, and 8, and set 2 contains customers 5, 6, 8, 10, 12, and 22, then Set 3 would contain customers 5, 6, and 8, since those records are in both Set 1 and Set 2.

Command: **Union**

Format: Union (*first set*; *second set*; *new set*)

Use:

This command combines the records from the first set and the second set into a new set. The same rules apply here that apply to Intersection: the new set can be a previously nonexistent set, a set that already exists, or even a replacement for the first or second set named. Duplicates between the first and second set are not duplicated in the new set. For instance, if the first set contains records 1, 2, and 3, and the second set contains records 3, 4, and 5, then the new set will contain records, 1, 2, 3, 4, and 5, *not* 1, 2, 4, 5, and two copies of 3.

Example:

The following routine performs an indexed search on the Last Name and ZIP Code fields to create two sets, then uses the Union function to contain all the records with either a Last Name greater than Larson or a ZIP Code greater than 50000. As you may remember, the Search by Index command does not allow the logical OR argument, which means you cannot do an indexed search that finds the records that meet one criterion OR another criterion. The Union function is a good way around this shortcoming.

```
Default File ([Customers])
Search by Index ([Customers]Last Name>"Larson")
'Load the current selection into "Above Larson" set.
Create Set ("Above Larson")
Search by Index ([Customers]ZIP Code>50000)
'Load the current selection into "Above 50000" set.
Create Set ("Above 50000")
Union("Above Larson";"Above 50000";"New Set")
'Make this new set the current selection.
Use Set ("New Set")
```

Command:	**Difference**
Format:	Difference (*first set*; *second set*; *new set*)
Use:	This command finds all the records in the first set that *are not in the second set* and puts them in a new set. For example, suppose you have a set of Macintosh owners called Mac Owners and a set of Apple IIGS owners called Apple GS Owners. If some of these people own both computers, they are in both sets. If you want to send out a special offer for Macintosh owners to get a good discount on an Apple IIGS, it wouldn't make sense to send the offer to people who own both computers. Thus, you would use the command Difference ("Mac Owners";"Apple GS Owners";"Mac Only Owners") to create a new set of people who own a Macintosh and *not* an Apple IIGS.
Example:	Assume you have two sets in memory: Under $5000, which represents companies in your Credit file with credit limits under $5,000, and Slow Payers, which contains the records of companies that consistenly pay their bills late. To create a new set, called Credit Offer, that contains the records of firms whose credit line you want to increase and that does not include the slow payers, you would enter Difference ("Under $5000";"Slow Payers"; "Credit Offer").
Command:	**Save Set**
Format:	Save Set (*string*; *name*)

Use:
: This command saves a special set to the disk with the document name you provide. For example, `Save Set ("New Set","Set One")` saves the set called New Set to the disk under the name Set One. If you do not provide a name, a dialog box appears for the user to enter the set name. You probably do not want this to happen, unless it is appropriate that the user enter some meaningful name.

Example:
: *See example for* **Load Set**.

Command:
: **Load Set**

Format:
: `Load Set` (*string; name*)

Use:
: This command loads a set that has been saved to disk back into the computer's memory. If the set belongs to a file that is not the default file, you should include the file name before the string. For example, if you want to load in Set Three, which was saved to the disk as Unique Set, you would type `Load Set ("Set Three";"Unique Set")`. If the file to which that set belongs — for example, Credit — is not the default file, you would enter `Load Set ([Credit];"Set Three";"Unique Set")`. The file name precedes the other two arguments.

Example:
: The following procedure creates a set of California customers, saves it to disk, erases it from memory, then loads it back into memory from the disk. Although not a very useful routine, it is a good demonstration.

```
Default File ([Customers])
Output Layout ("Customer Output")
Search by Index ([Customers]State="CA")
'make a new set
Create Set ("California Customers")
Alert ("I'm going to save California Customers to disk!")
Save Set ("California Customers";"CA People")
Clear Set ("California Customers")
Alert ("The set's gone now, but will be returning shortly.")
Load Set ("California Customers";"CA People")
'Load the set into the current selection, then display it.
Use Set ("California Customers")
'Asterisk is so output layout will be used, even if only one
'record shown.
Display Selection (*)
```

SUBRECORDS

When you learned about the user Environment, you found out how to create subrecords and the layouts that would accept or display their data. Subrecords are "owned" by parent records (just like a set is owned by a file), and they are most appropriate when you are not sure how many subrecords are going to be in a particular record. For the Customers database you have been working on, information on meetings is contained in subrecords, since some customers have been through many meetings with the company, whereas others have had only one or two.

In procedures, you have commands available to you to create, search, and sort subrecords, much as you do with parent records. An important difference is that you don't load and save subrecords. Because subrecords belong to a parent record, the loading or saving of the parent record automatically loads or saves accompanying subrecords.

Command: **Add Subrecord**
Format: `Add Subrecord (`*subfile name;string;*`*)`
Use: This command displays the subfile's input layout, creates a blank subrecord in memory, and lets the user enter that new subrecord as the current subrecord. If an Accept button in the layout is clicked, the subrecord is saved in memory. If a Don't Accept button is clicked, the subrecord is cleared from memory. Of course, a subrecord in memory has to be saved to disk, and this happens when the Save Record command is issued for that subrecord's parent.

Like the similar Add Record command, Add Subrecord cannot take input through variables. It can accept input only through the fields in the subfile's layout. When you enter this command, you need to follow it with the name of the subfile, the name of the layout to use, and—if you don't want the layout to have scroll bars or a zoom box—an asterisk.

Example: The command `Add Subrecord ([Customers]Meetings;"Meeting Input";*)` puts the Meeting Input layout on the screen without scroll bars or a zoom box and accepts a subrecord from the Meetings subfile whose parent is Customers.

Command: **Create Subrecord**
Format: `Create Subrecord (`*subfile name*`)`
Use: Like its counterpart Create Record, this command is useful for input with variables instead of fields. Using the Dialog command,

	you can display the layout you want to use to accept the subrecord input. Specify the subrecord you want to use by including the subfile's name within parentheses after the command.
Example:	To let the user create a new subrecord in the Meetings subfile, you would include `Create Subrecord ("Meetings")` in the procedure.

Command:	**Modify Subrecord**
Format:	Modify Subrecord (*subfile name;string;**)
Use:	Notice that the format for this command is exactly the same as that for Modify Record. Both commands do exactly the same thing: they bring the subfile's input layout to the screen and let the user enter subrecord data. The difference is that Modify Record includes the data from the currently selected subrecord in the input layout for the user to modify. If there is no currently selected subrecord, this command has no effect and the layout does not appear on the screen.
Example:	If you have a subfile called Products whose parent file is Companies, you can modify a subrecord in that subfile by typing `Modify Subrecord ([Companies]Products;"Product Input")`. An optional asterisk as a third argument prevents the scroll bars or zoom box from appearing in the input layout.

Command:	**Delete Subrecord**
Format:	Delete Subrecord (*subfile name*)
Use:	This command deletes the currently selected subrecord. If there is no current subrecord, nothing happens. The subfile name, within the parentheses, is necessary since 4th Dimension needs to know in which subfile to look for a selected subrecord. An important note here is that Delete Subrecord works only if the current record has been saved to disk with the Save Record command.
Example:	`Delete Subrecord ([Customers]Meetings)` deletes the current subrecord, if any, from the subfile called Meetings.

Command:	**All Subrecords**
Format:	All Subrecords (*subfile name*)
Use:	This command selects all the subrecords for the current record. This command does *not* select all the subrecords for the current selection, no matter how large it may be. Only the subrecords of the current record are selected.
Example:	To select all the subrecords in the Invoice Number subfile whose

parent is the current record in the Orders file, you would type All
Subrecords ([Orders]Invoice Number).

Command:	**First Subrecord**
Format:	First Subrecord (*subfile name*)
Use:	You are probably beginning to see how many parallel commands there are between subrecords and records. Like First Record, the First Subrecord function makes the first subrecord in the current selection of the subfile the current subrecord.
Example:	The following lines load in all the subrecords in the Meetings file and make the first subrecord the current subrecord.

```
Default File ([Customers])
All Subrecords ([Customers]Meetings)
First Subrecord ([Customers]Meetings)
```

Command:	**Last Subrecord**
Format:	Last Subrecord (*subfile name*)
Use:	This command makes the last subrecord in the specified subfile the current subrecord.
Example:	To make the last subrecord in the Complaints subfile the current record, you would type Last Subrecord ([Orders]Complaints).

Command:	**Next Subrecord**
Format:	Next Subrecord (*subfile name*)
Use:	This command lets the procedure move forward through sub-records, perhaps to let the user examine or modify them. The Next Subrecord command moves the subrecord pointer to the next subrecord in the current subselection of the specified sub-file. There is a helpful function called End Subselection, which returns a FALSE if there is at least one more subrecord following the current one or a TRUE if the current subrecord is the last one in the subselection.
Example:	The following procedure makes all the subrecords in the Meet-ings subfile the current subselection and moves through the subrecords one subrecord at a time. For each subrecord encoun-tered, 4th Dimension displays the value of the date field.

```
Default File([Customers])
First Record
i:=0
All Subrecords([Customers]Meetings)
```

```
First Subrecord([Customers]Meetings)
'Open a little message window.
Open Window(50;50;350;150;0;"Dates of Meetings")
'as long as there are meeting subrecords to be read
While (Not(End subselection([Customers]Meetings)))
      i:=i+1
      'Put a message in the window for each meeting date.
      Message("Meeting "+String(i)+" was on "+String([
      Customers]Meetings'Date))
      Next Subrecord([Customers]Meetings)
End while
j:=0
'pause for a while
While (j<100)
      j:=j+1
End while
```

Command:	**Previous Subrecord**
Format:	Previous Subrecord (*subfile name*)
Use:	This command is the opposite of Next Subrecord, because it moves backward through the current subselection, moving the subrecord pointer back one step each time it is used. The subrecord pointer determines the current subrecord; if there are no more subrecords left previous to the current one, the Before Selection function returns a TRUE instead of a FALSE.
Example:	The following procedure is a modified version of the one for Next Subrecord, except that it moves backward through a subselection instead of forward. Notice the new function Records in Subselection, which returns the number of subrecords in the subselection.

```
Default File([Customers])
First Record
All Subrecords([Customers]Meetings)
Last Subrecord([Customers]Meetings)
i:=Records in Subselection+1
'Open a little message window.
Open Window(50;50;350;150;0;"Dates of Meetings")
'as long as there are meeting subrecords to be read
While (Not(Before subselection([Customers]Meetings)))
```

```
                    i:=i-1
                    'Put a message in the window for each meeting date.
                    Message("Meeting "+String(i)+" was on "+String([
                    Customers]Meetings'Date))
                    Previous Subrecord([Customers]Meetings)
               End while
               j:=0
               'pause for a while
               While (j<100)
                    j:=j+1
               End while
```

Command: **Apply to Subselection**

Format: Apply to Subselection (*subfile name*;*statement*)

Use: This useful command can either read or affect the entire subselection. You can apply a one-line statement to a subrecord's selection, such as adding up order totals, making price changes, or modifying fields for whatever reason. For instance, if you increase prices across the board by 10 percent, you might issue the command Apply to Subselection ([Companies]Products; [Products]Items' Price:=[Products]Items'Price*1.1). This would take the price for each item, multiply it by 1.1 (which is a 10-percent increase), and place the result back into the Price field. This would apply to the entire subselection.

Example: Suppose you have a database of user groups, and the subfile name is Members. To change the Last Name field in that subfile so the last names are in all uppercase letters, you would enter the following procedure:

```
Default File [User Groups]
First Record
'as long as there are records to read from the User Groups
'file
While (Not(Last Record([User Groups])))
     'Select all of the members' subrecords.
     All Subrecords ([User Groups]Members)
     'Make their last name fields uppercase.
     Apply to Subselection ([User Groups]Members;
     [User Groups]Members'Last Name=Uppercase([User
     Groups]Members'Last Name))
```

```
'Go to the next user group record.
Next Record
End While
```

Command: **Search Subrecords**

Format: `Search Subrecords` (*subfile name*; *logical expression*)

Use: This command evaluates the current subselection and, based on the test of a logical expression, creates a new subselection from the old one consisting of subrecords that pass that logical test. You might want to find all the subrecords with ZIP codes of a certain value, customer numbers that are within a certain range, or dates that are in a particular season. The logical test you set depends on the fields that exist.

All the logical expressions that you already know can be used with this command. The AND symbol (&), the OR symbol (|), value tests (< for less than, > for greater than, = for equal, and so on) can all be used. In addition, the wildcard character (@) can be used for alphanumeric tests. The logical test can be quite complex, but for easier programming and debugging, it's usually best to keep it as simple as possible.

Example: The following procedure takes all the subrecords from the first record and selects those whose Date field is less than or equal to 7/15/88 (date values are surrounded by exclamation marks, which explains the unusual formatting). Once the procedure is through testing all the subrecords, the new subselection consists only of those records whose date is equal to or precedes 7/15/88.

```
Default File ([Customers])
All Records
First Record
All Subrecords ([Customers]Meetings)
Search Subrecords ([Customers]Meetings;
[Customers]Meetings'Date<=!07/15/88!)
```

Command: **Sort Subselection**

Format: `Sort Subselection` (*subfile name*; *subfile field name*; *operator*)

Use: This command sorts the current subselection into ascending order (> operator) or descending order (<). In the parentheses, specify the subfile name where the subselection is located, then the subfile field name that will be the basis for sorting, and the operator you want to use. The first record of the freshly sorted subselection is made the current record.

Example: The command Sort Subselection ([Customers]Meetings; [Customers]Meetings'Date;>) would sort the subselection of the Meetings subfile in ascending order, based on the value of the Date field.

PROCEDURES AND LINKS

A key component of a relational database is its ability to link files. The Customers database links the Customer Number fields of both the Customers and the Credit files. When a customer number is entered into a customer's record, the business name and the credit limit from the Credit file are loaded into the Customers file and made part of that record.

Linking with procedures is a rather advanced topic, but you should have a basic understanding of the linking commands and what they do.

Command: **Activate Link**

Format: Activate Link (*field to match*; *supplementary field*)

Use: This command is somewhat complex, so we will describe each component. First, it examines the field to match (the first argument) and goes to the linked file to find that same field. Next, it tries to match the value in that field in the current record to any of the records in the linked file. It might find one match, several matches, or no matches at all. If you don't specify a supplementary field, the first record that matches is pointed to.

Suppose you have a field called Product Name in the Orders file, and you want to get the linked record from the Product Descriptions file, which has the same Product Name field value. For simplicity's sake, assume that the Product Descriptions file has only four records:

Product name field	Product price field	Product number field
Widget	2,000	100
Gidget	3,500	207
Gidget	6,000	208
Thingamijig	2,000	312

Now assume that an order you have just entered has the product name Gidget. The line Activate Link ([Orders]Product Name) examines the contents of the Product Name field in the Orders file (Gidget) and looks in the linked file Product Descriptions to match those field values and have the Product Price and Product Number values ready to be used. Of course, the link has to be already established from the Structure window for Activate Link to work properly.

Notice, however, that there are two Gidgets. One is more expensive than the other, and their product numbers differ. If you do not provide a second field, 4th Dimension will load in the first Gidget record from the linked file. However, by including another field name, you can make 4th Dimension display all the possible choices so the user can choose.

The second field name is the one you want to show so the user can decide which of the possible linked records to use. In this case, the Product Number field probably would not be as good as the Product Price field, since it's easier to make a decision given a price than given some arbitrary product number. Therefore, `Activate Link ([Orders]Product Name;[Product Descriptions]Product Price)` would ensure that a list of possible choices is displayed. On the left side of the list would be the matches (in this case, Gidget and Gidget), and on the right side of the list would be the Product Price values (3,500 and 6,000). The user could examine that list and click the linked record that he or she really wants to use.

Understanding Activate Link is important to understanding how to program links in 4th Dimension. This command actually is not used as much as the other linking commands, since it does not change the current selection or the current record of the linked file, which you'll usually want to do. Activate Link is typically for more advanced programming, but it's important that you understand its function nonetheless.

Example: Assume you have two files: Contracts, which contains the names of firms that your business has contracts with, and Businesses, which contains information about the various businesses you have worked with in the past. When entering new contract information, you might want the Business field in Contracts linked with the Business field in the Businesses file. Further, since some businesses have the same name, you might want the City field from Business to be displayed in list form in case more than one match is found in the linked records. That way, if more than one match exists, all matching businesses and their correspond ing cities will be displayed for the user to select a single linked record. The command line in the procedure would be

```
Activate Link ([Contracts]Business; [Businesses]City)
```

Command:	**Load Linked Record**
Format:	Load Linked Record (*field to match*; *supplementary field*)
Use:	This is the most basic and commonly used linking command and acts very much like Activate Link. Load Linked Record finds the record in the linked file whose field value matches the value of *field to match*. This command looks through all the records in the current selection of the linked file and points to any and all matches there.

If a supplementary field is entered and more than one match is found, a list of matches is displayed along with corresponding values of the supplementary field. This lets the user choose from among the linked records that match.

The user can also use the wildcard character (@) in the linking field to have 4th Dimension automatically load in a variety of possibilities. For example, if the linking field is Last Name, and the user wants to see all last names listed in the linked field that begin with Sm, then the user can enter Sm@ in the linking field, press the Tab key to signify that the field has been entered, and let Load Linked Record find any Last Name matches in the linked field.

Load Linked Record works only the first time the linking field in a record is entered. This makes sense because once the link is made and the required information is found, there is no need for 4th Dimension to perform that link every time the record is displayed. Of course, if the linking field is modified, then Load Linked Record will be used since the correct linked record has to be found.

The converse of this command is Save Linked Record, which saves any modifications that have been made to the linked record. Its format is Save Linked Record (*field matched*), with the contents of the parentheses being the name of the field that was used to make the match.

Example:	Suppose you want to link the Customer Number field in Customers with the Customer Number field in Credit. You are confident that there aren't any duplications of customer numbers,

since the customer number has the Unique attribute. Therefore, you don't bother including a supplementary field, since you know any search of the linked record will recover either a single record with a matching customer number or no record at all. If a matching record isn't found, 4th Dimension will let the user create a new record. Nevertheless, the command you would enter in the procedure would be

```
Load Linked Record ([Customers]Customer Number)
```

Command: **Load Old Linked Record**
Format: Load Old Linked Record (*field to match*)
Use: When 4th Dimension saves a record whose linking field has been modified, it saves the modified record, and it also remembers what the linked record was before the modification was made. For instance, if a record had Customer Number 20 (which was linked to the Credit file), and the user changed the record to have Customer Number 47, then 4th Dimension would save the record as having Customer Number 47 and being linked to the appropriate record in the Credit file. However, 4th Dimension would also retain the fact that the last record it was linked to was the one for Customer Number 20.

Load Old Linked Record loads in the record previously linked to the linking record. This is useful if the previously linked record has to be modified or examined when the user changes the value of the linking field. For example, suppose you own a warehouse, and you have a file called Orders, which maintains all the orders placed, and another file called Parts, which keeps track of part numbers, product descriptions, and the number of parts in inventory.

Now say you receive a call asking for a quantity of ten part number 371. After you enter the part number in the Orders file, 4th Dimension would find the linked record for part number 371 and (assuming it was programmed to do so) would subtract 10 from the Stock on Hand field in the record for part number 371.

Suppose that, an hour later, the same customer calls back and says he meant to order a quantity of ten part number 731, not part number 371. You would open up the record for that order and, after you change the field for the part number, the linked record for part 731 would be loaded and a quantity of 10 subtracted from part 731's stock on hand. Next, 4th Dimension would use Load Old Linked Record to load in the linked record for part 371 (the one the record was *previously* linked to) and make the correction.

Think of Load Old Linked Record as 4th Dimension's "memory of how things used to be," in case you need to know the previously linked record for a linking record. Its converse, Save Old Linked Record, should be used to save any modifications made to the previously linked record. For instance, after adding 10 back to the Stock on Hand field, you would have to enter Save Old Linked Record ([Orders]Part Number) to save the modified old linked record back to the disk with the proper value.

THE EXECUTION CYCLE

Procedures can be either global procedures (programs that are universally usable) or file/layout procedures. File/layout procedures are those that are linked solely to a particular file or layout. They are basically a part of that file or layout, since they are used whenever their file or layout is accessed.

The execution cycle is a concept closely linked with file/layout procedures. The execution cycle is the current state of a file or layout. There are three phases in the input cycle and five phases in the output cycle. The input cycle consists of the following:

- **Before:** before a layout appears or before any input is entered into a file
- **During:** the phase in which information is being entered
- **After:** following the entry of information, such as when the user hits the Accept button to enter a record

The output cycle consists of the following:

- **In header:** commands to place something at the top of the page
- **Before:** commands to be executed before the output is displayed or printed
- **During:** commands to be executed while the output is being displayed or printed
- **In break:** the phase where results and totals can be computed and output
- **In footer:** commands to place something at the bottom of the page

The ability to issue commands at different phases of the execution cycle gives you a lot of power over how data are entered, displayed, and computed. You can control the appearance of information, make sure that values entered fallwithin a specified range, format printed pages, and in general execute commands at very specific times when a database is being used.

Command: **Before**
Format: Before
Use: This function is for the part of the execution cycle before a layout is displayed or printed. It is most appropriate to modify field values, check for the presence of data, or perform other functions that are necessary before the user sees anything displayed or printed in the Before phase. The Before function returns a TRUE in the following circumstances:

- when any layout or dialog is accessed, but before it is displayed
- just before a subrecord is going to be displayed
- before the printing of each record

After the statements in the Before phase are completed, the execution cycle goes to the During phase and the Before function returns a FALSE.

Example: Choose the Procedure item from the Design menu, double-click the File/Layout procedures title, then double-click the Customers file name, as shown in Figure 11-2. This gives you access to any of the file or layout procedures in a database.

Double-click the layout procedure for the Customer Input layout, and you will see three lines of the procedure already. These three lines load in the linked record based on the Customer Number field and provide the variables AG2 and AG9 with the values in Business Name and Credit Limit, respectively. These few lines are needed to load in the values from the linked record, and 4th Dimension created them automatically when you linked the Customers file to the Credit file and created the Customer Input layout.

Type in the last three lines of the following layout procedure (the first three are already there). These three lines simply tell 4th Dimension that before a record that uses the Customer Input layout is displayed or printed, the value of the Last Name field should be put in all uppercase letters. The Before phase is appropriate since the change should be made before the record is visible.

```
Load Linked Record(Customer Number)
AG2:=[Credit]Business Name
```

FIGURE 11-2. Choose the Customer Input layout procedure from this dialog box.

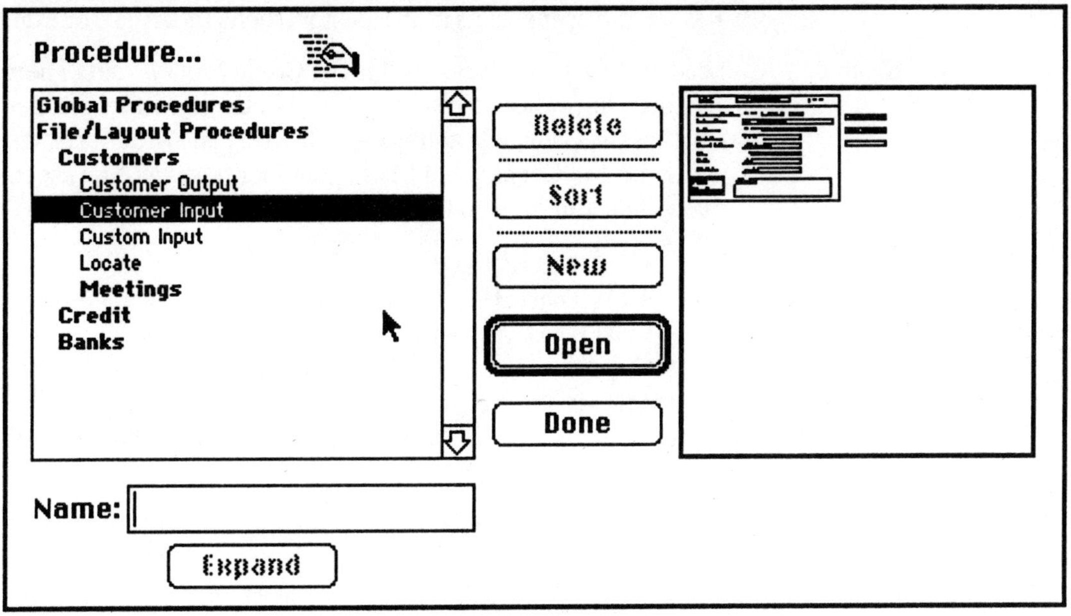

```
AG9:=[Credit]Credit Limit
If (Before)
     Last name:=Uppercase(Last name)
End if
```

Try out this procedure by going to the User mode and modifying a record. When the record appears on the screen, the last name should be in all capitals. This is true for any existing record that is displayed with Customer Input, although the value of the field itself is not saved that way permanently.

Command:	**During**
Format:	During
Use:	The function During returns a TRUE under any of the following circumstances:

- when the user modifies a field and moves to the next one
- when the user modifies a variable and moves to the next one
- when a button, radio button, or check box is clicked
- when Enter is pressed

- when the user is entering data in a subrecord
- when the user selects from a custom menu (not Apple or Edit)

Example: Load in the layout procedure for the Credit Input layout. There are three lines there already that load in the linked record that matches the Bank field and assigns the AM4 and AM5 variables, which are the Contact and Phone Number field values, respectively. Add four lines to this layout procedure, as shown:

```
Load Linked Record(Bank)
AM4:=[Banks]Contact
AM5:=[Banks]Phone Number
If (During)
 If (Modified(Credit Limit)
  Alert("Be sure you have your supervisor's OK on this change.")
 End if
End if
```

The procedure will now put the alert on the screen if the Credit Limit field is modified. While the layout is on the screen and is able to accept data, the During function returns a TRUE. If a modification of Credit Limit is detected, the alert is displayed to make sure the person entering data is being careful. You can see this layout procedure in action by going to the User mode and using the Choose File/Layout item in the file menu to use the Credit Input layout. Try modifying the credit limit of any record and watch the alert appear just as you programmed it to do.

Command: **After**
Format: After
Use: Once the user validates an entry for either a record or a subrecord, the After function returns a TRUE value. Clicking an Accept button or pressing the Enter key validates a record, whereas Cancel or Command-. cancels a record. Keep in mind that the After function is not used for output layouts, dialogs, or if the user doesn't change anything in the record.

Example: Go to the Structure window and double-click in the Credit file box to add a new field. Call this new field Limit and make it an integer with no special attributes. This field will hold the value of the two radio buttons (Net 30 and Net 60) that are in the Credit Input layout but that are not currently being used. Remember that even though the buttons are there, they do not do anything unless you enter a procedure for them.

Now load in the Credit Input layout procedure and modify it so it is identical to the following procedure. There are several changes you will notice. First, instead of If . . . Then controlling the execution cycle, the Case of command is used, since it is more efficient that several If . . .Then statements for Before, During, and After. Also, routines have been added to save the value of the radio button that has been turned on and to store the value of the month of the first order date into a variable called Month.

```
Load Linked Record(Bank)
AM4:=[Banks]Contact
AM5:=[Banks]Phone Number
Case of
 :(Before)
      'Find out what the stored value of the Limit field is.
  If ([Credit]Limit=60)
      'Turn the Net 60 button on.
    Credit60:=1
  Else
   If ([Credit]Limit=30)
      'Turn the Net 30 button on.
    Credit30:=1
   Else
      'Neither button should be on.
    Credit30:=0
    Credit60:=0
   End if
  End if
 :(During)
  If (Modified(Credit Limit))
   Alert("Please be sure you have your supervisor's OK on
this change.")
  End if
      'Is the Net 30 radio button on?
  If (Credit30=1)
    Limit:=30
  Else
      'Is the Net 60 radio button on?
```

```
If (Credit60=1)
 [Credit]Limit:=60
Else
   'Neither button is on.
 [Credit]Limit:=0
 End if
End if
End if
:(After)
      'Put the month of the first order date into a variable
      'called Month
Month:=Month of(1st Order Date)
```

Command: **In header**

Format: In header

Use: This function returns TRUE when 4th Dimension is printing the header of a layout. This is the area bounded by the top of the layout and the H line. You can put a page number, a title, a section name, or any other text or number at the top of the page. In Header's purpose is to make whatever assignments or modifications are necessary to the items that will be printed before they are actually printed.

In Header, just like Before, During, and After, is a phase of its own and should be used *only* in an output layout procedure. That's the only place where it makes sense to use it, since it is used basically to enhance printed output.

Example: The following short routine prints a special message at the top of each record printed that shows a credit problem. This is assuming there is a variable at the top of the page called SpecialMsg, which contains a message if there is a problem and contains nothing if there is no problem.

```
If (In Header)
   If ([Credit]Past Due>60)
      SpecialMsg:="* * * ALERT! Credit Problem! * * *"
   End if
End If
```

Command: **In break**

Format: In break

Use: This function returns TRUE when 4th Dimension is printing the area of a report between the D (detail) and B (break) lines as defined in the layout. The break area is used to print subtotals and grand totals, and the variables for these values must be set up in the break portion of the layout.

Command:	**In footer**
Format:	`In footer`
Use:	The converse of the In Header function, this function returns a TRUE if 4th Dimension is printing a layout's footer area, which is the area between the B (break) and the F (footer) lines. You can print page numbers, dates, and other information at the bottom of each page. Process the variables that will be printed during the In Footer phase, and the variables in the layout will be printed with their given values.

OTHER LAYOUT CONTROL COMMANDS

The remaining procedural commands can be used to gain greater control over the layouts. They aren't necessarily part of the execution cycle, but they are used most commonly in layout procedures.

Command:	**Go To Field**
Format:	`Go To Field` (*field name*)
Use:	Using this command is exactly like clicking on a field. Go To Field selects the field name you specify in parentheses.
Example:	Suppose you have a routine set up that requires the user to enter the Bank Name field first, even though it is not the first field in the layout. You might use Go To Field in the Before phase as follows:

```
Default File([Credit])
If (Before)
      Go to Field (Bank Name)
End If
```

Command:	**Highlight Text**
Format:	`Highlight Text` (*variable or field name*; *start*; *end*)
Use:	This powerful command can either place the cursor at an exact position inside a field or highlight a group of characters in a field. For instance, you might have a field called Name in which you want the user to enter his first, middle, and last names. You could

write a routine that, if the user enters only a middle initial, alerts the user that the whole middle name must be entered. Instead of making the user reenter the entire name, you could have 4th Dimension highlight the middle initial and its period so that the user could type in the full middle name, replacing those two characters.

There are many uses for Highlight Text. Use it anywhere you want to position the cursor at a precise point for the user or highlight some or all of the contents of a field or variable. The point of Highlight Text is to make a database easier to use and understand.

The three arguments enclosed in parentheses are the name of the field or variable you want to highlight, the beginning position in that field or variable where the highlighting should begin, and the ending position in that field or variable where the highlighting should end.

Example: If you want to highlight the third through seventh characters of the Name field, you would type `Highlight Text ([People]Name;3;8)`. Since the highlighting ends at character 8, that character is not included in the highlighting. If you just wanted the cursor placed between the second and third characters, you would type `Highlight Text ([People]Name;3;3)`. The integers given show what character the cursor will *precede*, so 3;3 would put the cursor just before character three and after character two.

Command: **Get Highlighted Text**
Format: `Get Highlighted Text` (*variable or field*; *variable 1*; *variable 2*)
Use: This is somewhat a reverse command of Highlight Text. When you issue this command, the position of the first character of selected text is placed in variable 1 (whatever name you give it), and the position of the last character of text plus one is placed in variable 2. If these numbers are equal, no text has been selected. If they are different, 4th Dimension can use this information to extract whatever the user has highlighted.

Example: The following routine gets the text that the user selected from the Name field and puts it into a variable called LastName. Suppose the first character selected is 5 (the variable strt) and the last character selected plus one is 11 (the variable stp). Last-Name would consist of a substring beginning at character 5 and ending 6 characters later (stp–strt).

```
Get Highlighted Text ([People]Name;strt;stp)
LastName:=Substring (String([People]Name);strt;(stp-strt))
```

Command:	**Execute**
Format:	Execute (*statement*)
Use:	The Execute command is like a command construction set for procedures. Using Execute, you can assemble and run a one-line procedure, with that procedure contained inside the parentheses. For example, suppose you have two variables, VAR1 and VAR2, and the procedure needed to add, subtract, multiply, or divide these two variables, depending on the circumstances. Instead of writing several If . . . Then statements, you can simply store whatever operator (+, -, *, or /) you want into a string called Op (or anything else you want to call it) and enter the command Execute ("Result:=VAR1"+Op+"VAR2). When the procedure encounters that statement, it will issue the command Result:=VAR1+VAR2 or Result=VAR1*VAR2 or whatever the line would be, based on the value of Op.
	Basically, any command you can construct in a string you can execute with this command. Execute gives you tremendous flexibility, since you allow the procedure to construct commands on its own, which means different commands can be issued for different conditions.

Command:	**Old**
Format:	Old (*field name*)
Use:	This command returns the value of the field specified before it was modified. It can do this since the old value of the field is still on the disk, and as long as you haven't saved the modified record to disk, the old value is still retrievable. This is helpful in undoing a change the user made in a particular field, which can be particularly helpful for difficult-to-enter fields like account numbers. Of course, modifying a record can be done only through the Modify Record command or the User environment.

Example: To replace the value of the field Account Number with its previous value, you could type `[Credit]Account Number:=Old([Credit] Account Number)`.

Command: **Reject**
Format: `Reject` or `Reject` (*field name*)
Use: The first format should be used in the During phase of a layout procedure. It rejects the entire entry just made by the user. The Reject command should be used, of course, only if the entry made is unacceptable and can't be quickly fixed by either 4th Dimension or the user. A good example given in the 4th Dimension command reference is if the Gender field equals Male and the Pregnant field equals Yes. Obviously, this is not a valid entry, so Reject is used so the user can reenter the record. The current contents of the record are cleared, and the blank layout is again available to the user for data entry.

A less drastic use of Reject is to make the user reenter a single field. This requires the second format, in which the name of the field to be reentered has to be specified. This is appropriate when the entry in a certain field isn't valid, as demonstrated in the following example.

Example: The short routine that follows rejects the entry in the Expense field if the expense reports exceed $10,000.

```
Default File ([Expense Reports])
If (During)
    If (Expenses>10000)
        Alert ("The limit on expenses is $10,000.")
        Reject (Expenses)
    End If
End If
```

If the user enters anything above $10,000 in the Expenses field, an alert dialog box states, "The limit on expenses is $10,000." After the user clicks OK, the entry in the Expenses field is cleared out so the user can type in a valid entry.

Printing, Debugging, and Customizing a Database

This chapter covers three important topics: (1) miscellaneous functions, which are a variety of math and time functions in 4th Dimension, (2) printing and how to write procedures to print reports, and (3) 4th Dimension debugging and utilities, which make creating a bug-free database easier.

MATH FUNCTIONS

The 4th Dimension procedural language supports a wide variety of mathematical functions. Some of those functions are basic (like Int, which takes the integer of a number), while others are quite complex (like Std Deviation, which takes the standard deviation of the values in a field). The various math functions fall into the categories of Computation, Statistics, and Trigonometry.

COMPUTATIONAL FUNCTIONS

Abs (*number*) computes the absolute value of a number. This function takes the absolute value of the number in parentheses. Whatever is given, a positive value of that number is returned. -10 becomes 10, 10 remains 10, and 0 remains 0. This function is helpful when it doesn't matter what the sign of a number is. For example, if you want to compute the number of days between one day and another, it doesn't make any sense to have a negative number. July 7 minus July 10 is -3, but what's important is that they are three (absolute value of -3) days apart.

Average (*field name*) computes the average of a field or a subfield. This function computes the arithmetic mean (all the values added together divided by the quantity of values) for a field or a subfield. There are two different ways to use Average, and different rules apply. The first way is to compute the average of a field in a current selection. This works in the In footer and In break phases of the print execution cycle, which means it is useful only in output layout procedures.

The second use of Average is to compute the average of a subfield in a subselection. For example, say you have a subfile called Orders whose parent file is Customers. The Orders subfile contains a subfield called Order Total, which is the numeric dollar total of the order. To determine the average value of the orders for the current record, you enter AvgOrd:=Average([Customers]Orders'Order Total). The average value of the subselection is stored in the variable AvgOrd.

Num (*number*) converts a numeric string into a numeric expression. If a variable x is equal to the string 1200, you might think that x is usable as a mathematical function, when in fact it is not. The string *x* is equal to the characters 1, 2, 0, and 0, but *x* does not represent the number 1200. To convert a numeric string into a real, usable number, use **Num**. If the string you specify has any alphabetical characters, 4th Dimension ignores them. For instance, b: = **Num** ("10 plus 20 equals 30") would make *b* equal to 102030. The example given for the Dec function shows one way **Num** can be used.

Dec (*number*) returns the decimal portion of a number. This function takes the portion of a number following the decimal. You can store the decimal part in a variable by entering something like DP:=Dec(3.48592), in which case DP equals .48592. Of course, a numeric expression like a variable could go within the parentheses. The following routine is a good example, because it allows for entry of a number and reports back if it is an odd or even number. If there is a decimal portion, the number is odd. If there is no decimal portion, the number is even.

```
i:=Request("Enter number, please.")
'Convert i into a usable number and place it in variable v.
v:=Num(i)
'Is there a decimal portion left over?
If (Dec(v/2)#0)
 Alert("This number is odd")
Else
 Alert("This number is even")
End if
```

Int (*number*) returns the integer (nondecimal) part of a number. Use the Int function if you want to use the nondecimal part of a number. If the number is positive, the value returned simply has the decimal portion removed. Thus, dc: = **Int** (502.9823) makes dc equal to 502, since .9823 is the unwanted decimal portion. Negative numbers are rounded off, so − 502.9823 is returned as − 503. Use Int when the decimal portion of the number is either inconsequential or unwanted.

Max (*field name*) returns the highest value found in a field or a subfield; Min (*field name*) returns the lowest value found in a field or a subfield.

Like the Average function, Max and Min work only during print time and only in the footer and break areas. Max finds the greatest value (for instance, the highest salary or the highest order received) in a field of the current selection, while Min finds the lowest value. Max and Min also work with subfields for the current subselection, and you don't have to be printing to use these functions with subfields

Mod (*number 1*; *number 2*) divides the first number by the second number and returns the remainder. The Mod function is used to get the remainder from a division operation. You don't have to include the division symbol (/); the semicolon separating the two numbers is sufficient.

Random returns a random number between 0 and 32,767

Although you probably won't need random numbers in a database very often, this function is available if you do need one. The line RN: = Random assigns the variable RN a random number between 0 and 32,767. If you want to narrow the range, use the formula

Mod(Random;high-low+1)+low

The value of *low* should be the low end of the range, and the value of *high* should be the high end of the range. For instance, to assign a number between 50 and 100 to the variable RN, type RN:=Mod(Random; 51)+50.

STATISTICAL FUNCTIONS

Each of the following functions follows the same basic rules. First of all, there are two syntaxes for each function, one of them for working with fields and the other for working with subfields. When you are computing fields, the function is valid only in output layout procedures, because the functions are intended only for the In footer or In break phase in the execution cycle. These types of functions can be used only when you are printing with the Print Selection command, which is discussed later in this chapter.

If you use a subfield name inside the parentheses, fewer restrictions apply. The functions then work with the current subselection in the current record.

Squares Sum (*field name*) computes the sum of the squares for a field. For example, for the values 3, 5, and 7 in a particular field, this function returns the sum of 3 times 3 plus 5 times 5 plus 7 times 7, or 83.

Std Deviation (*field name*) returns the standard deviation of a field. Unless you are creating a truly sophisticated database, you probably will not use this function. To learn more about standard deviation, consult any basic statistics text.

Sum (*field name*) computes the total sum of a specified field and is probably one of the more commonly used functions. You could use it to compute the total salary for a group, the total sales for a particular quarter, or the number of items in stock.

Variance (*field name*) returns the variance of the values in a field. The variance, like the standard deviation, is a statistical term best learned from a statistics text. This function computes the variance of the field or subfield specified.

TRIGONOMETRIC FUNCTIONS

The following functions work in basically the same way. Each function should be followed by a numeric expression inside parentheses. The function returns a value based on that expression. The trigonometric functions are Sin (sine), Tan (tangent), Cos (cosine), and Arctan (inverse tangent).

The remaining two functions, Exp and Log, are logarithmic functions. Exp raises the natural log base *e* by the number within parentheses. Exp (5), for instance, returns *e* to the fifth power. Log, the inverse function of Exp, returns the natural logarithm of the number inside the parentheses. Log(10) returns the natural logarithm of 10.

TIME FUNCTIONS

Nine 4th Dimension functions relate to the date and the time. These functions are helpful when you want to perform computations on dates or times, or when you want to automatically put the date or time in a particular field or variable.

Current Date returns the date from the Macintosh clock. This function returns the date, according to the Macintosh clock, in the proper 4th Dimension format (!mm/dd/yy!). For example, say you have a field called Orders, and you want the date of the order to be put in the record automatically. You would enter the following lines in the Orders layout procedure:

```
If (Before)
      Order Date:=Current Date
End if
```

Year of (*date*) returns the year in its full format from the date expression. If you want the year from a date expression, use the Year of function. For instance, if the variable DT is equal to !04/06/88!, then Year of(DT) returns the numeric value 1988.

Month of (*date*) returns a numeric value representing the month of a date. Month of does not return strings like April, January, or September. Instead, it returns a number that represents the month (1 for January, 2 for February, and so on) when provided with a date expression. This function is helpful if, for instance, you want to list all sales that took place in July (month 7).

Day of (*date*) returns the day of the month from a date expression. Like Month of, this function extracts the number of the date from a date expression. Day of (!04/17/89!) returns the value 17, since the date represents the 17th day of a month.

Day Number (*date*) returns the number of a day on which a date falls. This helpful function computes the day of the week (1 = Sunday, 2 = Monday, 3 = Tuesday, 4 = Wednesday, 5 = Thursday, 6 = Friday, 7 = Saturday) on which a date falls. The expression Day number (!02/27/88!) returns 7, since February 27, 1988, fell on a Saturday.

You could use this function, for example, in a stockmarket database. If the user requests a figure for a particular date, the database could indicate whether the stock market was open on that day. Of course, this function would not be able to compute holidays when the market was closed, but it could eliminate weekends. You could also use it to determine which days in a week are strong for sales.

Date (*string*) converts a valid string expression into a date expression. If a procedure contains a string that is in the valid date format of mm/dd/yy, the Date command converts that string into a usable date variable. The string itself can have date elements consisting of either one or two digits (July, for example, could be 07 or 7), and the character separating the date elements can be a slash (/), a space ( ), a period (.) or a hyphen (-). The elements must, however, be in the correct order of month, date, and year. For example, CD:=Date ("7 7 87") assigns CD the date value !07/07/87!.

Current Time returns the current time from the Macintosh clock. This function counts the number of seconds since midnight, which can range from 0 (midnight) to 86,339 (11:59:59 p.m.). This is a useful routine for performing such tasks as pausing for a certain number of seconds or timing a user who is entering data.

Time (*string*) computes the number of seconds between midnight and the time provided. The Time function can be used to compute how many seconds from midnight a certain time is. The string provided inside the parentheses must follow the format hh:mm:ss. For example, 7:32 and 21 seconds in the morning would be expressed as 07:32:21, while 7:32 and 21 seconds in the evening would be expressed as 19:32:21.

`Time String` (*second*) returns a string with the hh:mm:ss time. This function takes the numeric expression of seconds from midnight and converts it into the hh:mm:ss format. The number of seconds from midnight can range from 0 to 86,399. If you go over that, you get nonexistent times (like 25:20:30). Time string is typically used with the Current time function to determine the actual time in the proper format. The statement `CT:=Time String (Current time)` assigns the variable CT the string value for the current time.

PRINTING IN 4TH DIMENSION

The goal of a database is to store, organize, and analyze information, and to print useful reports based on that information. You already understand how to format the output, both in the display and on the printer, using the Output Layout command and the layout editor. You need to know several procedural commands to program the database to print.

`Print Selection` (*file name*; *) prints all the records in the current selection using the current output layout. You can use this command by itself without any arguments, in which case it displays the Print Settings dialog box, shown in Figure 12-1, and then prints the current selection of the default file.

If you specify a file name in the parentheses, the current selection of that file is printed. If you include the asterisk inside the parentheses (either by itself or following the file name and a semicolon), the Print Setting dialog box

FIGURE 12-1.   The Print Setting dialog box for the Imagewriter. A somewhat different one appears for the LaserWriter.

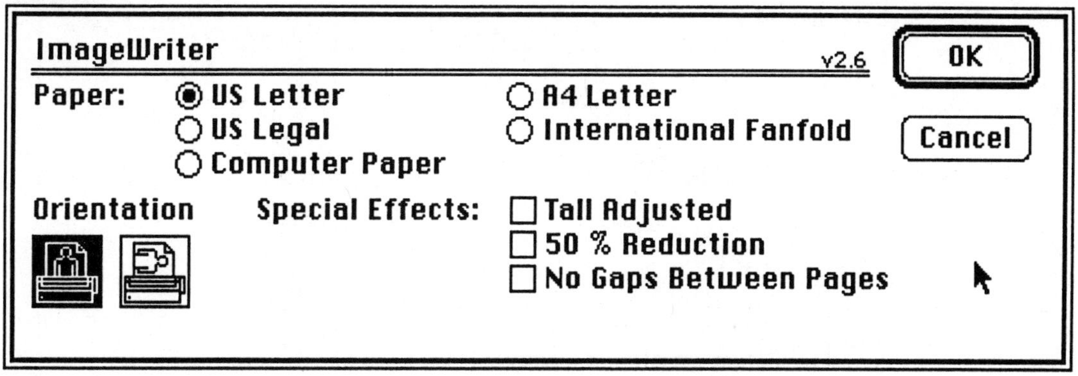

does not appear. You can use this if you don't want the user to be bothered or to be able to change the settings for printing.

Type in the next few lines, saving them as the global procedure Print-Cust. Next, add Print Customers to the File menu in the menu editor, as shown in Figure 12-2.

```
Default File ([Customers])
Output Layout ("Customer Output")
Print Selection (*)
```

Print Layout (*file name*; *layout name*) prints using the specified layout. Print Layout is a somewhat unusual command since it prints a layout with the current values of all the fields and variables in that layout. This command executes the instructions found in the Before and During phases of the execution cycle, but none of the other phases.

This command does not issue automatic form feeds after each layout is printed, so you can put several layouts on one page. You must be careful, however, to issue a Form Feed command after you are through printing with Print Layout so that the last page is printed. Otherwise, that layout stays in memory and is not printed.

FIGURE 12-2.   The menu editor, as it should appear for the File menu.

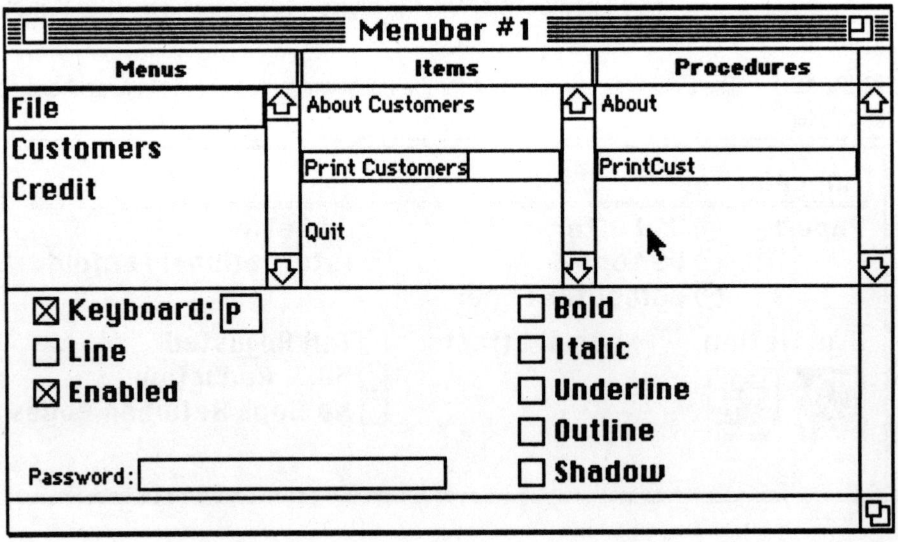

Form Feed causes the printer to push a blank page through the printer after the printing job is complete. Use Form Feed if you want to create a break in the printing of a report by issuing a blank page through the printer. You should also use Form Feed after a **Print Layout** command so that the printing takes place.

Print Settings displays the two printer dialog boxes for the user. There are two Printer dialog boxes: one for the page setup and another for the actual printing process. If you want to force these dialog boxes to appear (one after the other, of course, not simultaneously), issue a Print Settings command. This command is most commonly used before one or more **Print Layout** commands so the user can specify how to print the layouts. If the user clicks OK for both dialog boxes, the system variable OK equals 1. Otherwise, OK is set to 0, indicating that the user wants to cancel the printing process.

DEBUGGING AND CUSTOMIZING

As you have been entering and working with procedures, you may have been stopped by 4th Dimension because of a typographic or other error. 4th Dimension has powerful built-in tools and external programs to help you find and eliminate problems in a database. For example, if you are executing a procedure and 4th Dimension encounters a problem, it displays the dialog box shown in Figure 12-3 highlighting the error and giving its best description of what that error is.

FIGURE 12-3.   The error window shows where the error occurred and what the error was, and gives you the option to Abort, Trace, or Continue.

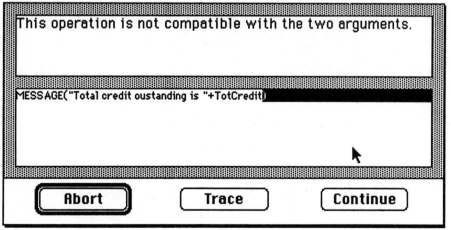

You can abort the procedure, which means it stops immediately and returns to wherever you were before the procedure was executed. You can trace the procedure, which means the Trace window is displayed every time a single statement is executed. Or you can click Continue, which makes the procedure go on despite the error.

You will usually want to abort the procedure so you can return to the Procedure editor and try to fix the problem. To get a better idea of what is happening in the procedure, however, you can click Trace, which brings a window like the one in Figure 12-4 onto the screen. The Trace window lets you execute a procedure one step at a time, so you can monitor where 4th Dimension is in the procedure's execution by noting the position of the check mark on the left side of the procedure listing.

Clicking Abort aborts the procedure, clicking No Trace turns off the Trace window, clicking Step makes 4th Dimension execute the next step of the procedure, and clicking View lets you see what is happening behind the Trace window. Trace can be a powerful tool in finding procedural bugs. To force the Trace window onto the screen while a procedure is being executed, hold down the Option key and click the mouse button once. The error window appears, and you can click Trace in that window.

The two procedural commands related to tracing are described in the following paragraphs:

FIGURE 12-4. The Trace window lets you monitor the progress of the procedure.

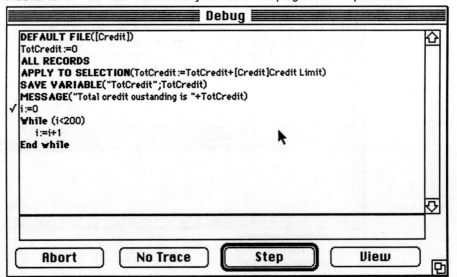

Trace puts 4th Dimension in Trace mode, which means the Trace window is displayed every time a single statement is executed. Trace remains in effect for *all* procedures until you turn it off.

No Trace turns off the Trace mode. When 4th Dimension encounters the No Trace command, it has the same effect as if the user clicked on the No Trace button.

EXPANDING YOUR SKILLS IN 4TH DIMENSION

I hope you have learned a lot about how to use 4th Dimension and what sorts of applications are possible with this amazing program. As mentioned at the beginning of this book, you should supplement and build on your knowledge by referring to the manuals that come with the 4th Dimension program package, especially the *Command Reference*.

The 4th Dimension package also comes with some helpful utilities, which you should learn as you become a more sophisticated 4th Dimension developer. Instructions on how to use these utilities is in the *Utilities and Developers Notes* booklet, which comes with 4th Dimension. These programs are as follows:

- **4D Tools** are used to clone databases, repair a damaged database, and develop a multi-user database.
- **4D Renamer** renames the files in the database folder that make up a 4th Dimension database. A sample screen is shown in Figure 12-5.
- **4D External Mover** converts 68000 object code into a 4th Dimension external procedure. A sample screen is shown in Figure 12-6.
- **4D xRef** is an extremely useful program that prints a report on your database, detailing the structure, procedures, layouts for each file, menubars, and all of the other components that make up your database. 4D xRef is a

FIGURE 12-5.   4D Renamer lets you change the names of database files.

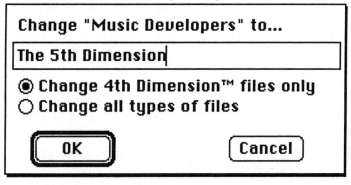

Change "Music Developers" to...

The 5th Dimension

◉ Change 4th Dimension™ files only
○ Change all types of files

OK   Cancel

FIGURE 12-6. 4D External Mover converts object code into an external procedure.

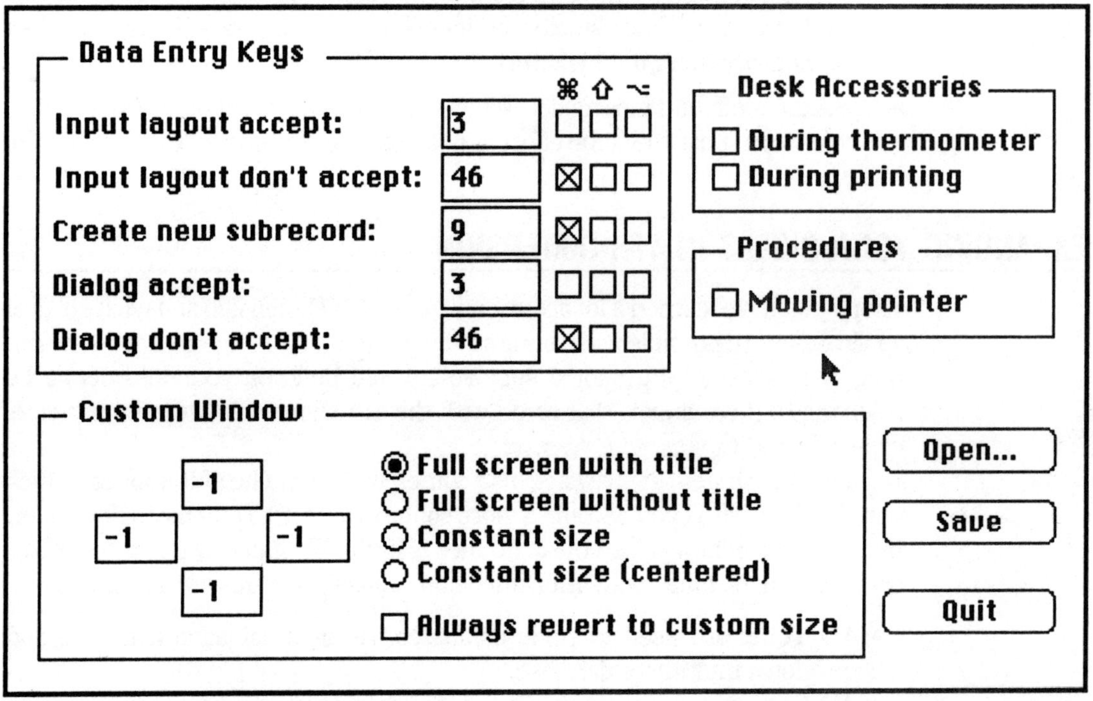

great debugging tool and is particularly useful if you want to impress your friends with the monstrous database you just finished. The dialog box for 4D xRef is shown in Figure 12-7.

- **4D Customizer** is used to adjust the 4th Dimension development environment. This is a fine-tuning program that can alter such things as the Custom window's behavior, the meaning of certain keys on the keyboard, and whether or not desk accessories are available while 4th Dimension is printing. Figure 12-8 shows a sample screen from 4D Customer.

Acius also sells a program called 4D Runtime, which is for people who want to use 4th Dimension databases developed by others, but who don't want to pay for the entire package. If you create and sell your own databases, you can distribute them to people who own either the whole 4th Dimension package or 4D Runtime, which is enough for using the database.

Whether you use 4th Dimension to create databases for yourself, as a commercial developer who wants to sell completed databases, or just because you're a Macintosh applications fanatic, I hope this book has helped you get started in 4th Dimension and to better understand all the program has to offer you.

FIGURE 12-7.   Dialog box for 4D xRef lets you specify what you want printed.

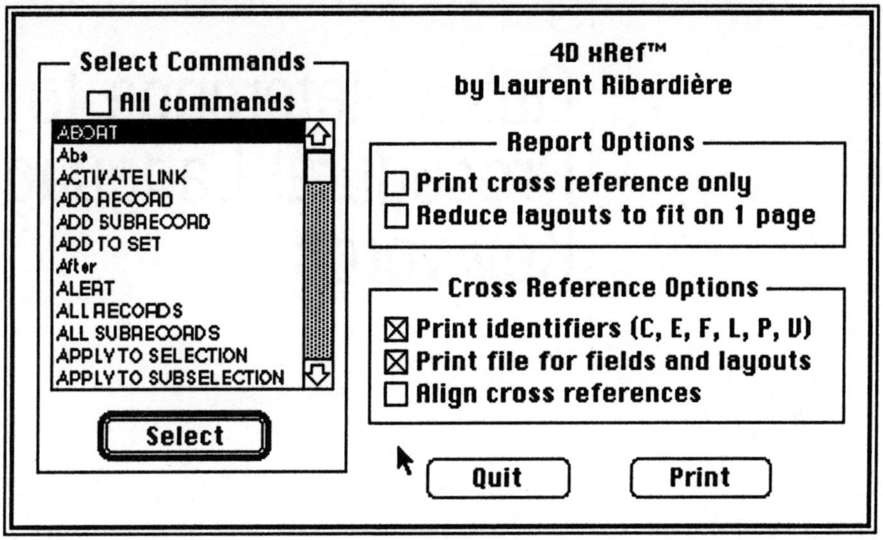

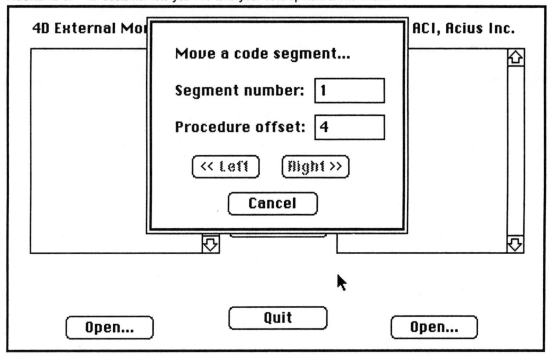

FIGURE 12-8.   4D Customer lets you fine-tune your development environment.

Quick Reference to Procedural Language Keywords

After
Returns a TRUE when the user clicks an Accept key or presses Enter while an input layout is displayed.

Before
Returns a TRUE before a layout is displayed.

DIALOG (*file name*; *string*)
Displays the dialog box you specify so the user can enter one or more pieces of data. A file name is optional.

During
Returns a TRUE during data input.

GET HIGHLIGHTED TEXT (*field name*; *first number*; *second number*)
Gets the first and last character positions of the text that the user has highlighted.

GO TO FIELD (*field name*)
Selects the specified field.

HIGHLIGHT TEXT (*field name*; *first number*; *second number*)
Places an insertion point within the text or highlights the text.

INPUT LAYOUT (*file name*; *string*)
Sets the default input layout. A file name is optional.

Modified (*field name*)
Returns a TRUE when the user modifies the field.

Old (*field name*)
Returns the value of the field before it was modified.

REDRAW
Updates the screen during input.

REJECT (*field name*)
Prevents the user from leaving the specified field, usually because the input is unacceptable.

DATA OUTPUT

DISPLAY RECORD (*file name*)
Shows the current record using the input layout. The file name is optional.

DISPLAY SELECTION (*file name;**)
Displays all the records in the current selection using the output layout. A file name and asterisk are optional.

FONT (*variable; number*)
Specifies a font for displaying a variable in a layout.

FONT SIZE (*variable; number*)
Specifies a font size to display a variable in a layout.

FONT STYLE (*variable; number*)
Specifies a font style to display a variable in a layout.

FORM FEED
Advances the paper one sheet in the printer.

GRAPH (*variable; number; string*)
Creates a graph based on values from a subfield or variable.

GRAPH FILE (*file name;number;first field name;second field name*)
Creates a graph based on the values from the fields. A file name is optional.

In Break
Returns a TRUE when a sort level changes.

In Footer
Returns a TRUE at the end of each page.

In Header
Returns a TRUE at the beginning of each page.

Level
Returns the current break level.

MODIFY SELECTION (*file name;**)
Displays the selection so the user can modify one or more records. A file name and asterisk are optional.

PRINT LABEL (*file name;**)
Prints the current selection in label format using the output layout. A file name is optional.

PRINT LAYOUT (*file name;string*)
Prints the layout specified with the values stored in its fields and variables. A file name is optional.

PRINT SELECTION (*file name;**)
Prints the records in the current selection using the output layout. A file name and asterisk are optional.

REPORT (*file name;string*)
Prints a report. A file name is optional.

Subtotal (*field name;number*)
Returns the sum total of the items in a field for the current break level. A number is optional.

EXTERNAL COMMUNICATIONS

DELETE DOCUMENT (*document name*)
Deletes a document from disk.

EXPORT DIF (*file name; document name*)
Write current selection to a DIF file. A file name and a document name are optional.

EXPORT SYLK (*file name; document name*)
Writes current selection to a SYLK file. A file name and a document name are optional.

EXPORT TEXT (*file name; document name*)
Writes current selection to a text file. A file name and a document name are optional.

IMPORT DIF (*file name; document name*)
Reads the DIF file and makes it the current selection. A file name and a document name are optional.

IMPORT SYLK (*file name; document name*)
Reads the SYLK file and makes it the current selection. A file name and a document are optional.

IMPORT TEXT *(file name; document name)*
Reads the text file and makes it the current selection. A file name and a document name are optional.

LOAD VARIABLE *(document name; variable)*
Loads a variable into memory from the disk.

ON SERIAL PORT CALL *(string expression)*
Defines the procedure to be called as activity occurs with the serial port.

RECEIVE BUFFER *(string variable)*
Assigns the value from the serial buffer to a variable.

RECEIVE PACKET *(string variable; number)*
Assigns delimited ASCII strings from a document or from the serial port.

RECEIVE RECORD *(file name)*
Reads the serial port or document specified to get a 4th Dimension record. A file name is optional.

RECEIVE VARIABLE *(variable)*
Reads the serial port or document specified to get a 4th Dimension variable.

SAVE VARIABLE *(document name; variable;*)*
Saves a variable to the disk.

SEND PACKET *(string expression)*
Writes ASCII strings to a document or a serial port.

SEND RECORD *(file name)*
Sends a 4th Dimension record to a document or serial port. A file name is optional.

SEND VARIABLE *(variable)*
Sends a 4th Dimension variable to a serial port or a document.

SET CHANNEL *(number one; number two)*
Creates, opens, or closes a document.

USE ASCII MAP *(document name)*
Loads an ASCII map into memory for character transposition.

LINK COMMANDS

ACTIVATE LINK (*field name one; field name two*)
Searches the linked file for a value matching its field argument and then creates a link to the linked file. A second field name is optional.

CREATE LINKED RECORD (*field name*)
Creates a new linked record in the linked field.

LOAD LINKED RECORD (*field name one; field name two*)
Finds the linked record, loads it into memory, and makes it the current record. A second field name is optional.

LOAD OLD LINKED RECORD (*field name*)
Finds the specified record using the old link and loads it into memory.

Old
Returns the value of a field before it was modified.

SAVE LINKED RECORD (*field name*)
Saves linked record.

SAVE OLD LINKED RECORD (*field name*)
Saves the record pointed to by the old link.

MULTI-USER COMMANDS

CLEAR SEMAPHORE (*string*)
Clears a flag from the network.

LOAD RECORD
Loads the current record into memory to check whether it is locked.

Locked
Returns TRUE or FALSE based on the read-only and read-write status of a particular record.

READ ONLY (*file name*)
Assigns read-only state to a file's records. A file name is optional.

READ WRITE *(file name)*
Assigns read-write state to a file's records. A file name is optional.

Semaphore *(string)*
Returns TRUE if network has a flag with the same name as given in the argument.

UNLOAD RECORD *(file name)*
Removes a record from memory. A file name is optional.

PROGRAMMING

ABORT
Stops program execution.

Case of...Else...End Case
Case statement.

CLEAR VARIABLE *(string)*
Clears one or more variables.

EXECUTE *(string)*
Executes a string of commands.

If...Else...End if
Branching statement.

LOAD VARIABLE
Loads a variable from disk.

NO TRACE
Turns off the trace debugging function.

ON ERR CALL *(string)*
Establishes instructions for when an error occurs.

ON EVENT CALL *(string)*
Establishes instructions for when a certain event occurs.

ON SERIAL PORT CALL *(string)*
Establishes instructions for when serial port activity occurs.

SAVE VARIABLE
Saves a variable to the disk.

TRACE
Turns on the debugging Trace function.

Undefined (variable)
Returns TRUE if the variable has not been assigned a value.

While...End While
Loop statement.

RECORD COMMANDS

ADD RECORD (file name;*)
Adds a record to a file; a file name and asterisk are optional.

ALL RECORDS (file name)
Makes the current selection all of the records in the file. A file name is optional.

Before selection (file name)
Returns TRUE if user tries to move record pointer before first record of current selection. A file name is optional.

CREATE RECORD (file name)
Adds a blank record to a file and makes it the current record. A file name is optional.

DELETE RECORD (file name)
Removes the specified record from a file. A file name is optional.

End selection (file name)
Returns TRUE if pointer is beyond the end of a selection. A file name is optional.

FIRST RECORD
Moves pointer to first record in a file.

LAST RECORD
Moves pointer to last record in a file.

MODIFY RECORD (file name;*)
Loads record into memory for modification by user. A file name and asterisk are optional.

NEXT RECORD
Moves pointer to next record.

ONE RECORD SELECT (*file name*)
Makes the current record the current selection. A file name is optional.

POP RECORD (*file name*)
Loads the record from the top of the record stack into memory. A file name is optional.

PREVIOUS RECORD
Moves pointer to previous record.

PUSH RECORD (*file name*)
Pushes current record onto the file's record stack. A file name is optional.

SAVE RECORD (*file name*)
Saves record to disk. A file name is optional.

SEARCH (*file name*; *expression*)
Searches through the records in a file that meet certain criteria. A file name and an expression are optional.

SEARCH BY INDEX (*field name*;*)
Searches through the records in a file using an indexed field as the basis for the search. A field name and asterisk are optional.

SEARCH SELECTION (*field name*; *expression*)
Searches through the current selection for records that meet certain criteria. A field name is optional.

SELECTION COMMANDS

APPLY TO SELECTION (*file name*; statement)
Applies the statement you provide to the records in the current selection. A file name is optional.

DEFAULT FILE (*file name*)
Makes the specified file the default file. A file name is optional.

DELETE SELECTION (*file name*)
Deletes all of the records in the selection. A file name is optional.

MODIFY SELECTION (*file name*;*)
Displays the current selection using the output layout and lets the user select one or more records to modify. A file name and asterisk are optional.

`Records in file` (*file name*)
Returns the number of records in a file. A file name is optional.

`Records in selection` (*file name*)
Returns the number of records in the current selection. A file name is optional.

`SEARCH` (*file name; expression*)
Searches through the records in the file specified to find which records match the criteria you have provided. A file name is optional.

`SEARCH BY INDEX` (*expression;**)
Searches an indexed field based on the criteria provided. An asterisk is optional.

`SEARCH SELECTION` (*file name; expression*)
Searches through the current selection for records that match your criteria. A file name is optional.

`SORT SELECTION` (*field name; expression*)
Sorts the current selection of the file into ascending or descending order based on the field(s) you specify.

`SORT BY INDEX` (*field name; expression*)
Sorts the records in a file based on a single indexed field.

SET COMMANDS

`ADD TO SET` (*file name; string*)
Puts the current record in the set. A file name is optional.

`CLEAR SET` (*string*)
Deletes a set from memory.

`CREATE SET` (*file name; string*)
Creates a set that comprises all the records in the current selection. A file name is optional.

`CREATE EMPTY SET` (*file name; string*)
Creates an empty set. A file name is optional.

`DIFFERENCE` (*first string; second string; third string*)
Places the unique elements of the first and second sets into a third set.

`INTERSECTION` (*first string; second string; third string*)
Places the common elements of the first and second sets into a third set.

LOAD SET (*file name; string; document name*)
Loads a set from disk. A file name is optional.

Records in set (*string*)
Returns the number of records in a set. A string is optional.

SAVE SET (*string; document name*)
Saves a set to disk.

UNION (*first string; second string; third string*)
Creates a third set that comprises all the records from the first and the second set.

USE SET(*string*)
Creates a current selection made up of all the records in a set.

STANDARD FUNCTIONS

Abs (*number*)
Returns absolute number.

Arctan (*number*)
Returns inverse tangent.

Ascii (*string*)
Returns ASCII code for a character.

Average (*field name*)
Returns average of the values in the field.

Char (*number*)
Displays character corresponding to given ASCII code.

Cos (*number*)
Returns cosine.

Current date
Returns current date.

Current time
Returns current time.

Date (*string*)
Returns date expressed in 4th Dimension standard format.

Day number (*date*)
Returns the day's number (Sunday = 1, Monday = 2, and so on).

Day of (*date*)
Returns the day's number from the date string given.

Dec (*number*)
Returns the decimal portion of a number.

Exp (*number*)
Returns exponential of the number.

Int (*number*)
Returns ineger of the number.

Length (*string*)
Returns length of the string.

Log(*number*)
Returns natural logarithm of the number.

Lowercase(*string*)
Returns string in all lowercase.

Max(*field name*)
Returns maximum value found in a field.

Min (*field name*)
Returns minimum value found in a field.

Mod (*first number*; *second number*)
Returns the remainder of a divide operation.

Month of (*date*)
Returns the month number from the date given.

Num (*string*)
Returns the numeric value extracted from a string.

Position (*first string*; *second string*)
Returns position of the first occurrence of one string within another string.

Random
Returns random integer between 0 and 32,767.

Round (*first number*; *second number*)
Returns number rounded to specified number of places.

`Sin`(*number*)
Returns sine.

`Squares sum` (*field name*)
Returns the sum of the squares of the values in a field.

`Std deviation` (*field name*)
Returns standard deviation of the values in a field.

`String` (*number; string*)
Converts number into a string. A string is optional.

`Substring` (*string; first number; second number*)
Returns the specified portion of the string.

`Subtotal` (*field name; number*)
Returns total for the given break level. A number is optional.

`Sum` (*field name*)
Returns the sum of the values contained in a field.

`Tan` (*number*)
Returns the tangent of a number.

`Time` (*string*)
Returns the number of seconds from midnight to a particular time string.

`Time string` (*string*)
Returns a time string in hh:mm:ss format from the number of seconds since midnight.

`Trunc` (*first number; second number*)
Returns the argument truncated by a certain number of places.

`Uppercase`
Returns the string in all uppercase letters.

`Variance` (*field name*)
Returns the variance for the values contained in a field.

`Year of` (*date*)
Returns the year number from the date given.

SUBRECORD COMMANDS

ADD SUBRECORD *(subfile name; string; *)*
Creates a blank subrecord in memory and makes it the current subrecord, then displays the input layout for user entry. An asterisk is optional.

ALL SUBRECORDS *(subfile name)*
Makes all of the subrecords in a subfile the current subselection.

APPLY TO SUBSELECTION *(subfile name; statement)*
Applies the statement to all the subrecords in the current subselection.

Before subselection *(subfile name)*
Returns a TRUE if the pointer is before the first subrecord in a subselection. A subfile name is optional.

CREATE SUBRECORD *(subfile name)*
Creates a blank subrecord and makes it the current subrecord.

DELETE SUBRECORD *(subfile name)*
Deletes the current subrecord.

End Subselection *(subfile name)*
Returns a TRUE if the pointer is beyond the end of the subselection. A subfile name is optional.

FIRST SUBRECORD *(subfile name)*
Moves the pointer to the first subrecord. A subfile name is optional.

LAST SUBRECORD *(subfile name)*
Moves the pointer to the last subrecord.

MODIFY SUBRECORD *(subfile name; string;*)*
Loads the subrecord into memory for modification. An asterisk is optional.

NEXT SUBRECORD *(subfile name)*
Moves the pointer forward one subrecord.

PREVIOUS SUBRECORD *(subfile name)*
Moves pointer back one subrecord.

Records in subselection *(subfile name)*
Returns the number of records in the subselection.

SEARCH SUBRECORDS *(subfile name; expression)*
Searches the subrecords.

SORT SUBSELECTION (*subfile name*; *subfield name*; *expression*)
Sorts all the subrecords in the current subselection.

USER INTERFACE COMMANDS

ALERT (*string*)
Displays Alert box to the user.

BEEP (*number*)
Generates a tone for the duration specified. A number is optional.

BUTTON TEXT (*button variable*; *string*)
Defines the text that will be contained in a button.

CHECK ITEM (*first number*; *second number*; *string*)
Places a check mark next to the menu item specified.

CLOSE WINDOW
Closes the Custom window.

CONFIRM (*string*)
Displays a Confirmation box for the user.

Current password
Returns the current user's password.

DISABLE BUTTON (*button variable*)
Disables button specified.

DISABLE ITEM (*first number*; *second number*)
Disables menu item specified.

ENABLE BUTTON (*button variable*)
Enables button specified.

ENABLE ITEM (*first number*; *second number*)
Enables menu item specified.

ERASE WINDOW
Clears the contents of the custom window.

GO TO XY (*first number*; *second number*)
Positions the cursor at the specified point within the Custom window.

INVERT BACKGROUND (*variable*)
Inverts the background of the variable specified.

MENU BAR *(number)*
Puts up the specified menu bar.

Menu selected
Returns the most recently selected menu and menu item.

MESSAGE *(string)*
Displays a message to the user.

MESSAGES OFF
Turns standard messages off.

MESSAGES ON
Turns standard messages on.

OPEN WINDOW *(first number; second number; third number; fourth number; fifth number; sixth number)*
Opens a window. Fifth and sixth numbers are optional.

REQUEST *(first string; second string)*
Presents a dialog box to the user to get information. Second string is optional.

Screen height
Returns the height of the screen in pixels.

Screen width
Returns the width of the screen in pixels.

SET WINDOW TITLE *(string)*
Gives the window the specified title.

INDEX

Here's how to receive your free catalog and save money on your next book order from Scott, Foresman and Company.

Simply mail in the response card below to receive your free copy of our latest catalog featuring computer and business books. After you've looked through the catalog and you're ready to place your order, attach the coupon below to receive $1.00 off the catalog price of Scott, Foresman and Company Professional Books Group computer and business books.

✂ — — — — — — — — — — — — — — — — — — ✂ — — — — — — — — — —

❏ YES, please send me my *free* catalog of your latest computer and business books! I am especially interested in

❏ IBM
❏ MACINTOSH
❏ AMIGA
❏ COMMODORE

❏ Programming
❏ Business Applications
❏ Networking/Telecommunications
❏ Other _____

_____

NAME (please print) _____

COMPANY _____

ADDRESS _____

CITY _____ STATE _____ ZIP _____

Mail response card to: Scott, Foresman and Company
Professional Books Group
1900 East Lake Avenue
Glenview, IL 60025

✂ —

PUBLISHER'S COUPON   NO EXPIRATION DATE

S A V E $ 1 . 0 0

Limit one per order. Good only on Scott, Foresman and Company Professional Books Group publications. Consumer pays any sales tax. Coupon may not be assigned, transferred, or reproduced. Coupon will be redeemed by Scott, Foresman and Company Professional Books Group, 1900 East Lake Avenue, Glenview, IL 60025.

Customer's Signature _____